NEWALS 458 4574

DATE DUE NEWALS 458-4574

APR 1 0			
GAYLORD			PRINTED IN U.S.A.

VOLUNTEERS FOR MENTAL HEALTH:

Undergraduate Psychology
Students as Mental Health
Paraprofessionals

A Book of Readings

Edited by
Philip Ash, Ph.D.
University of Illinois
at Chicago Circle

MSS Information Corporation
655 Madison Avenue, New York, N.Y. 10021

This is a custom-made book of readings prepared for the courses taught by the editor, as well as for related courses and for college and university libraries. For information about our program, please write to:

MSS INFORMATION CORPORATION
655 Madison Avenue
New York, New York 10021

MSS wishes to express its appreciation to the authors of the articles in this collection for their cooperation in making their work available in this format.

Library of Congress Cataloging in Publication Data

Ash, Philip, 1917-   comp.
    Volunteers for mental health.

    A collection of articles previously published in various journals.
    1. Volunteer workers in mental health--Addresses, essays, lectures. I. Title. [DNLM: 1. Mental health services--Collected works. 2. Voluntary workers --Collected works. WM35 A819r 1973]
RC439.A93   362.2'04'25   73-10368
ISBN 0-8422-5121-9
ISBN 0-8422-0322-2 (pbk.)

This book of readings is dedicated, with respect and love, to Elaine Govostis, who started the whole volunteer program and kept it going during all the years of her undergraduate work. Without her, this book of readings would never have come into being.

CONTENTS

PREFACE

In 1970 one of my favorite undergraduate psychology majors, Elaine Govosits, elected Volunteer of the Year in the city of Chicago for her volunteer work at Chicago State Hospital, approached me about the possibility of obtaining course credit for volunteer activities—for a field practicum in mental health. The idea seemed meritorious and I agreed to be the faculty "front". Since then, the "course" has, one way or another, been on the books every quarter, including summers. It has become one of the most popular courses among psychology majors, and one which elicits a very high degree of enthusiasm and commitment. Originally run as an "independent study" course on a generic course number, it has been institutionalized as a formal separate course, *Field Work in Applied Psychology*. To no small degree, the approval of the course by the College of Liberal Arts and Sciences was promoted by very commendatory letters from mental health institutions which utilize the services of our volunteers. When we first offered the program we had to scrounge among mental health agencies to locate volunteer openings. By 1972 we were known throughout the Chicago-land area, and strongly solicited for more volunteers than we could provide.

The practicum is patient-contact and treatment-oriented; students interested in research are referred through other channels.

First, it is run by the students, with largely pro forma faculty supervision. To administer the course, there are one or two student coordinators, who are responsible for all aspects (assignment, site review, speaker recruitment, grading) of the program.

Second, the basic commitment of a registrant is to work a minimum of eight hours a week in a mental health setting. A poor attendance record (one or more absences on a scheduled volunteer day) results in automatic withdrawal.

Third, a two-hour biweekly colloquium is scheduled with local mental health practitioners (psychiatrists, psychologists, social therapists, etc.) which registrants are expected to attend. And attend they do! An exceptionally gung-ho group of students, they have frequently kept interesting professionals long past the 5 p.m. - 7 p.m. period into almost midnight.

Fourth, at the end of the quarter each student is required to submit a *Field Clinical Report*, which describes the student's experience and indicates how it could be improved.

Fifth, at the end of the quarter, each student is responsible for obtaining, from his or her supervisor, a detailed evaluation of their work in the agency. Failure to obtain (mailed by the supervisor directly to me) this evaluation automatically results in an "Incomplete" grade.

Sixth, the student is required to fill out a detailed evaluation of the agency, where he or she worked, and to indicate whether (a) the agency is OK, (b) would be OK if they agreed to certain changes in dealing with volunteers, or (c) should be dropped.

The program of *Volunteers for Mental Health* is one of the most exciting and gratifying any faculty member could be involved in. Furthermore, it clearly serves a need in the "world out there". The volunteer is today, with shrinking mental health budgets, a last resort in the provision of mental health care. All the evidence shows that the volunteer can meet this challenge.

Philip Ash, Ph.D.
Professor of Psychology
University of Illinois
at Chicago Circle

INTRODUCTION

On the one hand, the quest for "relevance" has encouraged innovations in education that bring students into contact with some form of "reality"; on the other hand, mental health manpower budgets are not large enough—and they are shrinking even further—to provide enough mental health workers to meet the needs of patient populations. The confluence of these two trends has led to the creation of a new treatment resource: the undergraduate psychology student volunteer. Some treatment modalities—behavior modifications and token economy, for example—require a very high service personnel-patient ratio. Store-front crisis intervention facilities require round-the-clock manning if they are to meet human crises when they occur. Half-way houses of all kinds require more "helpers" than their budgets permit.

In all these settings, the psychology undergraduate has come to play an ever-larger role, as a volunteer mental health worker.

On sum, it has become clear that such programs have been successful, and have yielded rich dividends to the patients, the institutions which serve them, the community, and the volunteers themselves. There are also problems and questions to be resolved, however. Among them are such issues as:

How should a mental health institution best be organized to utilize volunteers?

What kinds and levels of training should volunteers be given—and by whom—to make them effective?

What factors in an institutional setting facilitate the use of volunteers, and what factors inhibit or frustrate their use?

What should be the role of the sponsoring academic institution, and the college professor responsible for the course under which volunteering is made possible, if that framework of the activity is followed? Where course credit is given, how should responsibility for evaluation of the student volunteer's performance be shared between the college and the mental health institution, or indeed should this be the responsibility of only one of the two agencies involved?

What effects do the volunteers have on the patients or clients served?

What effects, if any, does the volunteer experience have on the volunteer?

As Gene C. Gruver, in the first paper in this collection, observes in his concluding summary, "The use of nonprofessionals in general and college students in particular offer promise in the effort to provide more complete mental health services to an ever increasing population. However, researchers must move quickly with sound research designs to establish a firm empirical basis for justification of the paraprofessional as well as for student development in working with distressed individuals."

This collection of readings has been assembled primarily for use in courses in which the volunteer activity is coupled with an academic framework that includes periodic meetings of the volunteers, to share experience and to provide a substantive base that hopefully helps the student gain insight into the way in which his or her particular service fits into mental health practice more generally, and into the scientific psychological underpinnings (if any!) of particular therapeutic modalities and intervention strategies.

The papers have been grouped into five categories:

I.   Overview — a review of the literature on the college student volunteer.

II. The Contribution of the Student Volunteer — the effect of volunteer programs on various client populations

III. Comparisons of Student Volunteers with Other Groups — principally a comparison between students and credentialled professionals.

IV. The Effect of the Volunteer Experience on Students — in terms of personality change in the student, changes in attitudes toward mental patients and distressed individuals, and substantive learning changes.

V.   Other Paraprofessional Assistance — assistance rendered by others than students, such as secretaries.

Section summaries or commentaries have been omitted: let the papers speak for themselves. These readings are presented, not to answer the questions set forth above, but, *first*, to provide the volunteer with a framework in which he can share experiences with other volunteers, and second, hopefully to establish a starting point for further research and development on the use of the volunteer in mental health settings.

COLLEGE STUDENTS AS THERAPEUTIC AGENTS

GENE GARY GRUVER [1]

The mutually beneficial effects of college students working as therapeutic agents with individuals in a variety of mental health settings are reviewed. Studies based primarily on observation and clinical impressionism suggest that college students may be useful as therapeutic agents, and, at the same time, students involved in a helping relationship exhibit personality changes not unlike those effected by more traditional psychotherapies. There is evidence that many unresolved issues will require further empirical investigation before the widespread use of nonprofessionals in psychotherapeutic settings can be sanctioned.

Albee's continuing investigation (1959, 1967, 1968) of professional manpower resources in the mental health fields has made apparent the severe current shortages and, further, has suggested the probability of even greater future shortages. It has been established that with present methods and models in the mental health field it is simply not possible to satisfy the ever increasing social demands for professional personnel.

A second aspect of the mental health manpower dilemma is that even if there were sufficient numbers of professional personnel, present mental health ideology would prevent many of those needing help from receiving it (Arnhoff, Rubinstein, & Speisman, 1969). This fact is most evident in the notorious lack of success mental health professionals have had working with the poor (Grosser, Henry, & Kelly, 1969; Pearl & Riessman, 1965). Other groups such as drug abusers, alcoholics, and juvenile delinquents have also been neglected by the mental health professionals primarily because professional contact with them has been, for the most part, fruitless. On the other hand, Blau (1969b) reported that nonprofessionals appear to have had a great deal of success in working with these groups. Particularly effective have been programs such as Alcoholics Anonymous and

Synanon (Volkman & Cressey, 1964; Yablonsky & Dederich, 1963).

In addition to the success of nonprofessionals working directly with these individuals, another kind of role for the nonprofessional may be useful to mental health conceptualization. Reiff (1967) and Pearl and Riessman (1965) have suggested that one of the most important uses of nonprofessional personnel is a "bridging" function, that is, a link between professionals and their target populations. In order to be an effective "bridge," the nonprofessional must be indigenous of the target population and speak the vernacular of both the target population and the professional. His interclass communication and mediation skills can facilitate communication between the two groups, and, thus, he will be able to discuss the needs and goals of each group with the other.

Other groups go untreated, not because mental health professionals are less successful in treating them, but rather because professionals choose situations that are more challenging and may prefer to utilize their time working with individuals who manifest dramatic change more rapidly. Nonprofessionals may be able to fill this void by working effectively with some of these neglected groups, such as retarded children and geriatrics. In this way, nonprofessional mental health personnel may be the key to providing more complete coverage in terms of mental health services to the entire population.

More provocative is the evidence that some nonprofessionals are more effective than their professional counterparts in working with

[1] An earlier draft of this paper was submitted to the University of Arizona in partial fulfillment of the preliminary requirements for the PhD degree. I wish to thank Peter Madison for his direction and suggestions. I also wish to thank R. Wrenn, R. A. Ruiz, C. Trafton, and R. Pool for their helpful comments.

PSYCHOLOGICAL BULLETIN, 1971, vol. 76, no. 2, pp. 111-127.

some populations which are presently receiving professional focus. Zunker and Brown (1966), for example, found that student counselors were more effective in counseling college students than were the professional counselors. Poser's (1966) college girls produced more positive changes in hospitalized chronic schizophrenic patients than did the professional staff. If indeed nonprofessionals are more effective than professionals in dealing with certain populations, then part of our professional mental health manpower resources is being wasted!

It is necessary to take a new look at traditional conceptualizations in mental health, to examine the parameters of professional involvement in social problems, and to set goals for the future. All aspects of the manpower dilemma must be investigated to insure maximum utilization of present resources as well as seeking out new sources of mental workers.

Attempts at amelioration of the manpower dilemma in psychology have included subdoctoral education (Albee, 1968; Arnhoff & Jenkins, 1969; Hoch, Ross, & Winder, 1966; Knott, 1969), the examining of new models for psychology (Albee, 1968; Hoch et al., 1966), and the utilization of volunteers or nonprofessionals (Christmas, 1966; Holand & Voss, 1968; Reding & Goldsmith, 1967; Savino & Schlamp, 1967; Wahler, Winkel, Peterson, & Morrison, 1965).

Volunteers or nonprofessionals with varying levels of training, motivation, and socioeconomic status have been used in a variety of situations. Two investigations by Stover and Guerney (1967) and Patterson and Brodsky (1966) have utilized mothers as therapeutic agents for their own children while Rioch, Elkes, Flint, Usdansky, Newman, and Silber (1963), Nichtern, Donahue, O'Shea, Marans, Curtis, and Brody (1964), and Donahue and Nichtern (1965) have trained mature women to act as therapists for the children of others. Hirsch (1968) and Zimmerman and Zimmerman (1962) have shown that teachers can be effective as therapeutic agents. Even grandparents and retired individuals have been put to work as psychotherapeutic agents (Cowen, Leibowitz, & Leibowitz, 1968; Johnston, 1967). Hartog (1967) has described the work of volunteer enlisted men consultants in a

United States Army hospital, while Fellows and Wolpin (1969) and Perlmutter and Durham (1965) have described the use of high school teenagers in mental health programs. Grosser et al. (1969) have reported on the Conference on Nonprofessionals, which dealt primarily with the use of indigenous personnel in health and welfare fields.

The present review centers around college students who act as volunteers or nonprofessionals in various mental health facilities. The focus upon college students is relevant not only because they appear to have qualities and characteristics which may suit them to work with troubled individuals but also because such work appears to have a positive developmental influence upon their own personalities. Because of gross methodological deficiencies in most of the studies involving college students as therapeutic agents, these impressions and this review are based primarily upon conceptual analysis of present day mental health issues, its logic, and clinical observation. The justification of nonprofessionals and the issue of college student development need more study before widespread use of college students in mental health settings can be sanctioned. The function of this review, then, is to identify and structure important areas which require further empirical investigation.

Observers have postulated many unique characteristics of college students which make them especially desirable as mental health workers. Greenblatt and Kantor (1962a) suggested that college students are more successful than "volunteers of a more senior station in life," that is, ladies auxiliary and the traditional friends of mental hospitals, because they manifest less resistance to and more motivation for face-to-face contact with patients. Whereas more mature adults tend to hesitate at the door of the ward and restrict their service by selecting duties that keep them some distance from the patients, the college students courageously plunge into the ward and usually are able to make direct long-term contact with even the very severely regressed patients. Also, student volunteers appear to have a sense of personal conviction to their work that the staff of other volunteer workers cannot duplicate. Umbarger, Dalsimer, Mor-

12

rison, and Breggin (1962) suggested that the reason for student success with patients results primarily from three factors. First of all, they are crusaders who feel the exhilaration of finding a worthwhile cause. Further, they are revolutionists engaged in a struggle against mental illness, the toll of which can be seen in mental hospitals. Finally, an element of altruistic novelty characterized the students observed by Umbarger et al. (1962).

Mitchell (1966) posited that in working with children "college students seem to have a particular talent for finding the child in his own world [p. 311]." He further suggested that the casual dress of the college students, their idealism, and, in particular, their spontaneity and enthusiasm are all disarming features which enhance the effectiveness of their role. In his argument against equating behavior of college girls in mental hospitals with psychotherapy, Rosenbaum (1966) reasoned that college students, particularly young girls, are successful because mental hospital populations who have been rejected by our culture "will respond to young, vibrant people who are humane and extend warmth [p. 294]."

Similarities such as residing in a developmental institution and seeking life changes may create a bond between college students and inmates of mental hospitals and constitute a further basis for the reported success of college students working with troubled individuals. Keniston (1967) pointed out that both college students and psychotic patients reside in "developmental institutions," the common characteristics of which include stimulating, supporting, and confirming the development of each resident (college students would certainly see even more similarities between the two institutions). Sanford (1962) also compared college students to mental hospital patients in that they are both seeking personality change.

The fact that there is a reduction of social distance between college students and those seeking help may facilitate the establishment of a working relationship between the therapeutic agent and patient. Certainly, the distressed patient might expect more empathy from a college student who, like himself, is struggling with his identity, competing for financial and employment security, and who

also sees the locus of control outside himself. The professional therapist, on the other hand, may appear as though he long since attained identity, security, and control of self and thus cannot recall the intensity of his own struggle. If then, as some authors suggest (Rogers, 1957; Truax & Wargo, 1966), accurate empathy is the single most important therapist characteristic in determining outcome of therapy, then the college student instantly and automatically has an advantage over his professional counterparts via his social status. Furthermore, if feeling closer to the therapist in terms of social status does facilitate "instant felt empathy," then college students should be even more effective working with other college students, adolescents, and children.

Because they cannot rely on professional training or the professional facade, college students are forced to use a naive, commonsense approach to their encounter. Perhaps the fresh approach of these young people has an effect on depressed or disturbed individuals that the trained professionals have difficulty duplicating. Rogers (1957) has postulated that theoretical wisdom is not a necessary ingredient for a helping relationship, and, to expand Rogers' contention, it may be that theoretical wisdom is actually detrimental to some therapeutic encounters because it restrains and constricts the variety of approaches available to the therapist. College students, on the other hand, are free of this theoretical constraint and are less inhibited in trying new approaches. As a result of their ignorance they may uncover effective new approaches considered inappropriate or too illogical by professionals. The present author is not advocating disregarding all theory but simply suggesting that we may be able to learn from the fresh approach of untrained college students.

Reiff and Riessman (1965) have postulated that greater flexibility in terms of appropriate and accepted behaviors on the part of the nonprofessional may be a special asset. Whereas a college student may take his charge to the zoo or be invited to a party by the patient, the professional, by virtue of his role prescription, would not engage in these activities. Poser's (1966) college girls could play "Drop-the-

Hanky" with their patients, but the professionals in the study would not have dared such activities.

A final advantage of using college students as therapeutic agents and a further reason for their apparent success particularly in settings outside the hospital is that there may be less stigma involved for the client. Whereas a parent may be concerned about the stigma attached to sending his child to a psychologist, he may be less inhibited about his child seeing a college student given, of course, that therapeutic effect is roughly similar. To sum, it appears that college students may have an advantage in working with some populations by virtue of their *not* having prior training or professional status.

Personality theorists who are particularly interested in college student development (Madison, 1969; Sanford, 1962) suggest that college students have a significant potential for change, and there is a continuing search for ways in which the personality development can be facilitated. Evidence suggests that working part time in a community mental health facility may serve as an instrument of personality change. College students who work in mental hospitals, psychological clinics, or other mental health settings manifest significantly more positive changes in self-acceptance and moral judgments in sexual and aggressive acts than do control groups (Holzberg, Gewirtz, & Ebner, 1964) and also greater self-understanding (Reinherz, 1962; Stollak, 1969; Umbarger et al., 1962). Increased self-confidence and enhanced identity formation are further personality changes effected by working in a mental health installation (Scheibe, 1965; Umbarger et al., 1962).

Even if college students possessed none of the above characteristics which make them particularly desirable as therapeutic agents, the discovery of a large untapped pool of volunteer workers in mental health would be welcome news. The suggestion that they do have characteristics and qualities which make them particularly suited to working in a mental health setting, as well as evidence that working in mental health may foster desirable personality changes, makes the topic not only more interesting but also worthy of theoretical attention and of a review.

COMPANION PROGRAMS

Companion Program is a term used to describe situations in which college students spend a certain amount of time each week as "companions" to patients in mental hospitals. Companion Programs may be structured or unstructured, provide training or no training, provide monetary remuneration or no monetary remuneration, but they share the common feature that individuals from the community are brought into regular face-to-face contact with individuals evidencing behavior problems.

The first Companion Program originated in 1954 at Harvard University and provided service to the Metropolitan State Hospital (Umbarger et al., 1962). By 1962, the idea had spread to such an extent that a book describing one program was published (Umbarger et al., 1962), and a conference was held to discuss the impact of the programs (Kantor, 1962). The Companion Program idea is continuing to expand and is usually met with enthusiastic response from students, staff, and patients alike (Spoerl, 1968).

The program at Metropolitan State Hospital has been the model for subsequent Companion Programs, although not all new programs have been so ambitious as the original in which 2,000 students had been in contact with mental patients during the first 7 years of operation. At Metropolitan State Hospital there are four separate areas in which the students might choose to work. Each situation is formulated to bring students and patients together under fundamentally different conditions. First, there is the ward improvement project in which a group of students go onto a ward with severely regressed patients to paint the ward, hang paintings, hold parties, but most importantly, interact with patients. A second area of work is the children's unit, which includes both group and individual activities. Organization of a basketball team, academic tutoring or just going for walks are among the services performed by volunteers on the children's unit. The third area is the case-aide program in which students work in a one-to-one relationship with individual patients under professional supervision and control. Six years after the original program had

14

begun, the fourth work area was initiated. Wellmet, Inc., is a halfway house for patients in transition between the hospital and the outside community. All of these four programs at Metropolitan State Hospital are loosely structured, provide training in the form of group meetings held once a week during the time students are entering services, and provide no monetary remuneration.

Using whatever measure one chooses, the program at Metropolitan State Hospital has been an overwhelming success. The effects on patients and student volunteers alike have been, for the most part, positive. Measures of success on the ward improvement projects were subjective and consisted of the students' accounts, which were written in the *Adult Unit Diary* and also included the recording of "landmarks," which were considered important advances in patient group behavior. One of these landmarks, for example, was the opening of doors between the women's "violent" ward and its male counterpart.

The measure of success in the case-aide program is not only more objective but more startling. By the end of the first year, 11 of the 14 patients who had been visited by case-aide volunteers had been released from the hospital with a readmission rate of less than 28%. Improvements in the other three patients could be measured by their transfers to less secure wards and by other idiosyncratic achievements.

In a follow-up study of the chronic psychotic patients seen by college case-aide volunteers, Beck, Kantor, and Gelineau (1963) found that of the 120 case-aide patients who had been seen from 1954 to 1961, 37 (or 31%) had left the hospital while working with students. Of these 37, 28 were still out of the hospital at the time of the follow-up, an average of 3.4 years after they left the hospital. Seven more patients left the hospital a few months after their case-aide work and were all out at follow-up, an average of 1.2 years each. The finding that 31% of a group of psychotics were able to leave a chronic service after "treatment" by college students appears to support the assertion that the program at Metropolitan State is successful, but a firm conclusion is not possible without controls.

As has been suggested, the measures of success of the program at Metropolitan State Hospital include not only the effects upon the patients but also the effects upon the student volunteers. All students in the program claimed "that they learned a great deal from the case-aide experience." Many felt that their relationship with a patient and the instruction of the group leader had taught them more about psychological theory and mental illness than had their courses at college. Some became interested in careers in mental health work. Moreover, "all claimed that they had gained insight into their own personalities and problems through their relationships with the patients and their own group [Umbarger et al., 1962, p. 54]."

Erikson (1959) suggested that the crystallization of professional goals is a major phase of the process identity formation. If this is true, then work in the case-aide section of the program can be said to have facilitated identity formation since Kantor (1959) and Greenblatt and Kantor (1962b) have shown that more than 70% of the students who were indefinite or undecided about career choices before participating in the case-aide program made concrete choices in the direction of mental health. In evaluating Kantor's findings, it should be noted that no control groups were used, and, moreover, students' career decisions during college years tend to be unstable. However, Kantor's essential conclusion that the project influenced the career choice of participants in the direction of mental health is probably valid.

As in most new areas of research, objective measures of college student success are scarce; however, a large body of relatively objective research, particularly concerning the student development aspect, has come out of the Connecticut Valley Companion Program, which was modeled after the one at Metropolitan State. In one of the studies (Holzberg & Gewirtz, 1963), a group of students who volunteered for the companionship program were compared to a control group of students who volunteered for other social service activities such as YMCA or the Big Brothers. On a questionnaire that was administered to both groups at the beginning of the academic year and again at the con-

15

clusion of that year, the subjects in the Companion Program shifted significantly in a positive direction in terms of their attitudes toward and knowledge of mental illness.

In another study at Connecticut Valley Hospital, a questionnaire measure yielded data suggesting positive effects on both patients and students (Holzberg, Whiting, & Lowy, 1964). Eighty-four percent of the patients said they enjoyed the relationship with the students, while the students reported that 71% of the patients showed improvement over the year. Ninety-one percent of the students themselves reported they became less anxious about working in a mental hospital, 90% reported a greater understanding of mental illness, 84% suggested feelings about mental hospital personnel had changed, and 97% of the students considered that their experiences had contributed to their personal growth. In another study (Holzberg et al., 1964), the effects of association with hospitalized mental patients on the personalities of 32 male college students were compared to a control group of 24 students who had not been involved with mental patients. Students in the Companion Program demonstrated significantly positive change in self-acceptance and in moral judgments concerning sexual and aggressive behaviors. Holzberg and Knapp (1965) have presented further evidence of positive effects upon Companions in their findings that after serving as Companions they are less frequently on academic probation and that they increase their introspective behavior.

More recently Holzberg, Knapp, and Turner (1967) have collected psychological test data so as to compare patients in the Companion Program with a group of control patients who were not. A relatively small sample of 13 Companion patients and 30 controls completed the Minnesota Multiphasic Personality Inventory (MMPI), Bender Gestaldt Designs, and Draw-a-Person before and after the program. Companion patients changed significantly on the Depression scale of the MMPI from pretest to posttest, and a similar difference on the Paranoid scale barely missed significance. The investigators are still studying data on the Bender Gestaldt Designs and Draw-a-Person to see if significant changes occurred in Companion patients on those instruments.

One may argue that college students volunteering for service as a Companion appear to change to a greater degree because they are more pathological at the time they volunteer than the average college student. Knapp and Holzberg (1964) have shown this not to be the case. A group of 85 male college students volunteering for service as Companions to chronically ill mental patients were compared to a group of 85 control students on a number of psychological tests administered during the students' freshman year. Tests included MMPI, Edwards Personal Preference Schedule, Allport-Vernon-Lindzey Scale of Values, the Scholastic Aptitude Test, and the Terman Concept Mastery Test. Students taking part in the Companion Program were shown not to be different from their control counterparts in any significant clinical respect, but there is evidence that the Companions are (a) slightly more religiously oriented, (b) more morally concerned, (c) more compassionate, and (d) more introverted than the control students. In a later study, volunteers were also differentiated from controls on academic variables such as their major area of study, frequency of disciplinary action, and fraternity affiliations (Holzberg et al., 1967).

Scheibe (1965) described a program which is similar to the Companion Program model except that students were assigned to work for a continuous 8-week period rather than once-a-week appearances over a year's time as required in the Companion Program. Students in the Service Corps Program of the State of Connecticut lived at the hospital and spent a normal working week with chronic patients for which they received $200 salary for the 2-month period. Students were not assigned to a specific patient but worked with all the patients on the ward in unstructured activities. Positive changes in the students' description of the typical mental patient were noted on Gough's Adjective Check List given at the beginning and at the end of the work period. In describing themselves on the Gough Adjective Check List, students exhibited significant gains in Achievement, Dominance, Self-Confidence, and Nurturance. There were no reported adverse effects on the college students as a result of working with the mental patients. Further, Greenblatt and Kantor's (1962b) findings were substantiated in that a crystallization of vocational goals appeared in a direction favorable to mental health.

Hersch, Kulik, and Scheibe (1969) subsequently published a more detailed study of personal characteristics of college volunteers in the Service Corps Program. One hundred fifty-one students serving in the Connecticut Service Corps and 142 controls enrolled in summer school at four Connecticut colleges were given a battery of tests and questionnaires including California Psychological Inventory, Gough Adjective Check List, Rotter Internal–External Small Scale, Marlowe-Crowne Social Desirability Scale, the Strong Vocational Interest Blank, and a biographical questionnaire. The striking personal characteristics of the college student volunteers were maturity and control, drive for independent achievement, and sensitivity to distressed individuals. On the Strong Vocational Interest Blank, their interests were similar to those in professions emphasizing social service. Autobiographical data further indicated that the college student volunteers were more service oriented and more dedicated to mental health service. The authors concluded that "data reported here suggest that participation in volunteer work is not motivated by overconcern with personal problems but rather is partly attributable to a controlled drive for independent achievement and sensitivity to human problems [p. 34]."

Lawton and Lipton (1963) reported on a project at Morristown State Hospital wherein six college students were employed full time. No training was given, but the students were instructed to devote all their efforts to creating highly personal relationships with individual patients. Based upon subjective reports of the students, positive changes were noted in individual patients.

Levine (1966) reported an investigation of the changes in attitude and behavior produced in students by a nonacademic, off-campus program which he suggested appeals to and puts to work the unenacted idealism of today's college youth. Recreational and social activities with the mental patients fostered more positive attitudes toward and increased interest in social action.

Poser's (1966) now classic study was designed to compare the effect of professional and untrained therapists. The untrained therapists were 11 college girls as well as two inpatients—none of whom had training in psychology. The professional therapists included psychiatrists, psychiatric social workers, and occupational therapists. Poser divided 343 male chronic schizophrenic patients into groups of 10 with each group matched as closely as possible with every other unit in terms of patient age, severity of illness, and length of hospitalization. Each of the groups were then assigned to a therapist picked at random. Each therapist met with his or her group for 1 hour each day, 5 days a week, over a period of 5 months. Both the trained and untrained therapists were free to conduct their therapy sessions as they wished. Results were interpreted using the difference in pretherapy and posttherapy scores on six different psychological tests. It was found that the college students achieved slightly better results than the professional mental health workers doing group therapy with similar patients.

Walker, Wolpin, and Fellows (1967) described a program which was a joint venture between Westmont College, Santa Barbara, and Camarillo State Hospital, Camarillo, California. Students received college credit for research and service activities involving direct contact with patients. Using a modified sentence-completion test for the students and subjective reports of the patients, they concluded that "we may be able to foster better personal developments as well as enrich school and college curricula while developing potential interest and entrance into the mental health field [p. 188]."

Spoerl (1968) reported on students from the University of Washington who volunteered to work on the psychiatric service of the University Hospital. In order to capitalize on the student spontaneity and imagination, no instructions were given except that the volunteers were to begin their relationship with patients on a peer basis. Volunteers could work with either individuals or groups. No objective evaluation of the student volunteer project on the patients is available, but questionnaires were given the ward staff and patients, and written reports were solicited from the volunteers. Most of the comments on the questionnaires and written reports were favorable to such an extent that the program has been enlarged to involve more volunteers and more patients.

Cowen (1969a) discussed an innovation in which college students are enrolled in a year-long seminar practicum in mental health. The first 2 months are used in examining current and past community mental health programs, and then the students, working in groups of six to eight each with a graduate student leader, begin service in one of three community settings: (a) a state hospital in which they encourage verbal and nonverbal interaction with chronic schizophrenic patients, (b) a school setting working with young students experiencing school adjustment problems, and (c) a settlement house with very young children who are exhibiting very slow social verbal development.

COLLEGE STUDENTS WITH CHILDREN

Many of the Companion Programs have special Children's Units, but, since children appear to be more malleable and become much more intensely involved with the student companion, volunteers for the Children's Units are usually subjected to a far greater amount of control than those working with adults. College students often prefer to work with children for a number of reasons. First, improvement in the younger patients is more easily observed even by naive volunteers. Also, students discover that in just a short time the children begin to respond positively to college students. Umbarger et al. (1962) reported that students working with the children felt less anxious about their own identity and more successful in their work than they did with the older patients. Students were apparently much more effective because they could act in a more relaxed and normal manner. Further, socially validated roles of big brother and big sister worked extremely well with the children while no such role was readily available with the adult patients.

Kreitzer (1969) used psychology majors who received course credit for their work with hospitalized emotionally disturbed children. Training consisted of completion of course work in psychopathology as well as a weekly 2-hour group supervision session. Measures included staff member ratings and teacher-rated changes in, or elimination of, inappropriate behavior. Many of the target behaviors were reduced or eliminated, and some of the student therapists involved called this the "highlight of their college experience."

Reinherz (1964) reported a project in which students from Radcliffe and Harvard volunteered for work at Massachusetts State Hospital working with children who were inpatients and who did not have severe behavioral problems. Volunteer college students spent one afternoon a week with the children after having met with a social work supervisor for 15 minutes ahead of time to receive a progress report of the child. During the first year of the program, ward psychiatrists reported improved functioning in three out of the four children in the program. In the second year, physicians reported change and progress in all seven patients, and, in several cases, psychological tests confirmed positive growth. At the end of the second year, two of the seven patients were ready for discharge, and a third had gone home on extended leave. Earlier, Reinherz (1962) had observed that some of the successes that college students have in working with emotionally disturbed children may be due to their having recently solved or left unsolved basic issues of maturation in their own lives. She noted that in late adolescence identity problems such as sex role and career choice are important developmental issues, and their successful resolution makes the difference between a productive and nonproductive adult role. Often it was observed that as the student aided the child in working out the problems of self-maturity, the student, too, appeared to be gaining a definitive solution for himself.

Fellows and Wolpin (1969) reported a project using teenage psychology trainees in a mental hospital. Four academically superior boys spent 4 days per week working with adolescent and preadolescent boys in a mental hospital. They were paid $50 per month for 2 months. Following a week of orientation at the hospital, the trainees began individual counseling on the adolescent male unit engaging in pilot conditioning procedures and conducting group therapy. Students were on their own except for 1 hour per day of permissive discussion with their supervisors. Measurement in the study was primarily subjective, with the authors reporting a particularly notable effect upon the patients in that the boys idealized the trainees and sought to copy whatever they did. More objectively, it is reported that a number of boys from this particular dormitory "have been placed in foster or group homes where they seem to be adjusting well, having learned some aspects of effective behavior from the trainees [p. 276]."

Heretofore the emphasis has been placed upon students working with an inpatient population in mental hospitals, but many day programs or outpatient programs have been initiated, particularly in caring for children. Belz, Drehmel, and Silvertsen (1967) suggested that volunteers are an essential ingredient in the ongoing functioning of a facility dedicated to the psychiatric treatment of children.

Brennan (1967) has shown that college students can be used as helpers in providing expanded mental health services for children. He pointed out that the attrition rate of children in guidance clinics has been found to be around 60% (Tuckman & Lavell, 1959). Although companionship may not replace certain diagnostic and treatment services, it does represent a service that parents and children will use. He based his suggestion on the low attrition rate of 12% for this particular study in which he used college students as Big Brothers. He concluded that college students may facilitate and enhance treatment of children with psychiatric problems.

Goodman (1967) has experimented with companionship therapy between college students and troubled boys. Male college students were trained in a 2½-day experimental workshop and were paid $1.40 per hour. After counselors were selected, they were divided into a "quiet" group an "outgoing" group, with half the quiet counselors being paired with boys evidencing quiet problems, that is, social introversion. The other half of the quiet counselors were paired with boys having outgoing problems, and the same procedure was followed for the group of outgoing counselors. Although only tentative findings are available, results suggest that boys with social introversion problems gain most from participating in the program. As in the Companion Programs, Goodman noted that his students manifested personality changes not unlike those reported by Holzberg (1963). Goodman's counselors showed a dramatic increase of interest in the behavior of children and in working with troubled people, and they reported that improvement occurred in the way they interact with friends. Differences between counselors and matched controls who did not participate in the Companion Program are significant. Nonparticipating controls were used so as to determine the effects on the counselor in working with children.

Mitchell (1966) has coined the term "amicatherapy" which he described "as a form of therapeutic intervention whereby layman volunteers relate in sustained friendship roles to troubled and disturbed persons under the guidance and supervision of professionals [p. 307]." He suggested that there may be advantages to using college students in amicatherapy since college students seem to have a particular knack for meeting the child in his own world. He postulated that this may be the case since students are not yet irrevocably committed to the adult world. After a student is chosen to work with a particular child, he sees a supervisor for an orientation interview and is instructed simply to make friends with the child. Clinical investigations of 74 children who participated in Mitchell's program have indicated "all of the children have benefited by their relationship with the student volunteers [p. 314]."

Stollak (1969) and Linden and Stollak (1969) have investigated the possibility of training college students as play therapists. In the former study, the students' role is modeled as closely as possible to that of a client-centered play therapist. The basic task is to be empathetic, understanding, nondirective, and to convey this understanding and acceptance to the child. Students were trained in 10 sessions during which they observed play therapy techniques and played with normal children. At the end of the tenth session, each student was assigned a child between the ages of 4

19

and 10 who were taken from the waiting list of the Lansing Child Guidance Clinic or the Psychology Clinic at Michigan State University. Stollak (1969) noted that undergraduates do significantly change their behavior during the sessions by increasing their reflection of content and clarification of feeling statements. Linden and Stollak (1969) concluded that communicated empathy is not an innate ability but must be taught. This has an important implication for the utilization of college students in mental health settings. If one adheres to the client-centered tenet that communication of accurate empathy is a necessary prerequisite for therapeutic movement, the turning loose of naive, untrained college students on a mental hospital is not as effective in producing therapeutic change as the same students might be if they were first taught to communicate the empathy they feel, that is, to make appropriate verbal statements.

Davison (1966) trained undergraduates as social reinforcers for autistic children at a private day care center; however, the results were less than significant when kind and degree of behavior change were used as the criteria for success. Less than 15 hours of the child's waking hours were spent in the program, and, since learning theory depends on environmental contingencies for factors that shape and maintain behavior, these results were not unexpected. One important finding which did emerge from this study, however, is that intelligent, motivated college students can be trained in a very short time to carry out a behavior control program that applies learning principles to the manipulation of psychotic behavior in children.

COLLEGE STUDENTS AS THERAPEUTIC AGENTS IN RELATED AREAS

Heretofore this study has focused upon college students as therapeutic agents in settings traditionally within the realm of mental health, that is, mental hospitals and psychological clinics. In recent years, however, mental health professionals have come to view other settings as legitimate surrounds for mental health workers. Cowen has headed a number of research efforts seeking prevention of emotional disorders in the school setting (Cowen, 1968; Cowen, 1969b; Cowen, Car-

lisle, & Kaufman, 1969; Cowen, Izzo, Miles, Telschow, Trost, & Zax, 1963; Cowen, Zax, Izzo, & Trost, 1966; Cowen, Zax, & Laird, 1966; Zax & Cowen, 1967). Cowen, Zax, and Laird (1966) selected 17 undergraduate volunteers to provide emotionally disturbed children with a meaningful relationship by pairing them with active, enthusiastic college students. Student volunteers had no training and were encouraged to foster a spontaneous, warm friendship with the child. For a variety of assumed reasons, none of the outcome measures discriminated between the experimental group of emotionally disturbed children. Certainly the short time the program was in effect (2 months) limited the number of contacts. Another reason there may have been no significant difference between the two groups is that the control group was simultaneously engaged in another program aimed at preventing emotional disturbance. There were significant changes among the volunteers, however, in that institutional concepts were no longer rated in a stereotypically positive way. Further, volunteers rated youngsters experiencing emotional difficulties in a more positive and accepting manner on a semantic differential. It will be recalled that similar changes toward more positive attitudes toward mental illness have been found to result from participation in Companion Programs (Holzberg & Gewirtz, 1963).

In another study, Cowen (1968) compared the effectiveness of two interventive programs —one using housewives, the other using college students. Both groups of volunteers worked with children experiencing emotional difficulties in a school setting. Two independent rating-scale evaluations were used to measure changes in behavior of the youngsters. Mean improvement scores of the two experimental groups combined were significantly greater than those of noncounseled control groups; however, only the group seen by the housewives was rated as significantly improved. Children seen by the college students were directionally better than controls, but the difference was not significant. Cowen postulated several reasons for this difference. First of all, the housewives were carefully screened, with the experimenter selecting only those applicants with attributes facilitating

20

interpersonal interactions with young children. The college student selection was based only on gross negative screening which eliminated the most obviously unsuited. Also, the housewives had 2 years experience in the schools, whereas the college students had no previous experience. Further, the housewives knew school personnel better and were generally better integrated in the school setting. Also, the schedules of housewives were more flexible, and they were available at a greater number of times than were the college students. The subjective impressions of school personnel were that these facts stacked the cards in favor of the housewives.

J. McV. Hunt (1969) discussed a model for psychology he called the Hall-Nebraska "Model" where students are involved in a "counselor-counselee" relationship with various kinds of people who exhibit a variety of problems of living in the community. Undergraduate college students became college pals to deprived children, teenagers, families, children in orthopedic hospitals, children in institutions for emotional disorders, high school dropouts, and juvenile delinquents. Undergraduate college pals established an ongoing relationship with an individual in one of the aforementioned categories and continued his contact throughout the school year. When the counselor left school, he introduced to his counselee a new counselor and observed and encouraged the new relationship. The college pal association has been particularly effective in the family project. This program deals with 21 children—7 in each of three families, each child having a "college pal." There is no control group other than the children of other families in the neighborhood. Children from the neighborhoods of these three families seldom complete high school, and one criterion of the success of the college pal project was the number of the children in the project who have completed high school. All students in this project who are old enough to have completed high school have done so. Further, all have had at least a try at college. As with other projects of this kind, a second measure of success is the effect upon the college student themselves. Hunt reported that not only does this type of project keep counselors from dropping out of college, but also the students are learning about human relationships by dealing directly with people who are having problems in the community. Moreover, they appear to be learning an amazing amount about research methodology, including the vernacular.

The Department of Health, Education, and Welfare (1966) has noted that students represent a large and relatively untapped source of volunteer manpower for institutions housing juvenile delinquents. It is suggested that college students may more easily break the psychological barriers that often separate juvenile delinquents from adult workers since alienated young people usually trust another young person more than they trust adults. In the probation program at Boulder, Colorado, college students are presently serving as tutors, interviewers, and discussion leaders for the delinquents.

Gorlich (1967) further postulated that the functions of student volunteers in institutions for delinquents are threefold. First, they prove to the delinquent that someone on the outside really cares about them. Also, college students provide the young person with a role model. Finally, the students can later help spread the word about institutional needs.

Zunker and Brown (1966) supported the idea that youth-to-youth counseling may be more effective than adult-to-youth counseling. A sample of 106 college freshman, half males and half females, received 6½ hours of academic adjustment guidance from same-sexed professional counselors. Trained under identical conditions, upperclassman student counselors gave equivalent guidance to all other beginning freshmen at Southwestern State Texas College. Student counselors also used identical guidance materials, followed identical counseling activity sequences, and were provided facilities equivalent to those used by the professional counselors. A matching sample of 80 men with 80 women was subsequently drawn from the freshmen receiving student-to-student counseling. Student counselors were found to be as effective as professional counselors on all criteria of counseling effectiveness; in fact, student counselors achieved significantly better results than did the professional counselors on the majority of variables used to measure the outcome of counseling. Furthermore, student counselors received a greater degree of acceptance from the counselees, and their counselees made significantly greater use of the information received during counseling as reflected by first semester grade point averages and residual study habits.

This review does not exhaust or should it limit consideration of the settings or situations in which college students can be used as therapeutic agents. Programs such as suicide prevention centers, groups for children of drug addicts or alcoholics, college sensitivity groups tutoring underprivileged children, teaching delinquent girls good grooming, visitations to the geriatric homes, and recreation therapy in schools for retarded children are all seeking motivated, sensitive individuals with innovative approaches who can fill their manpower need.

PROBLEMS OF USING STUDENT VOLUNTEERS

Not all of the literature concerning the use of student volunteers in the mental health field is positive. Umbarger et al. (1962) discussed the resistance of the mental hospital's ward staff to the student volunteer and attributed much of the resistance to staff jealousy; that is, students have time and opportunity for personal contact with the patients, whereas staff is kept busy with maintenance. An article in the *Pennsylvania Psychiatric Quarterly* (Volunteer Coordinators Resources, 1966) suggested that resistance to the volunteers occurs because of three reasons: (*a*) lack of information on the part of ward personnel, (*b*) insecurity on the part of the staff, and (*c*) the image of the volunteer as a nuisance rather than an intricate part of the program.

Haun (1968) raised a strong objection to the establishment of "lay administered ghettos for chronically ill," but Rioch (1966) suggested a flexible attitude and suggested that psychologists and psychiatrists are not exempt from feelings of jealousy.

If we have invested long years of hard work in achieving a high professional status, including many courses that were dull and many examinations that were nerve wracking, and we are told that some young bit of a girl with no training can do the job as well as or better than we can, it is natural that we should try to find some objections [Rioch, 1966, p. 291].

Reiff (1967) discussed the dangers of a power struggle between professionals and nonprofessionals and the tensions surrounding such struggles. Perhaps the power struggle has already begun as the problem of controls over nonprofessionals is considered by Blau (1969a). He suggested that professionals should begin now to ascertain kinds of control over nonprofessionals which can and should be established. He suggested that the controls would be not only to ensure protection of the service recipient but also to ensure the effectiveness of the service rendered.

Another practical problem concerning the use of college students as psychotherapeutic agents has to do with the kind and amount of training needed prior to student-patient contact. The question of training of nonprofessionals is a topic worthy of a separate review, and numerous experimenters have investigated the problem (Berenson, Carkhuff, & Myrus, 1966; Carkhuff, 1968; Felzer, Bullock, Kay, & Wolf, 1968; Hart, Kroll, Berkowitz, & Woolcock, 1968; Linden & Stollak, 1969; Parsons & Parker, 1968; Sines, Silver, & Lucero, 1961; Truax, 1967; Vesprani, 1969).

While their naiveté has previously been presented as a potential advantage of using college students, it also is possible that it will be a liability. The unsophisticated student could project his own difficulties onto his patients or burden the patient with his own personal problems. Without intending harm, the college student may be tempted to "play" at psychotherapy by asking personal questions and attempting to interpret the patient's verbalizations. An additional potential pitfall of using college students in the mental health setting is that they tend to be temporary participants who have a peak experience in a setting without future responsibility. Since they are not forced to realize or continue with the problems encountered by professionals, they may not feel the responsibility for the long-term welfare of the patient. A further possibility is that because they have nothing to lose, that is, professional status, they may exploit the position or relationship with the patient to satisfy their own needs.

There is also concern with the Hawthorne effect. There is no way of knowing to what degree the student's enthusiasm and dedication is a function of newness to the situation and/or professional attention. It is possible that the pessimistic institutional climate of the setting may serve to dampen the student's vigor after a few months. Not only the total efficacy of college students but their relative efficacy at the beginning and at varying periods of time should be investigated. If it is found then that the college student agents lose their enthusiasm after a certain period of time, the time each student is involved in a given program could be limited, thus giving the patients the advantage of only peak experiences of the student therapeutic agent. It is hoped, however, that the freshness and strengths of the college student will offset many of the inevitable difficulties created by their utilization. As Cowen (1967) reflected: "The mental health movement has probably suffered more from its errors of omission than from its errors of commission, and we would be well advised to begin to correct some of the former, even at risk of the latter [p. 431]."

SUMMARY

The most obvious findings of this review are that there are few studies dealing with college students as therapeutic agents, and, further, most of those investigations which have been conducted are so methodologically inadequate that it is impossible to draw firm conclusions about the relative effectiveness of college students as therapeutic agents.

The studies are plagued with inadequacies in design which are characteristic of psychological studies in general and of clinical studies in particular. But even more distressing is the fact that few of the investigations of efficacy of college students as therapeutic agents utilized even the basic necessities of scientific inquiry. For example, less than 25% boasted a control group of untreated counselees. Also, only 5 of these 19 studies used pre- and posttesting and only 5 of 19 used objective measures (Cowen, 1968; Cowen, Zax, & Laird, 1966; Poser, 1966; Zunker & Brown, 1966).

Another problem encountered in reviewing the literature in which college students are used as therapeutic agents is that few of the studies are similar enough in any respect to warrant conclusions in a given area. The populations of the studies are extremely diverse; for instance, Poser (1966) used chronic schizophrenics, Umbarger et al. (1962) used "chronic psychotics." Spoerl's (1968) population included hospitalized college students while Goodman's (1967) students worked with troubled boys. Stollak's (1969) play therapists worked with children of unstated diagnoses from Michigan State Psychological Clinic. Also among the studies there is little consistency as to the kind or the amount of training. College students in some studies were given no training (Ralph, 1968; Spoerl, 1968), while others were given very specific training (Linden & Stollak, 1969; Stollak, 1969; Zunker & Brown, 1966). Further, there was a great deal of difference in motivation among the students. Some students received monetary remuneration (Goodman, 1967; Poser, 1966; Scheibe, 1965); others received college credit (Umbarger et al., 1962); and still others received no extrinsic remuneration (Levine, 1966; Spoerl, 1968). There were also differences in the duration and frequency of students working. Some students worked one day a week (Spoerl, 1968; Umbarger et al., 1962) while others worked full time (Lawton & Lipton, 1963; Poser, 1966).

Although there are not enough data from well-controlled studies to warrant conclusions concerning the relative efficacy of college students as therapeutic agents to patients, there is sufficient evidence to conclude that the therapeutic relationship has a definite, positive effect upon the college student therapist. The studies supporting this conclusion are much more methodologically complete than those describing the effect of the student therapist on patients; for instance, more than 60% of the former studies utilized control groups of students who did not participate in mental health programs. Further, over 90% of the studies describing the effects upon student therapists as a result of working in mental health settings used pre- and posttests which were relatively objective.

Personality changes such as positive changes in self-acceptance and moral judgments of a sexual and aggressive nature, greater self-understanding, increased self-confidence, and enhanced identity formation have been noted by experimenters in college students participating in mental health programs. It is felt that these studies are valid and that working in mental health programs may foster personality development in students in college. It is expected that college students are not unique in manifesting these changes, but most studies of nonprofessionals in mental health, other than college students, have not focused on these personality changes. One explanation is that personality changes in noncollege student volunteers participating in a mental health program occur less frequently or are less intense than changes in student volunteers. It may be that college students are more open to change, since goals and interests have not yet crystallized.

Attempts to conceptualize and explain the personality changes which are not unlike those reported in psychotherapy have been undertaken by Holzberg, Knapp, and Turner (1966). They have presented four formulations. Their first formulation views the personality changes in the students as a function of a heightened sense of self-competence, while a second hypothesis suggests that changes occur as a function of an enlarged and more flexible system of personality constructs. The clarification of their self-concepts and identities is also seen as a basis for personality change. The fourth formulation suggests an "emotional catharsis." One of the interpretations presented of how catharsis takes place is that "certain emotions may be extinguished by saturation, just as certain persistent habits may be overcome through excessive practice [p. 404]."

Reiff and Riessman (1965) hypothesized that added responsibility for a meaningful job, as well as the satisfaction garnered from acquiring new skills, may account for positive personality changes in some nonprofessionals. There also may be an increase in status and prestige as a result of working with professionals which is incorporated into their self-concept. Furthermore, one may gain added stability and security by reasoning that one must be in good shape himself in order to be able to help others.

A final hypothesis to explain positive personality changes occurring in nonprofessionals is an enhanced self-concept from the knowledge that he can influence the life of others. The fact that he can effect positive change in others may be particularly important to the college student who often feels like a computer card in a multi-university. It should be pointed out that these formulations are preliminary and have value only if they can be stated operationally and submitted to a direct test under controlled conditions.

It is felt that college student volunteer programs in mental health serve a variety of functions, including the providing of meaningful educational experiences for college students, alleviating the manpower squeeze in mental health, enhancing student development programs, preparing future generations of American leaders for constructive roles in mental health, and last, but particularly important for the present, is the providing of students with an opportunity to effect real and meaningful changes in their environment —a constructive cause to which they can devote their energies.

A number of problems face college student volunteer programs in mental health. Acceptance by staff and even by professionals has improved, but resistance to college students acting as therapeutic agents still exists. Another very closely related problem is the definition of interaction appropriate to nonprofessional college student therapeutic agents. Still a third problem area for the college student mental health program is the question of the kind and amount of training. Most agree that some training is necessary even if it is in the form of weekly supervision meetings. Diversity of opinion abounds, however, on the question of the exact program of training. Further, there is the question of the kinds of controls to be established over the nonprofessionals— organizational and legal controls as well as supervisory controls.

The use of nonprofessionals in general and college students in particular offer promise in the effort to provide more complete mental health services to an ever increasing population. However, researchers must move quickly with sound research designs to establish a firm empirical basis for justification of the nonprofessional as well as for student development in working with distressed individuals.

REFERENCES

ALBEE, G. W. *Mental health manpower trends.* New York: Basic Books, 1959.

ALBEE, G. W. The relation of conceptual models to manpower needs. In E. L. Cowen, E. A. Gardner, & M. Zax (Eds.), *Emergent approaches to mental health problems.* New York: Appleton-Century-Crofts, 1967.

ALBEE, G. W. Conceptual models and manpower requirements in psychology. *American Psychologist,* 1968, **23,** 317–320.

ARNHOFF, F. N., & JENKINS, J. W. Subdoctoral education in psychology: A study of issues and attitudes. *American Psychologist,* 1969, **24,** 430–443.

ARNHOFF, F. N., RUBINSTEIN, E. A., & SPEISMAN, J. G. *Manpower for mental health.* Chicago: Aldine, 1969.

BECK, J. C., KANTOR, D., & GELINEAU, V. A. Follow-up study of chronic psychotic patients "treated" by college case-aide volunteers. *American Journal of Psychiatry,* 1963, **120,** 269–271.

BELZ, J. F., DREHMEL, V. W., & SIVERTSEN, A. D. Volunteer: The community's participant in treatment of schizophrenic children in a day care program. *American Journal of Orthopsychiatry,* 1967, **37,** 221–222.

BERENSON, B. G., CARKHUFF, R. R., & MYRUS, P. The interpersonal functioning and training of college students. *Journal of Counseling Psychology,* 1966, **13,** 441–446.

BLAU, T. H. The professional in the community views the nonprofessional helper. *Professional Psychology,* 1969, **1,** 25–31. (a)

BLAU, T. H. Psychologist views the helper. In C. Grosser, W. E. Henry, & J. G. Kelly (Eds.), *Nonprofessionals in the human services.* San Francisco: Jossey-Bass, 1969. (b)

BRENNAN, E. C. College students and mental health programs for children. *American Journal of Public Health,* 1967, **57,** 1767–1771.

CARKHUFF, R. R. Lay mental health counseling: Prospects and problems. *Journal of Individual Psychology,* 1968, **24,** 88–93.

CHRISTMAS, J. J. Group methods in training and practice: Nonprofessional mental health personnel in a deprived community. *American Journal of Orthopsychiatry,* 1966, **36,** 410–419.

COWEN, E. L. Emergent approaches to mental health problems: An overview and directions for future work. In E. L. Cowen, E. A. Gardner, & M. Zax (Eds.), *Emergent approaches to mental health problems.* New York: Appleton-Century-Crofts, 1967.

COWEN, E. L. Effectiveness of secondary prevention programs using nonprofessionals in the school setting. *Proceedings of the 76th Annual Convention of the American Psychological Association,* 1968, **3,** 705–706.

COWEN, E. L. Combined graduate-undergraduate training in community mental health. *Professional Psychology,* 1969, **1,** 72–73. (a)

COWEN, E. L. Mothers in the classroom. *Psychology Today,* 1969, **3**(7), 36–39. (b)

COWEN, E. L., CARLISLE, R. L., & KAUFMAN, G. Evaluation of a college student volunteer program with primary graders experiencing school adjustment problems. *Psychology in the Schools,* 1969, **6,** 371–375.

COWEN, E. L., IZZO, L. D., MILES. H., TELSCHOW, E. F., TROST, M. A., & ZAX, M. A preventive mental health program in the school setting: Description and evaluation. *Journal of Psychology,* 1963, **56,** 307–356.

COWEN, E. L., LEIBOWITZ, G., & LEIBOWITZ, E. The utilization of retired people as mental health aides in the schools. *American Journal of Orthopsychiatry,* 1968, **38,** 900–910.

COWEN, E. L., ZAX, M., IZZO, L. D., & TROST, M. A. Prevention of emotional disorders in the school setting: A further investigation. *Journal of Consulting Psychology,* 1966, **30,** 381–387.

COWEN, E. L., ZAX, M., & LAIRD, J. D. A college student volunteer program in the elementary school setting. *Community Mental Health Journal,* 1966, **2,** 319–328.

DAVISON, G. C. The training of undergraduates as social reinforcers for autistic children. In L. Ullmann & L. Krasner (Eds.), *Case studies in behavior modification.* New York: Holt, Rinehart & Winston, 1966.

DEPARTMENT OF HEALTH, EDUCATION, AND WELFARE. Welfare Administration: Antidelinquency project measures effectiveness of volunteers. *Welfare in Review,* **4,** March 1966.

DONAHUE, G. T., & NICHTERN, S. *Teaching the troubled child.* New York: Free Press, 1965.

ERIKSON, E. H. Identity and the life cycle: Selected papers. *Psychological Issues,* 1959, **1,** 1–171.

FELLOWS, L., & WOLPIN, M. High school psychology trainees in a mental hospital. In B. G. Guerney, Jr. (Ed.), *Psychotherapeutic agents: New roles for nonprofessionals, parents, and teachers.* New York: Holt, Rinehart & Winston, 1969.

FELZER, S. B., BULLOCK, S., KAY, D., & WOLF, A. Mental health training program for community workers. *Proceedings of the 76th Annual Convention of the American Psychological Association,* 1968, **3,** 711–712.

GOODMAN, G. An experiment with companionship therapy: College students and troubled boys—assumptions, selection, and design. *American Journal of Public Health,* 1967, **57,** 1772–1777.

GORLICH, E. H. Volunteers in institutions for delinquents. *Children,* 1967, **14,** 147–150.

GREENBLATT, M., & KANTOR, D. An introduction. In C. Umbarger, J. Dalsimer, A. Morrison, & P. Breggin (Eds.), *College students in a mental hospital.* New York: Grune & Stratton, 1962. (a)

GREENBLATT, M., & KANTOR, D. Student volunteer movement and the manpower shortage. *American Journal of Psychiatry,* 1962, **118,** 809–814. (b)

GROSSER, C., HENRY, W. E., & KELLY, J. G. (Eds.) *Nonprofessionals in the human services.* San Francisco: Jossey-Bass, 1969.

HART, N. J., KROLL, M., BERKOWITZ, D., & WOOLCOCK, J. Assessment of demonstration community mental health program by its nonprofessional workers. *Proceedings of the 76th Annual Convention of the American Psychological Association*, 1968, **3**, 713–714.

HARTOG, T. Nonprofessionals as mental health consultants. *Hospital and Community Psychiatry*, 1967, **18**, 223–225.

HAUN, P. The future role of state mental institutions. *Psychiatric Quarterly*, 1968, **42**, 1–16.

HERSCH, P. D., KULIK, J. A., & SCHEIBE, K. E. Personal characteristics of college volunteers in mental hospitals. *Journal of Consulting and Clinical Psychology*, 1969, **33**, 30–34.

HIRSCH, I. S. Training mothers in groups as reinforcement therapists for their own children. *Dissertation Abstracts*, 1968, **28**, 4756B.

HOCH, E. L., ROSS, A. O., & WINDER, C. L. Conference on the professional preparation of clinical psychologists: A summary. *American Psychologist*, 1966, **21**, 42–51.

HOLAND, M. W., & VOSS, F. H. Nontraditional assignments for volunteers. *Hospital and Community Psychiatry*, 1968, **19**, 221.

HOLZBERG, J. D. The companion program: Implementing the manpower recommendations of the joint commission on mental illness and health. *American Psychologist*, 1963, **18**, 224–226.

HOLZBERG, J. D., & GEWIRTZ, H. A method of altering attitudes toward mental illness. *Psychiatric Quarterly Supplement*, 1963, **37**, 56–61.

HOLZBERG, J. D., GEWIRTZ, H., & EBNER, E. Changes in moral judgment and self-acceptance as a function of companionship with hospitalized mental patients. *Journal of Consulting Psychology*, 1964, **28**, 299–303.

HOLZBERG, J. D., & KNAPP, R. H. The social interaction of college students and chronically ill patients. *American Journal of Orthopsychiatry*, 1965, **35**, 487–492.

HOLZBERG, J. D., KNAPP, R. H., & TURNER, J. L. Companionship with the mentally ill: Effects on the personalities of college student volunteers. *Psychiatry*, 1966, **29**, 395–405.

HOLZBERG, J. D., KNAPP, R. H., & TURNER, J. L. College students as companions to the mentally ill. In E. L. Cowen, E. A. Gardner, & M. Zax (Eds.), *Emergent approaches to mental health problems.* New York: Appleton-Century-Crofts, 1967.

HOLZBERG, J. D., WHITING, H. S., & LOWY, D. G. Chronic patients and a college companion program. *Mental Hospitals*, 1964, **15**, 152–158.

HUNT, J. McV. Message, potpourri and the Hall-Nebraska "model." *Clinical Psychologist*, 1969, **22**, 127–136.

JOHNSTON, R. Some casework aspects of using foster grandparents for emotionally disturbed children. *Children*, 1967, **14**, 46–52.

KANTOR, D. Inducing preferences for mental health careers. *National Association of Social Workers*, 1959, 75.

KANTOR, D. Impact of college students on chronic mental patients and on the organization of the mental hospital. *Proceedings of the College Stu-*

dent Companion Program Conference. Stratford, Conn.: Connecticut State Department of Mental Health, 1962.

KENISTON, K. College students and children in developmental institutions. *Children*, 1967, **14**, 2–7.

KNAPP, R. H., & HOLZBERG, J. D. Characteristics of college students volunteering for service to mental patients. *Journal of Consulting Psychology*, 1964, **28**, 82–85.

KNOTT, P. D. On the manpower problem and graduate training in clinical psychology. *American Psychologist*, 1969, **24**, 675–679.

KREITZER, S. F. College students in a behavior therapy program with hospitalized emotionally disturbed children. In B. G. Guerney, Jr. (Ed.), *Psychotherapeutic agents: New roles for nonprofessionals, parents, and teachers.* New York: Holt, Rinehart & Winston, 1969.

LAWTON, M. P., & LIPTON, M. B. Student-employees become companions to patients. *Mental Hospitals*, 1963, **14**, 550–556.

LEVINE, C. Impact of work with mental patients on student volunteers. *Journal of Human Relations*, 1966, **14**, 422–433.

LINDEN, J. I., & STOLLAK, G. E. The training of undergraduates in play techniques. *Journal of Clinical Psychology*, 1969, **25**, 213–218.

MADISON, P. *Personality development in college.* Reading, Mass.: Addison-Wesley, 1969.

MITCHELL, W. E. Amicatherapy: Theoretical perspectives and an example of practice. *Community Mental Health Journal*, 1966, **2**, 307–314.

NICHTERN, S., DONAHUE, G. T., O'SHEA, J., MARANS, M., CURTIS, M., & BRODY, C. A community educational program for the emotionally disturbed child. *American Journal of Orthopsychiatry*, 1964, **34**, 705–713.

PARSONS, L. B., & PARKER, G. V. Personal attitudes, clinical appraisals, and verbal behavior of trained and untrained therapists. *Journal of Consulting Psychology*, 1968, **32**, 64–71.

PATTERSON, G. R., & BRODSKY, G. A behavior modification programme for a child with multiple problem behaviors. *Journal of Child Psychology*, 1966, **7**, 277–295.

PEARL, A., & RIESSMAN, F. (Eds.) *New careers for the poor: The nonprofessional in human service.* New York: Free Press, 1965.

PERLMUTTER, F., & DURHAM, D. Using teen-agers to supplement casework service. *Social Work*, 1965, **10**, 41–48.

POSER, E. The effect of therapists' training on group therapeutic outcome. *Journal of Consulting Psychology*, 1966, **30**, 283–289.

RALPH, D. E. Attitudes toward metal illness among two groups of college students in neuropsychiatric hospital setting. *Journal of Consulting and Clinical Psychology*, 1968, **32**, 98.

REDING, G. R., & GOLDSMITH, E. F. The nonprofessional hospital volunteer as a member of the psychiatric consultation team. *Community Mental Health Journal*, 1967, **3**, 267–272.

REIFF, R. Mental health manpower and institutional change. In E. L. Cowen, E. A. Gardner, & M. Zax (Eds.), *Emergent approaches to mental health problems*. New York: Appleton-Century-Crofts, 1967.

REIFF, R., & RIESSMAN, F. The indigenous nonprofessional: A strategy of change in community action and community mental health programs. *Community Mental Health Journal*, 1965, Monograph No. 1.

REINHERZ, H. Group leadership of student volunteers. *Mental Hospitals*, 1962, **13**, 600–603.

REINHERZ, H. The therapeutic use of student volunteers. *Children*, 1964, **2**, 137–142.

RIOCH, M. J. Changing concepts in the training of therapists. *Journal of Consulting Psychology*, 1966, **30**, 290–292.

RIOCH, M. J., ELKES, C., FLINT, A. A., USDANSKY, B. S., NEWMAN, R. G., & SILBER, E. National Institute of Mental Health pilot study in training mental health counselors. *American Journal of Orthopsychiatry*, 1963, **33**, 678–689.

ROGERS, C. R. The necessary and sufficient conditions of therapeutic personality change. *Journal of Consulting Psychology*, 1957, **21**, 95–103.

ROSENBAUM, M. Some comments on the use of untrained therapists. *Journal of Consulting Psychology*, 1966, **30**, 292–294.

SANFORD, N. Higher education as a social problem. In N. Sanford (Ed.), *The American college*. New York: Wiley, 1962.

SAVINO, M. T., & SCHLAMP, F. T. The use of nonprofessional rehabilitation aides in decreasing rehospitalization. *California Mental Health Research Digest*, 1967, **5**, 254–256.

SCHEIBE, K. E. College students spend eight weeks in mental hospital: A case report. *Psychotherapy: Theory, Research and Practice*, 1965, **2**, 117–120.

SINES, L. I., SILVER, R. J., & LUCERO, R. J. The effect of therapeutic intervention by untrained "therapists." *Journal of Clinical Psychology*, 1961, **17**, 394–396.

SPOERL, O. H. An activity-centered volunteer program for university students. *Hospital and Community Psychiatry*, 1968, **19**, 114–116.

STOLLAK, G. E. The experimental effects of training college students as play therapists. In B. G. Guerney, Jr. (Ed.), *Psychotherapeutic agents: New roles for nonprofessionals, parents, and teachers*. New York: Holt, Rinehart & Winston, 1969.

STOVER, L., & GUERNEY, JR., B. G. The efficacy of training procedures for mothers in filial therapy. *Psychotherapy: Theory, Research and Practice*, 1967, **4**, 110–115.

TRUAX, C. B. The training of nonprofessional personnel in therapeutic interpersonal relationships. *American Journal of Public Health*, 1967, **57**, 1778–1791.

TRUAX, C. B., & WARGO, D. G. Psychotherapeutic encounters that change behavior: For better or for worse. *American Journal of Psychotherapy*, 1966, **20**, 499–520.

TUCKMAN, J., & LAVELL, M. Attrition in psychiatric clinics for children. *Public Health Report*, 1959, **74**, 309–315.

UMBARGER, C. C., DALSIMER, J. S., MORRISON, A. P., & BREGGIN, P. R. *College students in a mental hospital.* New York: Grune & Stratton, 1962.

VESPRANI, G. J. Personality correlates of accurate empathy in a college companion program. *Journal of Consulting and Clinical Psychology*, 1969, **33**, 722–727.

VOLKMAN, R., & CRESSEY, D. R. Differential association and the rehabilitation of drug addicts. In F. Riessman, J. Cohen, & A. Pearl (Eds.), *Mental health of the poor*. New York: Free Press, 1964.

VOLUNTEER COORDINATORS RESOURCES. Direction of change: Facets of volunteer resources. *Pennsylvania Psychiatric Quarterly*, 1966, **6**, 48–58.

WAHLER, R. G., WINKEL, G. H., PETERSON, R. F., & MORRISON, D. C. Mothers as behavior therapists for their own children. *Behavior Research and Therapy*, 1965, **3**, 113–124.

WALKER, C. E., WOLPIN, M., & FELLOWS, L. The use of high school and college students as therapists and researchers in a state mental hospital. *Psychotherapy: Theory, Research and Practice*, 1967, **4**, 186–188.

YABLONSKY, L., & DEDERICH, C. E. Synanon: As a program for training ex-offenders as therapeutic agents. In, *Experiment in culture expansion*. Sacramento, Calif.: California Department of Corrections, 1963.

ZAX, M., & COWEN, E. L. Early identification and prevention of emotional disturbance in a public school. In E. L. Cowen, E. A. Gardner, & M. Zax (Eds.), *Emergent approaches to mental health problems*. New York: Appleton-Century-Crofts, 1967.

ZIMMERMAN, E. H., & ZIMMERMAN, J. The alteration of behavior in a special classroom situation. *Journal of the Experimental Analysis of Behavior*, 1962, **5**, 59–60.

ZUNKER, V. G., & BROWN, W. F. Comparative effectiveness of student and professional counselors. *Personnel and Guidance Journal*, 1966, **44**, 738–743.

27

II. THE CONTRIBUTIONS OF STUDENT VOLUNTEERS

THE ROLE OF VOLUNTEERS IN COMMUNITY MENTAL HEALTH PROGRAMS

ABRAHAM A. CHAPLAN, M.D., JOHN M. PRICE, JR., M.D.
ISADORE ZUCKERMAN, M.S.W. AND JON EK, B.A.

Volunteers can be a valuable asset to a community mental health program. A training program is indicated to widen their usefulness and appreciation. Training should include didactic material relevant to areas where they will be working and it should also be used as an assessment of resources that are brought to the program by the volunteers. Volunteers should actively participate in program planning. There is some indication that "communication" between the volunteer and the community rather than the professional workers and the community is most effective. Professional time can be employed more usefully in supervision and in training of volunteers.

Volunteers have proven their importance in mental hospitals (Wolff, 1960). It is only recently that their role in guidance clinics has extended beyond clerical tasks. As Malamud (1955, p. 300) points out, "The concept of the volunteer in community mental health programs is less clearly defined."

THE QUEENS CHILD GUIDANCE CENTER

Since 1963, the Queens Child Guidance Center has been exploring the role of volunteers in their Community Psychiatry Division and some guidelines have been established for the effective utilization of volunteers.

The Queens Child Guidance Center is a group of outpatient child guidance clinics which provide service to the borough of Queens, New York City. The Center has been in operation since 1954 and is financed by voluntary funds and the New York City Community Mental Health Board.

Staff consists of child psychiatrists, psychologists, and psychiatric social workers. Services offered to children and their parents consist of dynamically oriented psychotherapy.

To reach larger numbers of children in need of help, the Center formed a Division of Community Psychiatry in 1963.

AIMS OF THE DIVISION

Services for a Wider Range of Problems

A large number of children were not amenable to usual clinic services. This group included children whose parents were not motivated to bring them to the clinic for services and diagnostic categories

COMMUNITY MENTAL HEALTH JOURNAL, 1966, vol. 2, no. 3, pp. 255-258.

with which the clinic could not cope: delinquent behavior, organic impairment, mental retardation, very young children, and children with specific learning disabilities.

A major goal of the Community Psychiatry Division was to embark on a program of preventive psychiatry aimed to intercept problems of youngsters before they became sufficiently developed to require clinical treatment. It was also felt that the Community Psychiatry Division could work with groups of youngsters as a preliminary to clinical intervention to assess need and motivation for treatment, and to serve in an educative role to youngsters and their families.

Mental Health Resource for the Community

Many organizations made up of both professional and lay groups are also developing programs in the community. The Queens Child Guidance Center coordinated its activities with these groups.

In this capacity, the Community Psychiatry Division functioned as (a) advisors to community organizations in focusing their efforts; (b) collaborators, by sharing with these organizations; (c) as a funnel for support, both in material and manpower for use in our own programs; (d) and finally as catalysts in bringing certain organizations into meaningful working relationships, sometimes by simply providing a neutral meeting ground for them.

A Channel for Other Disciplines

Working in a traditional guidance center where the focus is on the individual, there is little chance for an anthropologist or sociologist to apply their skills. Yet, their disciplines have much to contribute to understanding the community as a vital entity. With its focus on the community, the Division provided a meaningful framework within which these disciplines could operate. The assistance to the Division in understanding the organization, structure, and mores of the communities involved, permitted the clinical staff to assess the influences these factors might have on the youngsters' problems.

ROLE OF THE VOLUNTEERS

Malamud (1955, P. 301) defines a volunteer as "anyone who contributes services outside his regular job and without payment for these services beyond occasional expenses. Thus, the volunteer may be a lay person, a professional person outside the field of psychiatry, or a professional worker with specific training in any of the various psychiatric disciplines."

Volunteers in our program are drawn from a variety of sources. Philanthropically oriented women's organizations have involved themselves in direct service programs in the community for many years. These programs include teacher aides, remedial reading assistants, and rehabilitation of handicapped children.

To adapt this growing interest to the Community Psychiatry Division goals listed above, it was necessary to conduct an intensive training program for volunteers. This was adopted to make the program's operations more effective and to increase the scope of the volunteers' usefulness as well as their personal satisfaction.

The training program consisted of 15 two hour seminars which covered normal and abnormal child development, cross cultural differences, the effects of cultural deprivation on personality development, and a clarification of the goals of the Division to the participants. Many of the anxieties shown by the volunteers in anticipation of working with culturally deprived or disturbed children were dealt with in these seminars. These discussions were illuminating to the professional staff who had become accustomed to working with problem children. It was fascinating to see the many stereotypes that existed in the minds of intelligent participants who were preparing to work with children who were in need of help.

A common expression of anxiety was shown in their own self criticism. Every conceivable flaw they felt they had was examined to see if it would disqualify them from working with the children.

In retrospect, many difficult situations were avoided by "anticipatory guidance".

The ease with which these volunteers could subsequently adapt to the programs and their work with the children has given us reason to conclude that the time was well spent. It certainly enhanced the commitment of the participants.

Several of the volunteers were selected because they held key positions in philanthropic organizations (e.g., presidents and executive members of philanthropic organizations). Others were affiliated with a wide variety of organizations. A few were derived from the lay board of the Center. These volunteers, when trained, became resource people to their own organizations.

VOLUNTEER PROGRAMS

In keeping with the aims of the Division, the volunteers were introduced to key community leaders. These included the following: school superintendents; youth board staff; local community center staffs; board of education special programs representatives; and local ministers. The volunteers participated in discussions with these community leaders. Some of the contacts were made through field visits, some through invitations to the leaders to attend the seminars and to address the volunteers. This served two purposes: it gave the volunteers a first hand appraisal of the overall problems in the community; it also served to help them select a problem area where they would feel most effective and comfortable in which to work. Volunteers were then assisted in working out projects. These projects were developed with two major considerations:

1. Each project was viewed as a pilot program which, if successful, would serve as a model for other volunteer groups. Unique skills or unusual circumstances were avoided in order to facilitate duplication of these projects.
2. Each project was designed to draw volunteers from the community being served to work along with volunteers from the general community. This served to train leadership within the area which would eventually be able to carry the project on its own.

Implementation

Junior Guidance Program. The Junior Guidance Program in the Board of Education is a special program consisting of early detection of guidance problems and provides special classrooms for youngsters from grades two to six who are not amenable to regular classroom instruction. Three classroom teachers are provided for two classes thus allowing a certain amount of free time for the teachers to attend conferences and to provide individual attention. In consultation with the staff of this program, additional help in remedial reading was thought to be needed. Trained volunteers were then assigned to these classes throughout the borough of Queens and each volunteer worked directly with youngsters selected by the teachers. These volunteers were supervised by Board of Education personnel. Specific problems and questions arising in relation to the emotional needs of the youngsters were discussed with the community psychiatry staff at regular seminars.

Remedial reading program. The Community Mental Health Board was eager for the Center to begin community programming in the South Jamaica area, a low income Negro area in Queens. Although the Jamaica Clinic is near this area, there has been little utilization of clinic facilities by these residents. Community psychiatry programs in this area aimed to start projects related to the needs of the area and to increase the motivation of the residents to use the clinical services. The Bethany Baptist Church agreed to cosponsor a remedial reading program in the church for any of the youngsters in the community. This project was staffed by volunteers drawn from the adult congregation of the church in collaboration with outside volunteers.

Following the training program, 18 Negro volunteers and 18 white volunteers provided remedial reading instruction to a group of 36 youngsters from the church and the community. The program was supervised by the Division of Community Psychiatry, which undertook to provide the remedial reading expert and the technical staff to implement the project. Organizational details were handled by both the church staff and the volunteer staff.

The key to success of this program stemmed from the fact that this Negro community was readily "reachable" through their church affiliation. Many of the other programs which have been initiated in the area under the sponsorship of more official agencies—such as the schools —did not receive the same attendance or enthusiastic support. Reinforcement of the minister seemed to be crucial in gaining the acceptance and participation of parents to bring their children to the church for instruction. Liaison between this program and the schools was undertaken by the Guidance Center staff. There was a "working relationship" between this program and the youngsters' regular classroom instruction. Other churches and ministers in the area were invited to observe the project and in the near future similar programs will be started. This project served a secondary purpose of bringing Negro volunteers into a close working relationship with white volunteers.

Prekindergarten program. The Union Methodist Church in South Jamaica was seeking to establish a nursery program but was unable to do on its own. The National Council of Jewish Women, who were able to contribute the complete furnishings for a prekindergarten program, was put in touch with the church. The clinic was eager to have a nursery program to augment its own services. Thus, all three agencies were able to bring about a project that neither one could have effected on its own. While the present program caters to "normal" children, it will soon be made available to disturbed children (organically impaired and mentally retarded) through a new facility to be opened by the Queens Child Guidance Center. In this instance a community project facilitated the expansion of the clinical services.

The prekindergarten program also served as an area for training volunteers and mothers in early childhood development. During the early period of its operation, the Division of Community Psychiatry was instrumental in setting up this project and provided the administrative and teaching staff with the understanding that the church would assume the responsibility for the future administration of the project.

Thursday Club. The Junior Guidance Program staff described above were so impressed with the calibre of volunteers available that they asked us to set up an after school program for youngsters dismissed from school at 2:30 p.m.

We learned that the Forest Hills Chapter of the National Council of Jewish Women operated a "Golden Age Club" in Forest Hills, and that their facility was not used two afternoons a week. Chapter volunteers, with our aid, set up a Thursday Club for girls and began a homemaking class for them. The attendance was excellent. An esprit developed early and the school noted a difference in the general adjustment of the girls in the classroom. This program, once started, required minimum supervision of the Community Psychiatry Division and received a special commendation from the New York State Hygiene Department.

REFERENCES

MALAMUD, IRENE, T. Volunteers in community mental health work. *Ment. Hyg.*, *N.Y.*, 1955, **39**, 300-309.

WOLFF, K. *Ment. Hyg.*, *N.Y.*, 1960, **44**, 206-209.

Case Studies of Volunteer Programs in Mental Health

Leslie J. Cowne, Ed.D.

A critical need for health manpower exists in many communities. Our population is increasing more rapidly than our mental health training resources, and it is highly unlikely that professional and institutional education will be able to narrow the gap within the next ten years. Volunteers can be an important part of the total effort, very often providing far more than traditional professionals expect of them. Under professional supervision, well trained and carefully selected volunteers can assume major responsibilities for persons in distress. This source of manpower is still not being tapped fully.

In my survey of new approaches to mental health manpower problems last year, I obtained data on some 600 programs, including 200 programs using volunteers in the mental health field. Of these volunteer programs, six were selected for panel presentation at a Mental Health Manpower Showcase Conference in Washington, D.C. in February 1970, and a further twelve programs were presented in round-table discussions. These programs show how the educated volunteer can function in a variety of settings at a level comparable with professionally trained persons.

The Community Friend Project of the California Association for Mental Health provides someone in the community, either before the patient leaves the hospital or immediately upon arrival in the community, to establish a continuing, encouraging relationship during the first three crucial months of readjustment to community life. Making a successful adjustment to living outside the hospital demands of a person some of the very resources, strengths and initiative that have been reduced or crippled by his sojourn in the hospital—and requires these resources at a time when he may be least able to call on them. A volunteer can function in this role because he is not a social worker or some other professional with a heavy case load. He is working with only one patient. The volunteer is also seen differently by the ex-patient as compared to the paid worker.

The training program for the Com-

MENTAL HYGIENE, July 1970, vol. 54, no. 3, pp. 337-346.

munity Friend project was worked out during a year-long pilot project. Changes were made as needed. Training now takes place in five or six sessions before the Community Friend begins his job and he continues under ongoing supervision, both individually and in a group, with other Community Friends.

The Community Friend is supervised by a Mental Health Association supervisor regarding specific questions about the convalescent relationship and the program. Some of the volunteer supervisors are retired social workers, or others with supervisory experience in volunteer services. One of the most critical parts of the program is liaison with the hospital and constant contact with agency personnel at the adminstrative level.

Since 1968, when the program was started, 50 persons have been trained and used. There is opportunity for Community Friends to become supervisors, trainers, or to take part in other aspects of the administration of the project. However, many prefer to remain in the one-to-one, time-limited relationship of being a Community Friend.

The Mental Health Association experienced no real problem in establishing this service except for professional unfamiliarity with the "new" program, which is to be expected despite continued publicizing of it, and changes in the after-care procedures resulting from California's new mental health legislation which became effective in July 1969 and made acceptance of the program slow at first. Occasionally, problems have arisen when the carefully designed initial guidelines were not followed correctly.

Evaluation of this program is being carried out under the supervision of the Director of Research of one of the state mental hospitals. The four major demonstration programs will continue through June 1970. At that time, revised guidelines will be worked out to enable other Mental Health Association Chapters to undertake the Community Friend projects.

The Mental Health Case Aide Program at the Metropolitan State Hospital in Massachusetts started in 1964 and involved volunteers working under the supervision of social workers in the hospital. It is sponsored by the Mystic Valley Mental Health Association. The Case Aides chosen are mature, selected women volunteers who commit themselves to a minimum of one morning a week working on a one-to-one basis with chronic hospitalized mental patients to aid their re-socialization and, hopefully, their return to life outside the hospital. The social workers select and match patients to Case Aide volunteers.

There is no training prior to the Case Aide's meeting with her patient for the first time. However, there is continuous on-the-job supervision provided by the social workers during the group sessions which are held weekly after the Case Aides have spent time with their patients. The Case Aides meet in groups of 12 with their social worker for lectures, and sessions with other mental health professionals to discuss the progress they are making with their patients and the problems they are encountering. After each weekly meeting with the patient, the Aide writes a detailed report of activities, the topics discussed, and personal reactions. The Aide and the social worker evaluate these reports together in monthly conferences.

Since the inception of the program, 143 Case Aides have been involved; each for a minimum of one year, many for two or more years, and several for four to five years. Several Case Aides have gone on to graduate studies in the health professions

33

and many have taken full-time paid work in the field.

There were no significant obstacles in establishing the program. The hospital staff had been skeptical at the beginning, but was prepared to go along and see how it would work out. Since each step was carefully studied and planned in advance, the professional personnel of the hospital have become convinced that the program is an asset.

No formal evaluation procedures have been applied. The criteria for success were simply the number of patients worked with, compared with the number who have been able to leave the hospital and function satisfactorily in the outside world, and the feedback from the volunteers of their feelings concerning the value of the program to them and the incomparable experience that it offers. Because of the success of this program, it is expected that the State Department of Mental Health will provide some budget to the hospital so that this can become a permanent part of the hospital planning for the patients. The Case Aide Committee which now administers the program will then continue to operate in an advisory and supportive capacity to the social worker staff of the program.

The Home Training Program for young mentally ill children on the waiting list of the League School for Seriously Disturbed Children in Brooklyn, New York, involves the paid professional staff of the school, who work directly with the parents of the young mentally ill children. The parents function as volunteers. These "volunteers" observe the weekly demonstration teaching sessions of their own child and his specially trained teacher and thus learn effective methods of child rearing and behavior management which they are able to make use of on a day-to-day basis in their own homes. To help them clarify and generalize what they see, the parents also have weekly meetings in small groups with the director and the social worker. These discussions are developmentally oriented and attention is focused on self-help skills, socialization, speech and language stimulation, and pre-academic skills.

The number of programs for very young, very sick children is insufficient for the demands now generated and this program was initiated to provide services for such children on the waiting list for admission to the school. Frequently, children as sick as the ones currently served in this program, are excluded from programs designed for the mentally ill young. The only requirement for entry into the program is that the parents need these services, and that they agree to bring themselves and their child at the appointed times.

Since 1966, when the program was started, this service has been made available to more than 100 families. The success of this program can be gauged by the ability of these parents to function more effectively, not only with their difficult sick children, but with their healthy children as well. In many cases, it has freed the parents to the degree that they have been able to get jobs or return to courses of study.

This program has been funded by both the school, National Institute of Mental Health, and the New York City Community Mental Health Board. Evaluation was built into the design of the project. The children of both the control and experimental groups received thorough pre- and post-evaluation on a number of measures. As a result of exposure to this program, the improvements in the experimental group were significantly greater than the improvements made by the control group. Parents also reported increased self-assurance in handling their children.

34

Initially, there was considerable skepticism about the possible effectiveness of such short term intervention. However, because of its success, the program will be continued as an integral part of League School Community Service. It will also serve as the model for other similar programs.

The Community Lodge Treatment Program for Mental Patients—Michigan. Since its inception as an experimental project on the West Coast in 1963, this program has been imitated and implemented in other parts of the country. Research revealed that post-hospital adjustment of patients who remained out of the hospital longest was best for those who were employed and who had a socially supportive living situation within the community. Post-hospital adjustment was unrelated to hospital behavior, but was highly related to the post-hospital social situation in which the patient found himself.

The object of a community lodge society is to create a productive and supportive work-living situation and to provide a total community social sub-system for the rehabilitation of the patients. The three basic goals are to provide members with social support from the group of former patients who live with them, to create a feeling of responsibility among the members of the group for each other's welfare, and to develop a social situation which will promote autonomous decision-making on the part of each member. The essential characteristic of a "lodge" is that there are no "live-in" staff; only lodge staff that are on call. That is, only lodge staff members contact the hospital when the need arises; only technical skills or knowledge, where these are lacking within the lodge members, are requested from outside. An important criterion for selecting the patients for a community lodge program is that the therapeutic need of the long-term patients be balanced with the need to establish a desirable group composition. Thus, the selection of the lodge members is based on the patient's inability to live in the community without a socially supportive situation, and his inability to work in the competitive labor force. Members must have differing degrees of maladjustment. While some may have gross psychotic symptoms, others should be relatively symptom free. This allows leaders to rise from the less handicapped who can take charge of the group.

All members must be given a part in the lodge operation, with concomitant responsibilities and with attainable behavioral expectations (although some latitude is allowed for mild deviance from these expectations). There must be a feeling of group cohesiveness, and there must be free entry into, and exit from, the lodge without penalty.

Funding has been provided through federal, state and hospital monies. Community lodges are usually established after sufficient funds have been obtained to purchase a house in a section of town which will be accessible to both the hospital and the community which the lodge members will serve.

The obstacles to establishing such a program are usually financing, choice of location, selection of patients, and the selection of staff. The major problem among these is the selection of "staff" because of the change in roles demanded, i.e., from being a dependent hospital patient, to a directing, self-supporting, supervising and group-supporting person.

35

Future plans call for the expansion of this program so that the lodge will no longer be a "sheltered living-working facility", but rather an alternative community mental health care system, where the residents of the self-governing lodge would participate in making plans to provide each person with a social situation, within the lodge sub-system, which would allow him the maximum possible arena for personal and social adjustment on a flexible basis. Patients can then also be drawn from a Community Mental Health Center population as well as the hospital population.

The Volunteer Services of the Salt Lake County Comprehensive Mental Health Center in Salt Lake City, Utah. This program was started in 1961 and volunteers are used as case aides for individual patients, aides in therapy groups, leaders and/or aides in activity groups, and in a variety of miscellaneous roles that are expected of them connected with fundraising, public relations, office or administrative tasks. The volunteers are used in out-patient services, hospital services, crisis intervention, children's services, juvenile court, and research and evaluation.

Volunteers are carefully selected with regard to their individual capacity and functioning, specific talents and interests, capacity to relate, appropriatenesss of affect, and responses to anxiety-provoking situations. The coordinator of volunteer services makes the specific assignments of the volunteer to the place or person that needs help. Individual orientation and screening provide the initial training, then continuous ongoing training, are available under staff supervision. For example, in the Partial Hospitalization Unit, volunteer aides are always welcome at the daily 4 p.m. meeting of that unit, but the focus is on maintaining the spontaneity of the volunteer, and effort is made to ensure that they not act as "junior therapists".

Funding for the salaries for the professional staff is met by some county, state and federal funds and additional fund-raising through local volunteer activities.

The only obstacle to the acceptance of this program has been where professionals have not had experience working with volunteers. However, once a successful experience has been completed, subsequent acceptance of such volunteers has been easy. Occasionally, patients are reluctant to accept the help from volunteer case aides, but this resistance can be minimized with the assistance of the professional persons in contact with the patient.

S.E.R.V.E. (Serve and Enrich Retirement by Volunteer Experience) is a demonstration project for older volunteers in community service. Its aims are: to meet the increasing need for service volunteers in social, welfare, health, educational and cultural agencies in the community; to provide a satisfactory and meaningful role for retired persons; to help the older person maintain his feeling of worth and usefulness; and to broaden his scope of interest. The volunteers serve on one chosen day of the week in one selected agency.

Continuous in-service training is given through regular group meetings with directors of agencies and SERVE staff. During the past three years 560 volunteers were placed and trained, with 420 of these older volunteers still giving active service. Many volunteers have accepted more demanding responsibilities after entering their area of service.

The project has been funded through the combined efforts of: Health, Education & Welfare, matching funds provided by Community Service Society, and private foundations and individuals. Some initial unwillingness to accept volunteers in agencies was experienced, but that resistance has been eliminated with successful work from the volunteers.

Volunteer Case Aide Program of Canton, Ohio. This program was based on the premise that some of the problems of human need can be solved by intelligent use of volunteers to extend and give depth to the services of the professional in the field of health and welfare. After a screening process and 20 hours of training, volunteers are placed in a cooperating agency, where they are trained to work as part of a team. Placements have been made in Juvenile Court, city schools, the Community Mental Health Center, County Welfare Department, City Government Urban Renewal and Family Service Society.

This program has been funded jointly by United Fund and Junior League. The only obstacles to acceptance so far have been some unwillingness by professionals to supervise and use the volunteer effectively. The effectiveness of the volunteer and her satisfaction depend to a large extent on the attitudes of the professional staff.

Bluebelles of the Wichita Mental Health Association are teenage girls who serve senior citizens in nursing homes and the mentally ill in the Wichita Falls State Hospital. The girls have a choice of location and time but must give at least two hours of service a week. Their specific duties supplement the professional staff and fill obvious voids in the lives of the patients, but they may not be used as replacements for nursing staff, or maid service. A ten-hour training course is given and monthly reports of service given by Bluebelles are sent from the agencies where they are assigned. There is an award system for the number of hours given in service. The program is funded entirely by the monies the girls earn and they have a fund raising project to earn scholarship money for those girls who cannot pay the yearly dues. The major cause of losing Bluebelles is when staff people in nursing homes or hospitals think they can "shove off" their work on Bluebelles. There must be a close working relationship between the adult volunteers administering and supervising the program.

Big Sisters of Racine, Wisconsin. These women from all walks of life are volunteering their time and friendship to a young girl in need of better peer and adult relationships. After an orientation period the volunteers are screened and matched with the young girls according to interests and congeniality.

Funding is a community effort supported by dues, and gifts from individuals and organizations. There were few obstacles to establishing this program. Most institutions were very anxious for it to get underway.

The Student Volunteer Program of Marion County Association for Mental Health in Indianapolis was started to stimulate interest in mental health careers, educate the high school youth through the development of projects, and to provide service to the community. Primary emphasis has been devoted to service in state hospitals. The students use their special talents in; occupational and recreational therapy, children's and nursing services, escort service, care and comfort of infirm patients, and service in the maintenance programs. At the beginning there was some resistance on the part of the hospital staff to using high school volunteers, but this has been overcome with successful experiences.

Behavioral Analyst Training Program of Southern Arizona Mental Health Center. This program, which began in 1965, trains both paid workers and volunteers in the use of behavior modification techniques in the child's natural environment. It was started as a demonstration project with pre-delinquents and now extends to the treatment of a wide variety of behavioral disorders. In working with maladaptive behaviors the environment is altered so as to prevent rewarding misbehaviors and systematically reward increased approximations of desired behaviors. In addition, the analysts train parents and others to be agents of change.

Training, designed to teach specific skills necessary to perform the duties of a behavioral analyst, is conducted by staff at the Center. Formal training lasts six weeks, but continues with close supervision and in-service training. The program is funded by the State of Arizona. There was some initial reluctance on the part of many professionals to accept this new program, but as effectiveness has been demonstrated this resistance has been dissipated.

SWAP: Social Worker Aide Program utilizes volunteers to assist the school social workers in Portland Public Schools, Oregon. It was initiated in Jan. '68 to alleviate the results of a cutback on taxes which reduced the number of social workers from 31 to 12. Many volunteers are former teachers and social workers, and mothers whose children no longer need them full-time at home. Volunteers are interviewed by the supervisor of the School Social Workers and then scheduled for an afternoon work session. Additional training is given to each volunteer as she works. These Aides perform many time-consuming tasks that were formerly done by the social workers and so allow the social workers more time to work with those needing help. As soon as the Aides learn new tasks, they are allowed to assume new responsibilities, and many ex-volunteers have gone on to gain advanced training in social work. This program is sponsored by the Mental Health Association of Oregon and Special Services Department Portland Public Schools, Oregon. It is funded by The Jackson Foundation and additional private monies. This service has been accepted by all concerned and has been recently incorporated into the VIPS Program (Volunteers in Portland Schools). Thus many more volunteers will be trained by the school Social Work Department. There are now 300 in the entire program compared to the 12 trained in the first year.

A Training Program for New Professionals, Paraprofessionals and Volunteers is sponsored by the Young Adult Institute & Workshop, Inc. in New York. It provides in-service training at the Institute for college trainees and interns, community volunteers and Urban Corps Workers, but only the Urban Corps Workers receive a salary provided for under the Federal Work Study Program. This program began in 1964, and thus far, 175 persons have participated. It was initiated to answer the local college pleas for field training experience for students. The Institute realized that such a program would provide more intensive work with its mentally handicapped clients and would also tap the reservoir of capable community volunteers. The community volunteers and paraprofessionals are screened and many paraprofessionals participating have had at least a year's training. Each trainee is assigned to an appropriate segment of the Institute's Adjustment Center Program according to his interests and the amount of time he can

38

work. Under supervision, the trainees assist the group workers in involving the clients in the programmed recreational activities. Often, a trainee is assigned his own group or certain individuals for participation in specific activities. In the future, the Institute plans to set up a cooperative training program for paraprofessionals.

Foster Grandparent Program not only provides elderly adults with employment, but it enables institutionalized, hospitalized or dependent neglected children to experience a warm relationship with a mature adult who cares. This program began in May 1967, and is sponsored and funded by the Administration on Aging, of the Department of Health, Education and Welfare. The program provides a social service to adults 60 years of age or older, in that it gives them a meaningful and socially acceptable role in their mature years. Acceptance in this program requires the elderly men and women to be able to read and write, and more important, the candidates must have a warmth and understanding for children. Candidates participate in a 40-hour orientation. The first 20 hours include introductions, discussions and workshops dealing with children and their needs. The next 20 hours are spent at the host institution where the Foster Grandparent is assigned. Here he is briefed on procedures, purposes and goals of his assignment, and given in-service training. This program is to be expanded, and to insure this expansion, a Foster Grandparent program is to be incorporated into every Model Cities Day Care proposal.

The Social Club, Birmingham, Alabama was established to provide convalescing mental hospital patients with a pleasant place to make friends, an opportunity for assuming responsibility, a sense of belonging, some social rehabilitation, and a place where they could find something interesting to do.

Potential members are contacted through physicians, nurses, hospital personnel and the Mental Health Association. The club rooms are open six hours a day, five days a week.

Volunteers must be over 17 years of age and have an ability to relate constructively to members. They are recruited through churches, civic organizations, colleges, hospitals and the news media. In-service training is provided by the Social Club Director.

The program has been funded by the state through Vocational Rehabilitation and Community Chest. Major obstacles so far have been to obtain adequate funding, and the reluctance of some potential members to take the initial step of coming to the club.

Community Aides Program in Minneapolis was initiated as a result of a request made by the training Director of Pilot City Regional Center, which is a multiple funded agency that provides a variety of services for the city. The request was for background and training for untrained non-professional aides who are engaged in direct service in the community. The program, sponsored by Pilot City and the Minnesota Association for Mental Health, began operating in November 1969. It includes a two-hour weekly session, where a speaker makes a presentation and a discussion follows. These sessions are designed to provide the Aide with some insight into the problems they will face in the community. The Minnesota Association for Mental Health provided the funds for the initial work. Some of the Aides trained are on the payroll of the Pilot City Regional Center. Some professionals felt that they were being asked to help too often, but this is the only difficulty so far.

These eighteen volunteer programs which were presented during the conference, demonstrated conclusively that the manpower problem in the mental health field can be alleviated in some measure by such activities. It is hoped that other agencies and professional organizations will undertake further expansion of these programs in their own areas while waiting for the professionals and ancillary support personnel to be trained in the traditional fields.

Southern California Counselling Center, Los Angeles was founded as a community service for those who need mental health counselling but cannot afford it. Professional staff assume responsibility for screening counsellor applicants and training and supervising them in their subsequent work assignments, which include individual, family, and group counselling. The criteria used for selecting these "housewife counsellors" are: life experience, academic background less than advanced degree; personal therapy; sensitivity; empathy; non-possessive warmth; genuineness; detached-involvement; flexibility and a sense of proportion.

Counsellors commit themselves to one or two nights of counselling clients. They confer weekly with supervisors, and attend monthly weekend workshops as well as irregularly scheduled workshops. The two-year training program at the Center can be used to meet some state pre-requisites for licensing.

The Agency is a walk-in center. No limit is set on the number of appointments. No fee is required if the applicant cannot pay. The Center is non-sectarian. There is a 24-hour telephone service for referrals of emergencies to available counsellors.

The Center is funded by private contributions; original funding for basic operations was the major obstacle. Volunteers are self-referred. No recruiting is undertaken.

PROGRAMS LISTED

Student Mental Health Assistant
Mrs. Raymond Von Spreckelsen, Hospital Services Director
Mental Health Association in Marion County
615 N. Alabama Street
Indianapolis, Indiana 46204

Behavioral Analyst Training Program
Dr. Rachel Burkholder, Staff Psychologist
Southern Arizona Mental Health Center
1930 East 6th Street
Tucson, Arizona 85716

SWAP (Social Work Aide Program)
Mrs. Langdon Hedrick, School Social Worker Aide
SWAP
35 S. W. 88th Street
Portland, Oregon 97225

Training Program for New Professionals, Paraprofessionals and Volunteers
Young Adult Institute & Workshop, Inc.
Mr. Thomas Robert Ames, Executive Director
260 Park Avenue, South
New York, New York 10010

Foster Grandparents
Miss Anne Johnson, Director
Chicago Commission for Senior Citizens
203 North Wabash Avenue
Room 2000
Chicago, Illinois 60601

Social Club
Mrs. Nancy Fritz, Director of Day Activities
Jefferson County Association for Mental Health
3600 8th Avenue, South
Birmingham, Alabama 35222

Social Work Assistants
Mrs. Jean Carmel, Executive Director
Wellmet Project, Inc.
6 Newport Road
Cambridge, Massachusetts

Community Aides
Mr. Arthur L. Cunningham, Board of Directors
Minnesota Association for Mental Health, Inc.
45-10 West 77th Street
Minneapolis, Minnesota 55435

Community Friends Project
Mrs. Marvin T. Smith, Chairman
California Association for Mental Health
901 "H" Street, Suite 212
Sacramento, California 95814

Mental Health Case Aide Program
Mystic Valley Mental Health Association
186 Bedford Street
Lexington, Massachusetts 02173

Home Training Program for Young Mentally Ill
Children
Mrs. Nanette Doernberg, M.A., Program Director
League School for Seriously Disturbed Children
567 Kingston Avenue
Brooklyn, N. Y.

A Community Lodge Treatment Program for Ex-
Mental Patients
Dr. David H. Sanders
Associate Professor of Psychiatry & Psychology
Michigan State University
East Lansing, Michigan

Volunteer Member of the Treatment Team
Mrs. Joanne Smith & Mrs. Orla Shaw, Directors
Salt Lake County Comprehensive Mental Health
Center
156 Westminster Avenue
Salt Lake City, Utah 84117

S. E. R. V. E. (Serve & Enrich Retirement by Volunteer Experience)

Mrs. Janet Sainer—Staff Specialist
Community Service Society of New York
105 East 22nd Street
New York, New York 10010

Volunteer Case Aide Program
Mrs. Margaret Kirkpatrick, Executive Director
United Fund of Central Stark County
618 2nd Street, N.W.
Canton, Ohio 44703

Bluebelle Teenage Volunteers
Mrs. Patricia Looney, Executive Director
Wichita Mental Health Association
1511 D. Beverley Drive
Wichita Falls, Texas 76309

Big Sisters of Greater Racine, Inc.
Mrs. Ernest L. Macvicar, President
Big Sisters of Greater Racine, Inc.
6427 East Hoods Creek Lane
Franksville, Wisconsin 53126

Southern California Counselling Center
Benjamin Weininger, M.D. & Hans Hoffman,
Administrator
1022 South La Cienega Boulevard
Los Angeles, California 90035

COLLEGE STUDENTS AS COMPANIONS TO LONG-TERM MENTAL HOSPITAL PATIENTS:

SOME CONSIDERATIONS

EDWARD H. FISCHER [1]

Fifty-one student volunteers for a companionship program each visited a mental hospital patient one hour a week, for an average of 18 weeks. Students' ratings of certain aspects of patients' appearance and behavior correlated with psychiatric aides' ratings of patients' "contact." But only the behavior ratings (rather than appearance ratings) correlated significantly with students' liking for the relationship. Patients' sex, education, years of hospitalization, and age were the best predictors of students' interest in future companionship. Some implications are that the students' apparent discouragement in relating to chronic patients might be lessened if experienced students were assigned to long-term patients and if the period of companionship were shortened.

The potential value of introducing college student volunteers into the environment of a state mental hospital has been recognized for at least 50 years (Cummins, 1967). During the last decade college student companionship programs have taken wider scale status in various institutions (Holzberg, Knapp, & Turner, 1967; Umbarger, Dalsimer, Morrison, & Breggin, 1962) and have been favorably regarded by patients, staff, and students. At Connecticut Valley Hospital, the program has usually involved weekly visits by the student to one companion patient. Although, initially, students may feel anxious and diffident about interacting with a mental patient, they have shown sensitivity to patients' needs and are able to offer fresh approaches to getting a reluctant patient off the ward or involved in new activity.

Patients selected for the program are frequently those who spend most of their time on the wards (viz., chronic schizophrenic and geriatric patients) rather than those who are already active. The assumption is that the visits will have a more beneficial effect for the minimally sociable chronic patient, in that he must make some adjustments in regularly meeting the student which might generalize to other situations.

However, there is anecdotal evidence that students find it difficult to relate to long-term patients, particularly over the course of an entire school year. Such patients are generally considerably older, have less education, and may converse monosyllabically, if at all. It can be argued that some interpersonal strain on the student's part is well worth the possible gain for the patient. But there may be a boomerang effect if the student companion becomes so frustrated or bored that his negative attitude influences the rapport that does exist.

The present study attempted to look at some psychological aspects of prolonged interaction with a chronic patient. Its main concentration was on the student's view of the companion relationship and his attitude toward continuation in the program.

METHOD

Subjects

The volunteer companions were 16 female and 35 male students from colleges near the hospital. Each student visited his companion patient for about an hour, on a weekly basis. The median number of visits per student was 18 at the time of data collection.

The group of companion patients consisted of 23 women and 28 men. Most of these people had been asked to participate in the program because they lacked visitors or were very inactive. The median age of the patient group was 39, and the median years of formal education was nine. The majority of the patients were diagnosed as schizophrenic, and about half (24) could be described as "chronic" by

[1] The data for this study were collected with the help of Sue Orr and Gary Beck.

JOURNAL OF CONSULTING & CLINICAL PSYCHOLOGY, Dec. 1970, vol. 35, no. 3, pp. 308-310.

the criterion of having been hospitalized for more than three years.

Student and Aide Ratings

Toward the end of the program, the students were asked to complete a questionnaire which included three kinds of rating scales. One scale required S to designate how much he liked the relationship with his patient, on a 7-point scale. Next there was a series of bipolar adjective scales, which S was to apply to the companion patient. Each pair of adjectives is shown in Table 1. Four of the scales refer to physical appearance, while five concern personal or behavior qualities. The Ss then indicated their interest in forming another such companion relationship ("if the opportunity were to become available in the future"), on a 4-point scale.

Psychiatric aides who knew the companion patients rated them on the nine adjective scales as a control index of the student ratings. The aides also rated patients for their "degree of contact." At least two aides made independent ratings of each patient.

RESULTS AND DISCUSSION

Aides' and students' adjective ratings of the same patients tended to be moderately correlated (the mean coefficient was $r = .40$). For two of the adjective scales, dependent–independent and pleasant–unpleasant, the correlations between aides' and students' ratings were nonsignificant. However, apart from these two rather subjective scales, the student judgments reflected moderate agreement with the aides'. Closer agreement might not be expected since students' and aides' perspectives of patients are likely to be somewhat different.

Table 1 shows the correlations between student adjective ratings and (a) aides' ratings of the patients' contact, (b) students' liking for the companion relationship, and (c) students' willingness to form another companion relationship.

The data in Table 1 show that students' ratings of patients' appearance (i.e., sloppy–neat, clean–dirty) and behavior (i.e., pleasant–unpleasant, unfriendly–friendly, talkative–quiet) correlated significantly with aides' ratings of the patients' degree of contact. However, Table 1 indicates that patients' behavior, not appearance, was significantly related to students' liking of the companionship. Also, it may be pointed out that while terms such as "unpleasant" and "friendly" applied to the patient have a seemingly obvi-

TABLE 1

CORRELATIONS BETWEEN STUDENT RATINGS OF PATIENTS AND OTHER RATING SCALE DATA

Adjectives	Patients' contact (aides' ratings)	Students' liking for relationship	Students' interest in future companionship
Appearance			
Sloppy–Neat	.35**	.19	.12
Attractive–Unattractive	.03	−.20	.01
Fat–Thin	−.05	.01	−.19
Clean–Dirty	−.40**	−.17	.01
Behavior			
Dependent–Independent	.18	.05	.24*
Pleasant–Unpleasant	−.26*	−.38**	.08
Unfriendly–Friendly	.34**	.46***	.14
Interesting–Dull	−.23	−.51***	−.24*
Talkative–Quiet	−.34**	−.35**	−.26*

Note.—When scored, the scales were keyed to the second of the pair of adjectives, for example, the −.40 correlation between Clean–Dirty and Patients' contact indicates that patients perceived as "dirty" tended to receive poor contact ratings. The appearance and behavior adjectives were randomly ordered in the actual questionnaire.
* $p < .05$.
** $p < .01$.
*** $p < .001$.

ous correspondence to liking the companionship, these descriptions did not correlate significantly with interest in future companionship. What mattered for the latter evidently was the patient's perceived dependency, dullness, and reticence. Each of these three descriptive terms had a low but statistically reliable correlation with student interest in forming another companionship.

The last findings carry more meaning when the correspondence of patient demographic variables to student interest is examined. The patient variables of sex, years of formal education, years of hospitalization, and age all had low but statistically reliable correlations with students' interest in continuing with the program. Students were more likely to express interest in further companionship if their companion patient was female ($r_{pbis} = .35$, $p < .01$), or had completed high school ($r = .32$, $p < .025$), and less likely to be interested if the patient was older ($r = −.24$, $p < .05$) or had many years of hospitalization ($r = -.37$, $p < .005$). Each of these correlations appeared to be independent of the others; for example, while patients' years of hospitalization had the strongest correlation with ratings of interest in future companionship, similar correlations existed for the remaining three patient variables when *only* long-term patients were considered.

Student's sex and socioeconomic class of origin were examined to determine their possible influence on the ratings. Social class was measured by categorizing the education and occupation of the student's father, according to Hollingshead's (1957) system. Although there was some tendency for female companions to express greater interest in future companionship than males ($r_{pbis} = .20$), the correlation was not quite significant at the .05 level. There was no discernible relationship between social class of the student and his interest in future companionship ($r = -.01$). It was also determined that the finding linking patient's sex and student's intention to continue the program held for students of both sexes.

Both the descriptive ratings and the demographic correlates suggest that the variables of patient chronicity influence the student's inclination to become a volunteer companion at a future time. Other (informal) data were gathered which substantiated this. When asked why they had little interest in future companionship, students who had so indicated stressed the patient's seeming indifference or lethargy, and the apparent futility of continuing the relationship. It may be that students who had chronic patients as companions developed expectations that other patients assigned to them would behave quite similarly.

The results imply that some selective matching of patients with volunteers could be effective. For example, it seems easier for students to relate to chronic patients who are of an age or background closer to that of the student. More experienced and willing students might be sought out to visit the "hard core" chronic patients who seem to benefit from the relationship, but who do not have the apparent advantages of youth and/or education.

Also, the companionship period could be shortened. The present data were based on an average of 18 visits, and many of the students had been involved with one patient over the course of an entire school year. It is possible to terminate a relationship before the student becomes seriously discouraged. The companion students usually meet in groups with a psychologist or social worker immediately following their visit with the patient. If a student indicates he is disheartened and blocked in his efforts to further the relationship with a chronic patient, he might be asked to see a new patient, preferably in another unit or building. If the possibility for developing more than one companion relationship in a year were considered an integral aspect of the program and made explicit at the outset, there would be no sense of failure on the part of either student or patient when a change did occur. Because the program has many desirable effects according to both participants and hospital staff, it is quite worth trying innovations which may improve the morale of companions to long-term patients.

REFERENCES

CUMMINS, M. C. College volunteers in the state mental hospitals. Unpublished master's thesis, Catholic University of America, 1967.

HOLLINGSHEAD, A. B. Two factor index of social position. Unpublished manuscript, Yale University, 1957.

HOLZBERG, J. D., KNAPP, R. H., & TURNER, J. L. College students as companions to the mentally ill. In E. L. Cowen, E. A. Gardner, & M. Zax (Eds.), *Emergent approaches to mental health problems.* New York: Appleton-Century-Crofts, 1967.

UMBARGER, C. C., DALSIMER, J. S., MORRISON, A. P., & BREGGIN, P. R. *College students in a mental hospital.* New York: Grune & Stratton, 1962.

Volunteers as a major asset in the treatment program

EUGENE GENDLIN, Ph.D.
JOSEPH J. KELLY, M.A.
V. B. RAULINAITIS, M.D.
FRED E. SPANER, Ph.D.

The number of hospitalized psychiatric patients is so great that there will probably never be sufficient professional personnel to give each patient adequate individual attention. Among the visions for the future is one of putting professionals into the responsible supervisory role and arranging for motivated, ordinary citizens to provide, under such supervision, the personal relationships needed in the rehabilitation of patients. This seems an especially hopeful possibility for the future when we consider that what is called "mental illness" nearly always includes a breakdown in interpersonal relationships as part of a not yet fully understood total condition.

Providing each patient with an opportunity for a long-term personal relationship, of a depth and receptive quality sufficient to allow him to experience himself differently, has always seemed far beyond our resources. However, if we can plan to draw not only from the pool of professional people, but also from the vastly greater pool of interested lay people, then the problem assumes manageable proportions. That the general populace might have to be drawn into the treatment process has often been envisaged and is, after all, not strange. Hospitalized psychiatric patients have in some sense been rejected and segregated

MENTAL HYGIENE, 1966, vol. 50, no. 3, pp. 421-427.

45

by society, and a fully adequate solution to their problems will probably involve some major move by ordinary people to bring these patients back into society.

In this long-range context, some of the volunteers in today's programs in psychiatric hospitals can be considered a vanguard. Volunteers are just such ordinary people from the community who come to a hospital to help in the process of rehabilitating patients. But, until recently, volunteers were not expected to make a significant contribution to treatment of patients. They were expected to play cards with the patients and to make the "climate" a little more pleasant, but were encouraged to keep their relationships with them on a purposely superficial level and away from their areas of difficulty.

It is true that, in all hospitals at all times, some volunteers have always related meaningfully to patients and have played important roles in the rehabilitation of some patients. But, generally, this has been accidental or spontaneous, and seldom integrated into treatment programs. Only a few volunteers have recognized their accomplishments, achieved usually without training, supervision, or responsibility on the part of the staff.

A major advantage volunteers have over professionals is the very fact that they *are* volunteers. Even with a good deal of training and seasoning, the definitive characteristics remain: volunteers serve at the hospital without financial remuneration, assuming temporary, limited responsibility for patients while presuming none, not expecting themselves to know more than they do, and accepting the decisions and judgments of staff supervisors. The volunteer is one of those rare people who can afford to say, and say again, "I don't know."

This is a report of a program by which

46

volunteers were trained and supervised in developing meaningful interpersonal relationships with patients. They were encouraged to be helpfully receptive to the patients' expressions of their difficulties. It was felt that, in this way, volunteers could contribute to this most time-consuming and individualized aspect of the hospital's treatment program.

Precedents exist for giving training to nonprofessionals [1] and, in several instances, to volunteers.[2-6] If volunteers are to do more than relate superficially to patients, they must have some training, (though perhaps not a great deal), plus some experience with patients and, most important, supervision. Supervision for volunteers has two different, quite distinguishable, aspects; and distinction between the two made the present project possible.

One kind of supervision concerns day-to-day activities of the volunteer in the wards and clinics. In this, the individual volunteer is in the direct charge of the nurse or therapist. Each volunteer is assigned to a particular department or "service" and to a specific staff member in that department. All this is co-ordinated by the director of volunteers at the hospital. The supervision involved, which is supplemented by an assignment guide or job description, is no net drain on the hospital's resources, since the effective volunteers more than repay the investment of time and effort by adding to the total available manpower within the given department.

A second and different kind of supervision concerns, solely and specifically, the volunteer's interpersonal relationships with patients. Because the conventional mode of supervision is already provided and in operation, this second type requires much less time than one would imagine. In the

47

project reported here, it involved only two and a half hours per month. Yet, in that amount of time and within six months, it was possible to train volunteers to work with patients at a different level, by developing new attitudes, and teaching specific procedures—within the context of personal discussions of their problems and their experiences with patients.

Initially, six meetings on the general topic of interpersonal relationships with patients were held at the hospital with the consulting psychologist. More than forty volunteers were invited to these meetings by the director of volunteers. All except four had had prior hospital experience, and all were serving at least once a week in various patient-contact assignments. Most of them were attached to the nursing service. Different days of the week were selected for different meetings in order to make it as easy as possible for volunteers to attend at least once during their day of assignment. The size of each group was limited to about a dozen participants.

The consulting psychologist gave some informal talks, which were followed by discussions. This set the stage for a more formal program with a group of self-selected individuals who, with one exception, had attended three or more of the six meetings. Thirteen volunteers agreed to continue as a "closed" group for six additional monthly conferences. In addition to participating in discussions, they agreed to hand in at each meeting a one-page "process note" in which each had written a paragraph or so about one "good" and one "bad" (i.e., troublesome, problematic, difficult, or failing) experience they had had with a patient during the month. The subject matter of these notes was not referred to during the meetings unless the volunteer herself mentioned it. But it was possible, at later meetings, to bring up and discuss points relevant to these notes and likely to be of general interest. The notes also provided the consultant with some indication of the level of work and thought.

Typically, the sessions developed from group conversations about one or another volunteer's immediate problems with patients ("There is a patient, who . . .") to various possible modes of responding to patients, their deepening relationships, and methods for opening avenues for the patients' self-expression. The volunteer's own attitudes, fears, self-criticisms, and expectations were aired. Major emphasis was placed on the honest use of the volunteer's own self and current feelings, both with the patients and in the group settings.

The character of this training can best be conveyed by reproducing a typical session. During a recent national Veterans Administration Voluntary Service conference, the following group session was conducted, on a raised platform, before an audience of approximately three hundred and fifty persons, including medical professionals, officials of national service and Veterans' organizations, and volunteers from several Chicago-area hospitals. This was one of four, separate, 20-minute presentations given at this conference by four different Veterans Administration hospitals. The session was unrehearsed, except that each volunteer was asked beforehand to recall a previously unmentioned problem that she could bring up for discussion. The transcript * here reproduced is preceded

* Tape-recorded and transcribed verbatim, and published in "Report of the 1965 Annual Meeting," VA Voluntary Service National Advisory Committee, Office of the Chief Medical Director, Veterans Administration, Washington, D. C., June 1965, pp. 20–24.

by an introduction by the Chief of Staff of the Veterans Administration Hospital, Downey, Illinois.

Mental hospitals are changing from custodial care to a more active rehabilitation of the patients. In this rehabilitation process, volunteers can play an important role. There have never been enough professional personnel working in the mental hospitals.

The greatest need of mentally ill patients in a large hospital is to get more individual attention. . . . The patient needs more deep interpersonal involvement, not just a superficial social relationship. At Downey we have a project in which we are encouraging a group of volunteers to develop closer interpersonal relationships with individual, selected patients. We hope that, through these closer interpersonal relationships, the individual patient will have an opportunity to express his feelings. He will be able to compare his own attitudes with the healthy attitudes of mature volunteers. He will be able to see different ways of behaving, to get some common-sense advice from somebody who has been able to successfully manage his or her own life.

This role of the volunteer might be uncomfortable at first. Volunteers have been told so many times before, "Do not get involved, do not ask probing questions." Sometimes they have been afraid that they may harm a patient with what they say or do. To enable the volunteer to be more comfortable and more effective in this individual approach, Downey has been giving training in the form of group sessions. Once a month, a group of volunteers meets under the guidance of a psychology consultant and discusses problems which they, themselves, present. When discussing the problems in the group sessions, the volunteer learns how to deal with similar problems next time. They are learning what to say or not to say, how to draw the patient out, how to help him talk about what really bothers him, rather than superficial matters, how to help him help himself. The volunteer works under the supervision of the nursing staff.

In the next 15 minutes, a group of volunteers from Downey will demonstrate to you a very small segment of this group training.

DR. G: We thought we would present the kind of meeting that we usually have, just the same way as we usually have it so you could hear the sort of things we talk about and the sort of things that come up.

MRS. W: Doctor, I have a slight problem. I work in a building that has an open and closed ward. In our closed ward, we have one patient who is in his thirties and usually sleeps most of the time. Recently he has been joining us in a card game, and I know he is trying to talk to me because he looks directly at me, talks real fast, real low, and mumbles. How can I get him to stop and make him understand?

DR. G: I hear you've been waiting a long time for this patient to move toward you in some way. Now he is doing it, but you can't hear anything he is saying?

MRS. W: That's right.

DR. G: This patient she is talking about—she has waited for some months for him to make some sign that he notices her, make any sort of response. Now the patient is talking, looking right at her, but mumbling so badly and on purpose so as not to be audible.

MRS. W: I asked him to please slow down and talk so I could understand him. He looks at me and just keeps rattling on and taps me on the shoulder and talks some more.

DR. G: Is he trying to get something across to you? From the way you tell the story, it seems to me this patient isn't really wanting you quite to get it. He's talking right at you, but he's having difficulty making himself understood, is he? Is he feeling the trouble of not getting across to you?

MRS. W: Well, the way I understand it, he is just beginning to accept me in the ward and he is looking at me. He mumbles. They said he couldn't play cards. In fact, this is the best way I have found of communicating with him. By playing cards with him, the patient does communicate better. In this case he wanted to play cards and one of the aides said he couldn't; so he showed him he's one of the best ones there. During the game he mumbles to me constantly, pays no attention.

DR. G: Do you tell him you wish you knew what he was saying?

MRS. W.: Yes, I do.

DR. G: Because so often patients will do that. They will communicate without letting you know what they are saying, sometimes by mumbling and sometimes with their hand over their mouth.

MRS. F: Is it important that she knows what he is saying? Actually, the idea is that he is aware of her being there.

DR. G: I think it is very important that he knows that she wants to know what he is saying, that she would really like to know, that she knows that he's talking to her, that she doesn't dodge his eyes when he looks right at her. But if you say that you let him know that you wish you understood, then I don't think it's so important if he isn't ready to have her hear it.

MRS. L: I think the attitude of the patient is very important because, for a great length of time, he didn't speak to you at all, and now he at least acknowledges you with the mumbling.

MRS. H: Doctor, in the corridors and in the canteen, I am frequently asked, Am I a patient? Do I answer, "Yes, I am," and keep on going; or do I say, "No, I am not. May I help you?"

DR. G: Well, from your laughter, I can see that this happens to some of the rest of you. I would say that the question, "Are you a patient?" is an opening for a conversation. That's the way I'd take it. Are you a patient? Are you a social worker? Are you a psychologist?—any number of other things like that are openers for conversations. My feeling about it is to always answer openers honestly and then go ahead and make the conversation which is being invited.

MRS. O: I would like to ask about the patient who doesn't talk at all. It has something to do with what Mrs. L talked about. We've discussed it, and I've tried the method that we have discussed, but I'm not getting to first base. I sit next to him and I tell him that I would like to know what he's thinking. It's all right that he doesn't talk, but I am interested and I would come and see him again and sit next to him. But it seems like maybe there might be something more that I can do or something that I'm not doing that would help.

DR. G: (To audience): You can get from what's just been said that we've discussed this before. (To Mrs. O) Now that some of your feelings are building up, the ones that you've just expressed to us, you can also express to the patient and say, "Gee, I've been here a long time and I haven't heard anything from you. I guess it's all right if you don't say anything, but I am really getting bothered. Maybe, you know, I'm not helping you at all. I just really would wish you'd say something,"—which is much stronger because it builds up over a period of time that you have come.

MRS. O: I find that he is following me with his eyes. He watches me now around the room but he still won't come to me and he will not speak to me.

DR. G: Yes, and you can recognize that. Do you look back and recognize that? I mean are you able to get across to him that you know?

MRS. O: I believe I do.

DR. G: Well, then of course you're *moving*, so my feeling about that is, express your impatience but don't get too impatient, because you *are* moving. If he now knows you via eyes, you have a relationship with him, you have a conversation with him. It's much more important to have contact than what we say or do—it doesn't matter that much. So you've already got a conversation every time you come but it isn't yet in words. It isn't yet fully recognized. You can say some of these things like you said here to him, too.

MRS. O: Maybe I'm impatient or overanxious. I just want so much for the patient.

DR. G: But I want him to hear your feeling the way we are hearing it. You know, you're looking at me brightly with your eyes flashing, saying, "I so much wish." Does he hear it that way? Does he hear it that clearly?

MRS. R: I'm sure he does. Just knowing Mrs. O, I know he would.

MRS. G: I have a similar patient. She follows me with her eyes, too, and she won't utter a word. She crochets and knits and she does beautiful things. Every time I come in, she smiles and looks away and I always comment on what she has done. I speak to her several times a day, and she is always smiling at me and always getting something out to show me, but not once have I asked her anything about her talking. I have a feeling that one of these days she's going to forget herself and say something to me. I may be wrong, but she is looking forward to conversation.

DR. G: It's good to have these tentative, nonverbal conversations. . . . It's also good to say that you wish you could hear them, that you wish she would say something, that you hope that one of these days she will. I think that's important, too, just like you are telling me.

MRS. R: I just have to say that so many times we think of so much sadness in the world of mental hospitals and mental illness and there is so much that's so funny. I can go in and laugh and the patients will laugh. One day I was leaving, and I can't remember which patient now said, "Mrs. R, I think you come here to have fun." I said, "You know, sometimes you're right." It's just a good, easy feeling. Sometimes we're so worried about helping the patients and pleasing them. I think just being there sometimes helps—being yourself.

MRS. T: Don't you think a lot of this comes with time? I don't think we did this when we started, but maybe now our responses are a lot greater since we've gotten over our, shall I say, our testing period—and our patients do test us.

DR. G: Yes, we all agree, being natural comes later. It takes a long time to get back again to where one was before one started *working* in some careful fashion. To get back to being natural takes time.

MRS. C: I was wondering, Doctor, if you or any of the girls have any suggestions for me about how I can create an opportunity to talk to this particular patient that I have. This man is not in a closed ward; the only place I really have contact with him is in the canteen having coffee. Usually when I go in he's watching for me but he's at a table with two or three other people. He always asks me if I want to join them and we have to talk so generally and still he is watching for me. Have you any suggestions? It's hard for me to ask him if he wants to go over to another table, but I think maybe he'd like to.

DR. G: You work in the library, don't you?

MRS. A: Couldn't you speak to him about some books he would like and then see him in the library?

MRS. C: I do suggest that he come in, and occasionally he does. When he does come in, I notice he gets kind of dressed up, which is a good sign,

I think. We have plenty to talk about, if we could have an opportunity. Just once he waited for me. I wonder if I could just say, "Shall we go over here?"

DR. G: I certainly think you can. Whatever feels appropriate to you. If it feels appropriate in the canteen even to say, "You want to talk to me over here for a few minutes?" I'd certainly do that. I've used more corners, walls, and what not. I think it's important that you respond in some way to this that you're picking up, that he might want to talk more personally.

MRS. F: What I was going to say in regard to the library volunteer and the patient in the canteen was that, if you take him off to a corner, you'd better talk fast because you won't be alone with him long. Because then everyone comes in—especially when they see a volunteer. They're right in there. They want attention too.

DR. G: I think the important thing might be to respond to what this patient is saying with his eyes, which maybe is, "Here you are someone whom I might be able to relate to and then there are these other people here." So once she takes him to one side and even suggests this, I think the patient would then know that she had picked this up and was willing for this. And then, also, the other thing that you are mentioning is always a problem—the other patients' coming over. I think one should feel free to be able to say to the others, "I'm glad you came, too, you know. Have a seat. But I'm talking to Mr. Brown." You were pointing out that so often, when you are trying to be in a corner, others come.

MRS. F: I've had that happen so often.

DR. G: I think it's even good to have other patients stand and listen to the kind of thing we do.

MRS. T: Yes, but her man probably would resent it. He wants her alone.

DR. G: I agree, I think it's worth keeping a sharp lookout and I think, if he does resent it, then help him say so. "Do you wish Mr. Smith wasn't listening to us?" Then he can say, "Yes." . . .

Discussion

As yet the program here described lacks

an objective mode of evaluation. From the 14 meetings during a 16-month period, and from the written "process notes," it is possible to conclude that the volunteers in this program are not different from any other trainees who have had some experience and some supervision in relating to psychiatric patients. Their many expressions of increased confidence, success, and gratification have provided an important, though subjective, index.

The project has demonstrated that the pervasive need of psychiatric patients to regard themselves, through personal experience, as sensible, concern-worthy individuals in a human relationship *can* be met without major additional resources.

Currently, we are planning to refine and improve the program. We intend to bring in more than one trainer and, consequently, more than one set of procedures and attitudes. Thus, the volunteers may have the benefit of various approaches to hospitalized patients without sacrificing their freedom to choose, in practice, just which of the ideas, suggestions, procedures, and attitudes offered may help them to work most successfully.

The fact that one fully trained professional, utilizing only two and a half hours per month, was able to aid 14 volunteers to become a more therapeutic resource suggests that similar consulting relationships of two and a half hours monthly with five professionals (a total of only 20 professional hours, less than one-eighth of a full-time position), on a rotation basis, could provide both wider and more extensive training and supervision for up to seventy volunteers.

There are many precedents for psychiatric treatment using adjunct personnel in significant interpersonal relations, and it is not a new idea to enable such personnel to give patients more continuing and intense interpersonal relationships than hospitals could otherwise provide. However, in the past, such adjunct personnel have usually been reserved for the private hospital. The present program indicates that providing such personnel for every patient in the large, tax-supported hospitals is not at all beyond present and potential resources.

Judging from the volunteers' own reactions, it is also likely that many more volunteers will be attracted to the hospitals once it becomes known that training and function of this kind are available.

REFERENCES

1. Rioch, M. J.: American Journal of Orthopsychiatry, 33:678 (July), 1963.

2. Young, C. L.: Hospitals, 35:46 (November 16), 1961.

3. Ewald, V.: Psychiatric Studies and Projects, 2:16 (February), 1964.

4. "Milieu Therapy—A Dialogue," Mental Hospitals, 14:351 (June), 1963.

5. Spencer, S. M.: Saturday Evening Post, 230:90 (October 5), 1957.

6. Conte, W. R., and Liebes, E.: A Voluntary Partnership. Pamphlet published by the Hogg Foundation, Austin, Texas, 1960.

Student-Employees Become Companions To Patients

M. POWELL LAWTON, Ph.D.

MORTIMER B. LIPTON, Ph.D.

THE MAJOR PROBLEM facing large public mental hospitals is to provide patients with adequate *personal* attention. Since World War II, staffing problems have lessened somewhat, but no mental health profession can yet provide a sufficient number of personnel to satisfy the hospitals' needs.

However, volunteer programs have done much to provide individual attention for a limited number of patients. Student-companion programs have been especially successful because they use the ability of intelligent young people to give something of themselves to patients.

In the summer of 1962 Norristown State Hospital initiated a trial program which utilized college students as nonprofessional Mental Health Workers. This experiment differed from similar programs in that the students were employed full time, and devoted all their efforts to creating highly personal relationships with individual patients.

Any definitive evaluation of the Mental Health Worker program must await more experience and scientific observation, but this paper describes the structure of the program and includes subjective reports from some of the young workers.

The major purpose was to stimulate the patients socially and orient them toward reality, regardless of the type or severity of their disabilities. We postulated that there is something innately

MENTAL HOSPITALS, 1963, vol. 14, no. 10, pp. 550-556.

therapeutic in the person willing to devote time to a patient, and that his willingness is of primary importance, regardless of the type or amount of professional training he has received.

We sent announcements to six colleges and received approximately fifty applications for our six positions—a possible index of the existing degree of interest in such work. We selected six highly motivated students, both graduates and undergraduates; two were psychology majors and four were majoring in other fields.

During two weeks of intensive orientation, meetings were scheduled with all hospital departments with which the workers might have contact. There were seminars to introduce some of the fundamental concepts of mental illness, personality, the structure of the mental hospital, interviewing techniques, and psychological testing. Finally, group discussions were held to define what the actual work would be, and to differentiate the students' tasks from traditional psychotherapy. Since our goal was social improvement, we gave the Mental Health Workers the following criteria of improvement: a mute patient begins to talk; another patient emerges from lethargy; one shows interest in hospital activities; others are able to undertake regular intrahospital employment; some start to plan for vocational rehabilitation; others ask about post-discharge support.

The students were assigned to a building for chronic but quiet men and to one for chronic but fairly disturbed women. The building physicians were favorably disposed toward the idea and planned ward and personnel meetings to allow the psychologist, the physician, nurses, and aides to discuss the program before it started. The physicians then chose a list of patients classified as very regressed, moderately regressed, chronic, and convalescent. Each Mental Health Worker worked with eight or ten patients from this list, so that each one had examples of both the "best" and "worst" types of patients.

Each worker presented himself to the patients as a summer student in the psychology department, but they differed among themselves about how best to state their roles. Some simply said that they would like to be friends; others said little or nothing about their functions. Some mentioned the ultimate goals of social rehabilitation and discharge, others did not.

Each worker also spent time with two or three patients who were undergoing a rehabilitation routine. They developed spontaneous relationships with 10 to 15 other patients, who were, in a sense, "self-referred." Finally, each worker spent a week at a summer camp with 30 to 40 patients. During this week his regular contacts were suspended.

From the beginning the program seemed extremely successful. The workers were eager to learn from nurses and aides, and formed mutually beneficial peer relationships. At first we held supervisory sessions for the last hour of each working day, but during the last half of the summer these sessions were held only three times a week. We also held individual supervisory meetings with each of the workers.

At the group meetings the workers discussed specific problems, and occasionally one would present a case in detail. In retrospect, they wished these seminars had been more structured, instead of developing into problem-centered free discussion.

Their contacts with their patients were extremely varied. For the most part they saw each one from three to five times a week, some on the wards, others on the grounds. Frequently the workers accompanied patients to their hospital activities and jobs, working beside them and becoming a part of the working groups. They gave freely of their after-hours time, their cars, their pocket money, and in some cases even invited patients to their homes when such an invitation seemed to be a natural part of the relationship they were trying to build. Often they had to use all their resources simply to persuade a patient to remain with them, but not one worker gave up on any patient.

Some of the final reports of the workers themselves best show the nature of their experiences.

How Workers Saw the Tasks

Goals. "With patients who were very regressed and very sick, we just tried to make contact and hoped to make some sort of change in their hospital

60

routines, whether it was just a walk on the ward, an occasional walk outside, or stopping to say hello. With the patients who were verbal, our goals were clearer: We tried to get them moving toward a new job, to become their friends, to support them, and to destroy their feelings of inadequacy."

"We were told that one of the values that we could offer the patient was friendship, an individual friendship, which seemed to be a dire need around here. We thought we could direct the inquisitive patient or the patient who fel· the need into an appropriate program, such as industrial therapy or occupational therapy. We tried to establish friendships which would decrease the withdrawal of many of these patients, and hoped to motivate patients who were less withdrawn. We thought we could help some to take a step forward —to open just a crack in the door—to further their actual rehabilitation."

Workers Describe Their Activities

Methods. "Whether one prefers to call the Mental Health Worker's relationship with a patient that of a friend or merely that of a companion, it is characterized by time, attention, and sincere interest. Just listening and talking, that was the way we began, just getting acquainted. With some of the chronic regressed patients the relationship did not progress beyond simple social contacts, perhaps varying the patient's daily routine by walks and rides around the hospital grounds, or such things as a trip to the zoo. For example, I spent one morning in the beauty shop doing not only my own patient's hair, but some of the others', too. I tried to elicit some response, not necessarily a verbal one, to the environment. With the patients who were improving and those in rehabilitation, motivation was the goal—motivation toward a hospital job, toward a job change, and in some cases, toward getting a job outside the hospital. When feasible, working with a patient in industrial therapy proved effective in establishing and strengthening the relationship, perhaps because it indicated our willingness to participate in whatever he was doing. In the paring room, for example, the presence of two of us working with the patients snapping beans or husking corn seemed not only to facilitate individual relationships but to stimulate some kind of group reaction and interaction as well.

"The Mental Health Worker's role, as compared with those of other hospital workers, is certainly less disciplined, partaking a bit of each of the others' functions. For example, during mornings spent in the occupational therapy building I would work with the women, knitting, sewing, or painting, and with the men, woodworking and carpentering. In industrial therapy I would work with the patient, motivating him in his job, sometimes to the point of using persuasive and firm methods to get him interested. As compared to the other disciplines, we care not for the mind as the doctors do, nor for the physical daily needs as the attendants do. What we care for, specifically, is the well part of the patient. This is what I think we all tried to work with and appeal to during the summer. The Mental Health Worker represents a portion of reality that necessarily intrudes upon a patient in an institution. There is a possibility that other workers may have resented our function, but I think this was avoided in most cases. The relationships of each Mental Health Worker were entirely individual, and each of us worked in his own personal way. The relationship can be called friendship, I think, insofar as some measure of trust and confidence was exchanged, and this was what happened in most cases."

"We did simple things with patients, like looking at books, drawing pictures, or looking outside at the trees and birds. Most of us had pass cards and took the patients around the hospital grounds and to the farm to look at the animals. Occasionally we would just have to sit quietly while the patient stared off blankly, and we would hopefully look for some sign of contact, if only a simple 'hello' or 'get out of here.' With verbal patients we might play catch to get them active, play records, take walks, or visit the neighborhood zoo. We also tried to change their hospital jobs if they weren't happy with them. Finally, the group of patients who were nearly ready to leave the hospital needed a practical approach, and we tried to discuss practical problems that might arise. They had worries about leaving the hospital and going into the world outside, and we tried to calm these anxieties. We also tried to act as intermediaries between the doctors and the patients. Some of us contacted the relatives of the patients in the hope of stimulating outside pressure."

"At camp, one worker started five-o'clock bird walks. These were before breakfast, but the turnouts were surprisingly large. Every Thursday night there was a dance. Two Mental Health Worker girls used to get together the previous evening and conduct dancing lessons. In the camp environment it was much easier for us to communicate with patients because they did not look around and see stone walls. Also, it made our roles a little different; it was easier for them to see us as fellow campers than as fellow patients. Camp also gave us a chance to seek out patients whom we felt we could help. In the hospital we had been assigned a definite list of patients, but here we had nobody in particular with whom we had to form relationships. We were pretty much on our own, and it was really quite gratifying because we were able to make this free choice to talk to and be with anyone we felt we might be able to help."

Complementing the Efforts of Staff

Relations with Personnel. "The nurses and aides were very helpful in accepting us into the building and making us feel like part of the ward. They would discuss their feelings, tell us anecdotes about a lot of the patients, and occasionally tell us some of their own problems and ask for advice. They helped us just by talking to us in front of the patients. They also helped us to establish relationships with the patients by giving us information and advice, introducing us to the patients, and encouraging them to follow our advice when they were refractory. There was an occasional misunderstanding, but, on the whole, we tried to fit in, and to complement the efforts of the aides and nurses rather than conflict with them. We hope that they learned something from us; we learned quite a bit from them. The industrial therapy personnel were very generous in occasionally letting us take patients off the work line, and the occupational therapy and recreation personnel were interested in hearing our views and in helping to carry

63

out specific plans with the patients."

Results. "An example of a patient's views about the Mental Health Worker's role may be found from Angeline, my very regressed patient. She is very incoherent and you can't get too much out of her verbally. We used to write quite a bit. I would talk about the trees and so on, and Angie always wrote down exactly what I said. She would never ask anything or write down anything herself, and I once sat with her for an hour not saying a word just to see if she would write something down. She realized what I was doing, and I turned my head for a while. When I looked back, Angie had written down, 'a pencil of security,' and although I couldn't get an answer about what I had done for her or what our relationship together was, to her this was some kind of friendship. This was not a verbal answer but it was something I could actually feel—I felt quite good about this."

"Estelle was someone I could relate to and talk to quite easily. She told me that having us there was like changing night into day. She said it seemed to have lifted the morale of all the people. She said that the only thing she was afraid of was that when we left morale would go down again. Now of course this is quite an exaggeration, but this is what she told me. She said she felt that we were someone to talk to, not like a nurse or a doctor but like a friend. Another patient, Sarah, who has been in the hospital for 19 years, said she found it completely overwhelming to have someone take an individual interest in her, be with her every day just to talk to her, and go for walks or ice cream, or whatever we did. Sarah said she didn't know how to accept my interest in her. Jean said that for the first time she didn't feel alone; she had someone to talk to. It seems to me from what I've heard directly that this type of job is very necessary, for it fills the gaps of loneliness during the day and eases the insecurity that so many of these people are experiencing. Just the awareness that someone is around to talk to is helpful and at the same time therapeutic. Patients said our companionship made the summer very pleasant, and others said this should be an all-year-round thing. Still another person said that he was able to talk to someone about places and things he hadn't seen for a long time before he came into the hospital."

Enhance Chances for Rehabilitation

"In dealing with the patients we took steps to enhance their chances for rehabilitation. For the first time some went to jobs and to occupational therapy, and others were motivated to try other things, like checkers, painting, or reading. I gave one of my very withdrawn patients a spelling examination. You wouldn't know by talking to him that he knew anything, yet of 100 moderately hard words he missed only two. With another patient, our friendship has progressed in many ways, and now I can talk with him for maybe five or ten minutes without his walking off as before. Not many of the withdrawn patients suddenly became candidates for remission or extended visits—this wasn't the case, generally—but a lot of them seemed to come back a little more into our world. They became more interested in things and they were more talkative, more socially aggressive. The ultimate values of our relationships are very hard to estimate. I myself believe that if even a minute step forward is taken, and the patient has derived this from his relationship with a Mental Health Worker, that's enough to justify our presence."

Case Study. "Fanny became ill in 1937 and has been in the hospital ever since. She has had EST and a lobotomy, and during the last few years has pulled slightly out of her generally catatonic adjustment. When I first came to see her, she was obviously very hostile: She wanted to be left alone, said 'go away.' On the other hand, she did hang around the doorway when I looked in to see her, which indicated that there was some hope of communicating with her. However, it was a long time before she stopped being hostile. She said that I should go and work with the twenty-year-olds. She thought I was here to get a wife, or get a job, and said I was wasting my time with her. The first time I felt that we had made some kind of communication occurred on an evening when I stayed for two hours or more, and just sat there. I emphasized that if she didn't have anything to say we didn't have to talk, and there we sat. Finally, for the first time she began to talk with some spontaneity, recalling memories from childhood.

"She continued for quite a while to mistrust my motives. I would sometimes joke with her. If she said 'no,' I would just repeat it and joke about her saying 'no.' For instance, I wanted to take her to the store. She didn't want 'to hang around the men,' so she refused to go. Well, in spite of all her show of hostility, when I went down to where she works sorting clothes, she stopped working. She sat down on a laundry bag and kind of half indicated I might sit down on one next to it. Of course, if I had taken the lead and sat down first, she would not have sat down! I had let her take the lead. We sat down and talked, but I got into a fairly big argument with her because I was getting annoyed at all the hostility and I was becoming hostile, too. That didn't work at all, so after that I would just drop by and ignore her saying 'go away,' and so on. This seemed to work, and pretty soon she started to be gracious, offered me coffee, and so on. It helped that I was talking to her where she worked with all the other women, and I did a kind of group therapy. If Fanny wouldn't talk or would say she didn't want to go to the store, I would ask the others what they thought about the store.

"Finally, toward the end of the summer, I actually went into the ward and was able to talk with her for the first time outside her work stronghold. She began to talk about cafeteria work, and indicated that maybe she wanted to change. She quit that entirely as soon as I started pressing it, however, because she was very fearful of making any step forward. As she was getting more gracious and I was spending more time with her, she began to feel she was wasting my time and I had to reassure her that she wasn't and that she deserved every bit of it, but that when she said 'no,' she *was* wasting my time. If she would let me take her to the store, then she would not be wasting my time. This seemed to work.

"At the end of the summer, I finally persuaded Fanny to rejoin the remotivation class that she had stopped attending at the beginning of the summer. It turned out that she was the most verbal member of the group. When I took her and some of the others for a ride around the farm afterward, she continued to talk about harvest-time topics (the subject of the remotivation group) and pointed things out to others. So, in little ways our relationship became a lot more friendly, although if pressed, she would still come out with a hostile remark or two. Concretely, Fanny is back in remotivation and has made several visits to the store. I have also talked with the aide quite a bit about what we can do to get her moving. The aide is fearful that she will regress, and we talked this over quite a bit. Now we agree that perhaps pushing her into a different job, in spite of her saying 'no,' would be good for her, since she is capable of much more."

The foregoing shows how the Mental Health Workers saw their activity. Apparently, ward personnel and patients, too, have reacted favorably to the program.

As observers, we saw the Mental Health Worker constantly wrestle with the problem of reassuring himself that he was being useful in spite of the fact that his patients may not have gone appreciably further toward the goal of discharge. As mentioned earlier, our orientation stressed this ultimate goal more than the goal of providing patients with the immediate pleasure of spending time in social activity. Now, however, we are convinced that teleologic and immediate goals should be equally stressed. Appreciation of the intrinsic desirability of having a patient productively occupied is one basis of modern institutional psychiatry. We feel that this philosophy is centrally relevant to the best use of the Mental Health Worker. He must begin his task with an appreciation of the therapeutic potential of his willingness to give something of himself to the patient.

COLLEGE STUDENTS HELP CHRONIC PATIENTS

CONSTANCE B. NELSON, Ph.D.

FOR MANY YEARS the psychology department of the VA Hospital in St. Cloud, Minnesota, has used college student volunteers for technical procedures, such as collecting and analyzing data, but students had never worked directly with patients for the department until 1966. When I joined the psychology staff that year, the department chief asked me to organize and coordinate a volunteer program for undergraduate psychology students.

Like every large state and VA psychiatric hospital, the St. Cloud VA Hospital has a large chronic population, and many of the men have no family to visit or correspond with them. One problem with such patients is to keep hope alive, not only in them, but to some extent in the staff also. We thought the psychology students could help to do that, and so we called the project HOPE: Helping Our Patients Emerge.

During the first year 48 students, 42 men and six women, took part. Eighteen students from St. Cloud State College served for two and a half months, and 30 members of my abnormal psychology class at St. John's University in Collegeville participated for five months. Each student served at least one hour a week.

After the students were registered and given a preliminary briefing by the hospital's office of volunteers, I interviewed each one to find out his major

HOSPITAL AND COMMUNITY PSYCHIATRY, Dec. 1969, vol. 20, no. 12, pp. 394-395.

subject, vocational goals, interests, and hobbies. I then met with the staff of the geographical unit on which the students would serve, to discuss the project and get suggestions about which patients might be assigned to the volunteers; we tried to match those with similar interests. Only two of the patients we selected refused to participate. The biggest problem was to work out visiting times compatible with the students' complicated school schedules and the patients' treatment schedules.

I gave the students a brief orientation about the hospital, emphasizing the importance of confidentiality. I also was available after classes at St. John's for my students there, and at set times in my hospital office for the St. Cloud students. The ward staffs provided immediate supervision, and the Catholic chaplain gave special guidance to four students who were studying for the priesthood. All the students kept notebooks about the interaction with their patients; the notebooks helped determine their grades in their psychology courses.

The students had a few explicit rules to observe, such as not taking a patient off the ward unless he had a privilege card or his physician's approval, and always telling the nursing staff where they and their patients would be. The one rule the students felt was detrimental was the ban on taking patients off grounds in their cars. Public transportation into town is poor, and few of the students could afford the taxi fares. They felt they could have helped their patients more if they could have taken them to more places outside the hospital.

The students were conscientious about keeping their appointments with patients and letting us know if they would be unable to. We were impressed with their devotion, perseverance, and skill in trying to reach mute, withdrawn patients. They uncovered skills and interests in the men that we had not known of; some depressed patients who at first were hostile to the volunteers eventually became friendly with them and appreciative of their help. I recall one bitter veteran, long estranged from his family, who suddenly started writing to his college-age son. The unit staff came to enjoy and admire the students; many of them told me they hoped their own teen-agers would turn out as well as the volunteers. The staff also enjoyed serving as teachers and interpreters for the students, and they were stimulated by their eagerness and enthusiasm.

The students gained not only valuable experience to supplement their textbook learning but also the gratification of helping others. The project also helped them with their career plans; at least six said they decided to go on to graduate work to become social workers, psychologists, or psychiatrists. Equally important, a few learned they did not want such a career. The four seminarians said the experience would be invaluable in their work as priests.

Some of the students who later sought to enroll in graduate schools asked me for a letter of recommendation based on their work in the project, and then wrote to tell me the letter had helped them be accepted. All in all, Project HOPE produced benefits beyond the immediate ones to the patient, student, and staff participants. Both the hospital and the community derived gains from the more enlightened and hopeful attitudes the students acquired.

COLLEGE STUDENT VOLUNTEERS AS CASE AIDES IN A STATE HOSPITAL FOR CHILDREN

HELEN REINHERZ

ALTHOUGH volunteers have become well accepted in mental hospitals, their role has not generally included direct therapeutic work with patients. Since 1954, however, Harvard and Radcliffe student volunteers have been working with groups and individual patients at the Metropolitan State Hospital in Waltham, Massachusetts. Their work has been commended by the Joint Commission on Mental Illness and Health as a "contribution to reduction of the manpower problem in the helping professions," and a demonstration that "relatively untrained people can work with the mentally ill under supervision."[1]

In spite of the existence of a well-established, volunteer case aide program with professional supervision in the adult hospital, the Children's Unit began its case aide program only on a pilot basis in the fall of 1959. Five students were each to work intensively with an individual patient selected by the hospital staff with the following criteria: the child had not been assigned to a "professional" therapist, would be in the hospital for the remainder of the academic year, and did

AMERICAN JOURNAL OF ORTHOPSYCHIATRY, 1963, vol. 33, no. 3, pp. 544-546.

not present unmanageable behavior problems.

Acceptance of the case aside program by the hospital staff was a gradual process. However, co-operation was facilitated by regular communication with the staff, assurance of careful supervision by the group's professional leader and responsible performance on the part of the volunteers. (I have written elsewhere in detail about the salient aspects of professional leadership of the volunteers, as well as some of the content of the learning experience.[2]) By the second year, the children's case aide program had become an accepted ongoing part of the program of the hospital and is now well into its fourth year of continuation.

As had been traditional in all volunteer work with patients, the students thought of themselves primarily as socializing influences bringing the outside world to the patients and bringing the patients out into the world. In addition, as their work progressed, both the students and their professional leader defined the case aide role increasingly in terms of the special student-patient relationship.

By the end of the first year, the student role was delineated as ego-supportive, educative in the broadest sense of the word and parental in bringing healthy experiences in relationship and activity that are part of the normal maturation of a child in any community. Two of the children in the pilot group who had been most deeply deprived of the support of a steady adult figure began to show striking changes in growth and ability to relate, at first to their volunteers and later to other adult figures in the hospital.

As a result, the goals of the students enlarged from the more modest intention of aiding the children in socialization to more ambitious levels such as providing "a corrective emotional experience with an adult" and "helping to establish inner controls." An evaluation of the accomplishments of the program at the end of the first two years by students, professional leader and staff members most closely associated with patients and students indicated that the student had in most cases partially or wholly fulfilled the goals that they had set for themselves.

One of the important elements that makes any volunteer relationship with hospitalized mental patients unique is the fact that the volunteer is considered a representative of society at large, of the community outside the hospital walls. The volunteer case aides brought the children into the community as much as possible, trying to give the patients the kind of experience available to children "on the outside." Thus, the students had the opportunity to witness and the need to handle many of the difficulties the children had in dealing with the community outside the hospital, from unrealistic fears to lack of knowledge of how to behave in various situations. The difficulties had to be handled on the spot by the students, often with therapeutic results.

Another unique factor in the case aide relationship was that, as well as being community-oriented, it was activity-oriented. The activities not only had great ego-building values in themselves, but they also provided an easier way of relating for children who had much difficulty in verbalization. For some of the children in the hospital the case aide relationship provided the leeway and lack of spatial confinement necesary to help them slowly lose their distrust of adults and begin to relate to others. One of the hospital staff members said that he felt that the case aides contributed in a major way to the child who had in the past been unready to form the kind of relationship and trust that would enable him to use traditional forms of therapy. Through the case aide program, which seemed less threatening to the children, the ability to relate meaningfully developed and the children became receptive to other forms of psychological help.

The youth of the college volunteers, mainly in their early twenties, made them highly suitable as figures for identification by the children. Of special interest was the marked identification with their volunteers of two early adolescent boys. In both cases ward personnel and psychiatrists noted a rapid maturing and meaningful growth during the period of "case aide therapy."

Some of the positive results that college students have had in working with emotionally disturbed children may well be related to the fact that college students have just resolved or are in the process of solving many of the basic issues facing the maturing individual. In late adolescence, identity problems, particularly those associated with sexual role and career choice, are among the most pressing issues besetting the individual. The emotionally disturbed child is also grappling with the many problems of identity, on a different level. Thus, the college student is in a position to be particularly sensitive to many of these struggles and needs in the disturbed child. In many cases as the student aided the child in working out a problem involving self-concept and maturity, the student, in turn, seemed to be achieving a definitive and positive solution for himself as well.

An evaluation of the impact of the volunteer case aide program must include an acknowledgment of changes in the hospital milieu during the first two years of the program. There was an increased ratio of staff to patients and a resultant improvement in hospital morale during a period in which the total staff was attempting to improve the treatment and milieu. However, our assessment of the case aide program was based on the clinical judgment of the hospital staff.

After the first year's program, it was reported by staff physicians that three out of four children seen for the full year's period showed improvement in functioning. For the second year, when patient selection was more informed, the staff physicians reported change and progress in all seven of the children seen by volunteers. In several cases, when psychological tests were done on patients, positive growth was confirmed.

It seems clear that many of the goals and achievements of "case aide therapy" are identical with the sound therapeutic aims of professionals and nonprofessionals involved in the difficult task of working with the emotionally disturbed child. Both volunteers and members of the hospital staff can supplement one another's efforts toward their common aim—the achievement of growth and appropriate maturity by the child.

REFERENCES

1. Action for Mental Health: Final Report of the Joint Commission on Mental Illness and Health. **1961.** Basic Books. New York, N.Y. : 253-254.
2. REINIIERZ, H. **1962.** Leadership of student volunteers. Mental Hospitals **13**(11): 600-602.

Volunteers Help Build Patients' Self-Esteem

ARTHUR N. SCHWARTZ, Ph.D.

T OO OFTEN the assistance given to patients in an institution is based on the staff's priorities, capacities, and needs rather than on the patients'. Help is not really help unless it is relevant to the patient and can be used by him. Because of our concern with that problem at the Veterans Administration Center Domiciliary in Los Angeles, we undertook a survey three years ago to determine the needs of the 150 men in our restoration program. We wanted to understand how each man characterized himself: that is, what his needs were, how to help him articulate them, and how we could respond appropriately to his particular needs and priorities.

From that survey we found that the patients shared several characteristics. The men were lonely: they had a strong sense of personal, social, and vocational failure; they felt vulnerable, inadequate, powerless, and apprehensive; and they had a strong fear of further failure. In short, our patients were "losers"—not necessarily born losers, but, over the years, vocational, social, and marital losers. Despite many medical, counseling, and vocational efforts to help the men, they continued to show a marked lack of self-esteem; that appears to have contributed at least partially to the high readmission rate of those who were released.

One problem that some of the men discussed with a staff member was their need to meet and to deal effectively with "nice" women. Their problem

Betsy Hardie, M.A., director of volunteers at the domiciliary, is co-author of this article.

HOSPITAL & COMMUNITY PSYCHIATRY, March 1970, vol. 21, no. 3, pp. 87-89.

74

was not really where to meet such women or what to talk about; all of the men were reasonably able conversationalists. Rather, their sense of inadequacy made them apprehensive about initiating a social relationship with women they considered worthwhile and attractive human beings. We felt that an appropriate response to such a fundamental need was not to refer them to social clubs or a Dale Carnegie course, or to teach them the elements of small talk, or even to give them formal psychotherapy, in which we merely talk about self-esteem.

We felt the men's underlying sense of inadequacy must be met head on by giving them opportunities to experience success in associating with "nice" women in a relatively "safe" social situation. By "nice" we meant women who were trustworthy, straightforward, humane, and warm in spirit; by "safe" we meant a situation in which each individual could socialize at his own pace, without fear of being overwhelmed by social expectations or penalized for social errors.

Through our volunteer service we recruited attractive young women with the desired qualities to meet once a week with a group of patients who had expressed the need for such interaction. We selected the volunteers quite carefully, seeking those who were not only active and straightforward, but also warm, friendly, easy-going, and poised enough to respond to most social errors and ineptness with kindness. We wanted good listeners as well as good talkers.

To date, 29 women have participated for four weeks to 14 months; they included five airline stewardesses, nine office workers, seven housewives, three sales clerks, two professional models, a writer, two artists, and a student. (Several other women participated only a few times, and were classed as visitors.)

A IRLINE stewardesses make fine participants but not unexpectedly they are the least reliable in attendance because of their variable schedules. And when the meetings were changed from late afternoon to evening for the convenience of the men who worked during the day, the housewives with children began to drop out. Thus, over the three-year period there has been a complete turnover in volunteers, but gradual enough so that fairly good continuity has been maintained. The women recruited through our volunteer service have friends they in turn recruited to participate.

We do not attempt to give the volunteers a lengthy formal orientation, but concentrate on acquainting them with the general goal of the group. We avoid the usual cautions about not becoming too personal and about avoiding discussions of religion, sex, or politics. We believe that the women, no less than the men, should be allowed to be themselves and to deal with situations spontaneously; we feel that the women we select are responsible adults who are able to deal capably with even potentially difficult situations.

During the past three years, about 62 patients have taken part, on a voluntary basis. The original participants were five men who made the first inquiries about how to meet women, and attendance grew as word spread about the program. The median length of participation is five months; only 18 per cent have come to fewer than four meetings. To date, 26 of the men have returned to the community, and five of them still maintain occasional contact with the group. About 12 eventually dropped out of the program without explanation. Although we had a peak average attendance of 21 men and seven volunteers during part of 1968, the current average attendance is nine men and four volunteers.

The group meets each Tuesday evening for two hours, starting about 7 p.m. The volunteers and men assemble in a comfortably furnished staff room, and usually by 7:30 all participants have arrived and are engaged in twos and threes in conversation. A sideboard holds coffee prepared by one of the men and pastries furnished by the volunteers, and people help themselves at will.

ONLY RARELY do we present a formal topic of discussion. Once we announced that we would discuss loneliness, and the response was guarded. However, as various members began disclosing their feelings, the group became increasingly engrossed in the discussion. When one of the stewardesses said she felt lonely at times, the reaction was astonishing, almost as if a dam holding back feelings had collapsed. Later several of the men indicated that they had suddenly realized that they had no corner on loneliness; perhaps even more important, the open discussion of such a sensitive subject had made them feel closer to the group.

Usually conversational exchanges begin spontaneously, with two or three members discussing a subject that intrigues and gradually involves the entire group. For example, when one of the volunteers brought her eight-year-old son to a meeting, the men were very pleased. They joked with the boy and began asking the mother questions about his activities. In short order the entire group was discussing children's sensitivity to feelings, the members' own childhood experiences, and the values and risks of expressing feelings. On another occasion the "way out" dress of one of the women led to a discussion of hippies, dropping out, and cultural norms.

Despite the obvious pleasure the participants took in these exchanges, it was still evident after a few months that some constraints were operating. One concerned my role as a staff member, even though I have attempted as far as possible to be just another member of the group. I also usually leave the meeting just before it disperses; I found that when I left too early, some of the participants suspected that I was not personally interested in the group, and if I stayed to oversee the departure of the members, I seemed to be a staff chaperone.

Another problem was that the men were all too aware that the volunteers came to them in the institution, and that increased the men's feelings of being inmates. As their need emerged to meet with the women on neutral ground, at least occasionally,

77

we began to explore possibilities. I discussed the matter with the group, and with their enthusiastic support enlisted the help of our volunteer service director. She contacted several service organizations and obtained cash donations, to be used for monthly outings for the group.

We canvassed local restaurants until we found one willing to serve the group a complete dinner at cost. The group meets for dinner one evening a month, either at a restaurant or elsewhere outside the institution, such as at a volunteer's home or on picnics at a park or beach, with costs met from the special fund. At our first dinner we encountered the ticklish problem of whether or not the men could order a predinner drink; a number of them have drinking problems, and several classify themselves as alcoholics. When the question arose, I explained candidly that we had only enough money to buy the dinners; those who wanted to order a drink would have to pay for it. About four or five of the 18 participants elected to buy one. Our experience so far has been that several members will order a drink at the table, and we have never lost anyone to the bar. The alcoholics have never ordered drinks, although they joke about it.

The success of the group is shown in the men's comments about it and their improved behavior and attitudes. We frequently hear such comments as, "I really enjoy the group—I feel so comfortable." And not long ago, one of the men asked me wistfully, "Do you think I can ever learn to get along with people, with. women?" I asked him how he thought the group felt about him, and he replied, "Well, I think they like me; at least they make me feel good."

AFTER THE FIRST two months of the group, it was no longer necessary to send the men reminders about the meetings. We feel that they will continue to participate voluntarily as long as the group offers them some incentive. The primary incentive is the opportunity to engage in safe, pleasant socializing with mentally and physically attractive women. In addition, if a member misses a meeting, he is not chided or asked a reason; instead, he is usually greeted the next time with "We missed you."

The group enables the men to learn new social skills through an imitating and testing-out process. As they experience success with interpersonal exchanges in the group, they begin to show changes in their attitudes and behavior. Some of the changes appear quickly, particularly in the matter of dress. Probably because they have little incentive to do otherwise, most of the domiciliary patients dress casually, even sloppily. However, the men in the group take pains to be neatly dressed and groomed for the meetings. And when one participant refused to modify his crude language, the other men pressured him into not returning. The courtesy and consideration they show each other and the women have been exemplary, including such gestures as helping the women with refreshments, lighting their cigarettes, and escorting them to their cars after the meeting.

O NE QUESTION that arises is whether the men are more interested in the unmarried than the married women. Although a few men have made dating overtures to some of the single volunteers, we have noticed that the men respond principally to the warmth, kindness, and interest shown by the volunteers, regardless of marital status.

The relationships among the men have improved as well. My experience has been that the men in the domiciliary tend to look down on one another; each seems acutely aware that he is surrounded by losers. However, the men in the group have learned to have more respect for one another. For example, at one meeting where the men outnumbered the women four to one, a man who had been conversing at length with two other men remarked to me, with some surprise, "You know, some of these guys are really interesting."

The women also gain personal satisfaction from the group, and they show it by their participation and through special gestures. When our special fund ran out near the end of 1968, we were afraid we would have to forego the group's Christmas dinner. Instead, we enjoyed a fine dinner at a fashionable inn, paid for by our senior volunteer, a young matron; the party was her husband's Christmas gift to her, and her only stipulation was that her largesse remain anonymous. Another woman, with her husband's consent, shared her birthday cake with the group, and recently one woman asked me how she could get practical-nursing training so that she could enlarge the sphere of her volunteer work.

Although the group is not an end-all for getting the men back into the community as capable, productive citizens, it does fill an important gap in the range of rehabilitative modalities by meeting a need that the men consider a priority. We encourage those who leave the domiciliary to maintain regular contact with the group, because we feel that they can be effective models and supports to those who still need sheltered care.

THE USE OF HIGH SCHOOL AND COLLEGE STUDENTS AS THERAPISTS AND RESEARCHERS IN A STATE MENTAL HOSPITAL

C. EUGENE WALKER

MILTON WOLPIN and LLOYD FELLOWS

The problem of attracting many more mental health workers into the field is becoming increasingly more acute (Albee, 1960). Along with this growing challenge demands are increasingly being felt for more meaningful experiences in education. Students need a chance to interact directly with the excitement of the real world rather than the dry abstractions of textbooks. Clearly, students today care greatly about what happens around them. The volunteer mental health programs seem to be a natural as something to be built into the formal educational structure.

The present report suggests that colleges and high schools might readily implement such programs. Our results are consistent with those reported by Schiebe (1965) and others.

The Program for College Students

This program was initiated in September, 1964, as a joint venture between Westmont College, Santa Barbara, a small (600 students) liberal arts college and Camarillo State Hospital, Camarillo, California, a large (4600 patients and 25 psychologists) state hospital. The college offers two three-unit psychology courses open, by consent of the instructor, to upper division (junior and senior) students from any academic area.

In one course each student is assigned to a psychologist at the hospital for whom he serves as an assistant four hours per day once every week. The student works on a research project conducted by the psychologist and is given as much responsibility and freedom in carrying out his part of the project as he is capable of handling. Students in this course share in the responsibility of searching the literature, planning the research, gathering and analyzing data, and writing the final article. So

far two articles have been published in this fashion (Wolpin and Pearsall, 1965 and Wolpin and Raines, 1966) and others are currently in preparation. A weekly one hour class is held on the campus to provide further supervision and informal discussion of problems as they develop.

The second course emphasizes service activities involving direct contact with the patients. Students lead re-motivation groups, talk to individual patients on a "friendship" basis, direct activity groups with children, teach school on the adolescent ward, work in art therapy with regressed patients and get involved in a wide range of activities. The supervision, reading assignments, and class meetings are handled as above.

For a rough evaluation all students completed a sentence completion test modified from one originally developed by Lindgren (1952). There has been general agreement among the students that the practicum course was one of the best and most exciting experiences of their undergraduate education. Typical comments were: *"The value* . . . is in being in a situation where academic learning may be acted upon." *"The best* . . . part of the course is learning by doing . . . part was being able to go down to the hospital and really participate." *"What I liked most* . . . was finding out what being a part of psychology is actually like." *"What I liked most* . . . was learning how to accept a mental patient as a human being, learning about abilities I didn't know I had." *"Research in psychology* . . . is more interesting to me because of my experience at Camarillo . . . is exciting, interesting, and enslaving; as well as being never ending . . . is slow but interesting and presents problems that are just hard enough to maintain interest in solving them."

A few students felt that the experience had been useful in helping them decide on a vocational choice. Some were influenced positively and others negatively: *"Since I have taken this course* . . . I'm a little more sure of the type of work I want to do." *"The influence of this course on my vocational goals*

PSYCHOTHERAPY, THEORY, RESEARCH & PRACTICE, 1967, vol. 4, no. 4, pp. 186-188.

81

. . . is I'm pretty sure I wouldn't like to do this all the time."

One frequently made comment was that much more responsibility was given the student and much more was expected of him in this situation than he was accustomed to in his ordinary classroom experiences, e.g.; *"The practicum would be better if . . . there had been more orientation." "I really didn't expect . . . to be treated so much as an equal by the staff."* However, as they adjusted to this situation, it became a source of considerable reward and they were happy for it: *"What I like most . . . has been the opportunity to develop responsibility in a professional situation."*

The major disadvantages of the course had to do with practical problems in traveling to and from the hospital (the trip is fifty miles one way).

The Program for High School Students

A high school program grew rather naturally out of the experiences with college students. In the spring of 1965 we contacted a local high school, detailed the experience we had had working with students at the college level, and asked if they were interested in developing a pilot program for the summer. Cooperation at all levels at the high school was very good.

For this program we selected through school recommendations and personal interviews four boys who excelled academically and in extracurricular activities.

These youngsters were required to spend four full days a week for eight weeks at the hospital, where they were assigned to work on the adolescent and pre-adolescent boys units. They were paid $50 a month for the two months, on a par with domestic peace corps work. We expected and received strong commitment in time and energy.

Following an initial week of orientation to the hospital and discussion of general principles of psychology and mental health, the trainees began to work on the adolescent male unit. The first two weeks required almost the full time of the one psychologist involved in the program. It was the most demanding time for the supervisor. The following weeks required a diminishing amount of time, so that by the end of the first month the teenage trainees were fairly well on their own. The permissive discussion hour was important in allowing the students to ventilate their feelings concerning various experiences, and to learn additional behavioral dynamics from the supervisor. Initially the supervisor needed to suggest programs and activities which might be carried out by the trainees. As they became familiar with the types of activities which were considered helpful, they planned for themselves and became adept at implementing their plans, despite the administrative complexities of a large mental hospital.

The high school trainees attended various lectures at the hospital along with staff members, including psychiatric interviews, staffings, and team meetings on the adolescent unit. They were involved with patients individually and in group therapy with a leave planning group. They did counseling and tutoring in basic skills with academically retarded adolescents, and engaged in therapeutic conditioning procedures. They organized and supervised social activities and outings such as beach parties, camp-outs, social dances, hikes and swimming. They ran sports events including baseball, basketball, volleyball and football.

A typical day included running a club group therapy session, taking a group swimming, eating with some boys in the patients' dining hall, tutoring at the school, and reading in the professional library about subjects that interested them.

Intensive inquiry with staff, patients and students has failed to elicit negative comments of any consequence. There is much enthusiasm for a larger project in the future.

Effect on Hospital

For the patient, these programs mean more personal care and the opportunity to interact with an attractive young person interested in helping. Many of the patients have commented favorably regarding their student "therapists."

Their effect upon the patients was particularly notable with one dorm of 13 boys on whom the high school students concentrated. Many of the boys idealized the trainees and sought to copy whatever they did. The trainees were held in a kind of "big brother" esteem and respect. In the months since the summer program closed, a number of the boys from the dormitory have been placed in foster or group homes where they seem to be adjusting well, having learned some aspects of effective behavior from the trainees.

This sort of program seems to be an effective means of overcoming some of the problems in mental hospitals.

DISCUSSION

From the present writers' experience, it is not surprising that the final report of the Joint Commission on Mental Illness and Health should contain a recommendation that this type of program be extended and expanded (1961).

Many questions are raised by the seeming success of such programs and many innovations remain to be attempted.

Can youngsters bring a breath of fresh air and hope into the lives of the older, and somewhat infirm? Would a similar approach work in reform schools, jails and clinics? Would it work with a population of persons in acute distress, as compared to those we know best in state hospitals, the chronic? Must we rely on youngsters who are clearly among the more adequate and capable or can juvenile delinquents, for example, be deliberately introduced into such a setting, by coming over daily from their own institution, with the explicit expectation they have something to offer and can help others? Would deliberately fostering such expectations result in a positive experience on both sides?

By reaching students early, we may be able to foster better personal development as well as enrich school and college curricula while developing potential interest and entrance into the mental health field. The fact that many of these young people will someday be leaders in their community enhances the value of their having a background regarding the problems and possibilities in the area of psychological research and service to the emotionally troubled.

REFERENCES

ALBEE, G. W. The Manpower Crisis in Mental Health. *Amer. J. Pub. Health,* 1960, **50,** 1895-1900.

DOHAN, J. L. in: GREENBLATT, M., LEVINSON, D. J., & WILLIAMS, R. H. *The patient and the mental hospital,* Glencoe, Ill.: The Free Press, 1957.

GREENBLATT, M. & KANTOR, D. "Student Volunteer Movement and the Manpower Shortage." *Amer. J. Psychiat.* 1962, **118,** 809-814.

Joint Commission on Mental Illness and Health. *Action for Mental Health.* New York: Basic Books, 1961. (pp. 88-93 and 253-254).

LINDGREN, H. C. The incomplete sentences test as a means of course evaluation. *Ed. Psych. Measurement,* 1952, **12,** 217-225.

SCHIEBE, K. E. College students spend eight weeks in a mental hospital: A case report. *Psychotherapy: Theory, Research and Practice,* 1965, **2,** 117-120.

SIEGEL, B. A. Students as professional aides in direct patient relationships in a state hospital. *Unpublished Paper,* presented at APA Convention, 1966. Mimeographed copies available on request.

SIEGEL, B. A. The use of pre-professional and non-professional personnel as a partial solution to the manpower shortage. *Symposium,* presented at the California State Psychol. Assoc. Convention, Jan., 1966. Mimeographed copies are available on request.

UMBARGER, C. C., DALSIMER, J. S., MORRISON, A. P., & BREGGIN, P. R. *College students in a mental hospital.* New York: Grune and Stratton, 1962.

WOLPIN, M. & PEARSALL, LESLEY. Rapid de-conditioning of a fear of snakes. *Beh. Res. & Ther.,* 1965, **3,** 107-111.

WOLPIN, M. & WALKER, C. E. An undergraduate practicum program in psychology offered by Camarillo State Hospital and Westmont College. *Quart. of Camarillo,* 1965, **1,** 29-32.

WOLPIN, M. & RAINES, J. Visual imagery, extinction and expected roles as factors in reducing fear and avoidance behavior. *Beh. Res. & Ther.,* 1966, **4,** 25-37.

Psychology Students
Work with Retardates

ZEV W. WANDERER, M.S.

MANNY STERNLICHT, Ph.D.

PSYCHOLOGY DEPARTMENTS, by and large, tend to shy away from volunteer programs, because it is difficult to use amateur workers in a highly technical field. However, at Willowbrook State School, N.Y., the largest known institution for the mentally retarded, a successful volunteer program has been operated for nearly three years.

This volunteer program started in 1960. It followed, quite unintentionally, a tour we made of neighboring universities in an endeavor to bring our department to the attention of graduate psychology faculties at Columbia, New York University, and Yeshiva University in Manhattan. Faculty members were impressed with the massive research potential offered by our 6000 patients, including nearly 1000 in the pediatric wards. A number of students requested tours of our facilities, and we were able to establish an ongoing psychology internship program.

By the summer of 1961, a large number of candidates, most of them working toward their master's degrees in psychology, applied for volunteer work. They came from the same schools in which our recent interns were completing their doctoral training. We could accept only four of the applicants that first year. We did not demand actual work experience, but we did require that our volunteers have excellent classroom knowledge of the theory and practice of clinical psychology and sufficient motivation to study intensively to acquire the needed skills. The relatively low rates of absenteeism and tardiness among our volunteers seemed to confirm

MENTAL HOSPITALS, 1964, vol. 15, no. 5, pp. 271-272.

the validity of the choices made at the screening interviews.

The psychology volunteers saved little if any of our time, nor did they lighten our workload, mainly because of the supervisory and training time required. But an intangible gain resulted—the stimulation of dealing with inquisitive, skeptical, inquiring young people who could not be placated by classroom platitudes and vagaries. Members of the regular staff gained new experience in teaching and supervising, which added zest to their daily routine.

To enable these student psychologists to gain a frame of reference in dealing with mentally retarded patients, we assigned them to work on the wards for several days under the supervision of an attendant. This experience was followed by a week of rote-learning of the most commonly employed tests, after which the volunteers spent another week observing the staff administering these tests. Questions were welcomed at scheduled and unscheduled conferences. During the third week, the volunteers were encouraged to ventilate their feelings about dealing with patients and to discuss various interpretations.

Assignments Varied

By the fourth week, these volunteers were administering intelligence tests and at the same time taking didactic courses in administering and interpreting projective techniques. One or two were already sufficiently well trained to need only a minimal amount of supervision. Although our interns participate in psychotherapeutic procedures under close supervision, the volunteers' contact with psychotherapy was confined to theory.

Two of the volunteers were later assigned to a clinical research project then being carried on by the psychology department. Their tasks consisted mainly of reviewing the literature in a given area, and executing certain experimental procedures. One tabulated raw data into workable form.

We included all volunteers in all staff conferences, and they had contact with other members of the staff both in groups and individually. They were required to attend all medical conferences open to the psychology department. We held individual conferences to discuss plans for their own professional advancement, such as their choice of a doctoral program, preparation for their fall examinations, internship opportunities, and possible areas of specialization. The chief psychologist occasionally discussed their personal problems with them.

Rapport with Social Workers

Volunteers were invited to use staff dining and recreational facilities, where they exchanged views with members of the other disciplines. It was not uncommon for a volunteer to stay overnight at the staff house. Since psychology and social service share the same corridor at Willowbrook, the volunteers were able to observe the contributions of the social workers at firsthand and to discuss them personally with the social workers. The joint psychology-social service coffee breaks were usually scenes of lively and stimulating exchanges.

At the conclusion of their volunteer work, the students summed up their experiences on a questionnaire as "profitable," "exciting," "an excellent firsthand learning experience." They had experienced being "inside" a large state school and hospital, had been confronted by a wide array of patients, and had learned that one serves best when one masters the art of viewing patients objectively while relating empathically. They had been exposed to a vibrant, growing psychology department, and absorbed the philosophy that psychology is a science as long as research continues, and is an art as long as practice is being continually refined. They had sensed some intrastaff problems, experienced "the tyranny of the trivial" that besets any organization of sensitive people, and observed the steps taken to increase understanding and harmonious interaction. They had seen how administrative machinery can blend efficiency with understanding, and had learned some things about state institution policies and programs.

At the end of the two summer months, nearly all had served a total of 270 hours. Each volunteer had made some decision about his career and had started on his chosen course. The psychology department ended the summer by giving a "recognition luncheon" for the volunteers.

86

Quick Placement for Volunteers

A few months after the completion of the summer program, we became curious about what our former volunteers were doing. We made inquiries and learned that one young man, thanks to his experience at Willowbrook, had immediately obtained a part-time position as clinical psychologist with Catholic Charities, while pursuing his doctoral studies. Another was immediately appointed as Senior Guidance Counselor in a Long Island school system, with a $2000 raise over his last presummer position, presumably because of his newly learned skills in testing children. A third volunteer, who had served only one full month, decided to become a school psychologist, and was accepted full-time in the Rochester public school system. The fourth, a young lady, was surprised to learn that she had now qualified for a research assistantship at Yeshiva University, where she was pursuing her doctoral studies in clinical psychology. She accepted the appointment.

During the fall of 1961, one of our former volunteers called and stated that she could spare one day a week and would appreciate it if we would accept her, as well as a fellow graduate student, for additional volunteer service and training during the winter. After screening the new candidate, we extended the volunteer training program throughout the winter months for one day a week. The full-time program resumes every summer, and this year Willowbrook is preparing to accept three or four new student volunteers.

III. COMPARISONS OF STUDENT VOLUNTEERS WITH OTHER GROUPS

Comparative Effectiveness of Student and Professional Counselors

VERNON G. ZUNKER

WILLIAM F. BROWN

A sample of 160 beginning freshmen, half males and half females, received six and one-half hours of academic adjustment guidance from same-sex professional counselors. Upperclassman student counselors gave equivalent guidance to all other beginning freshmen at Southwest Texas State College. A matching sample of 80 men and 80 women was subsequently drawn from the 316 freshmen receiving student-to-student counseling. Age, sex, measured scholastic ability, measured study orientation, and high school academic achievement were employed as matching variables. The four professional and eight student counselors completed 50 clock hours of identical pre-counseling training, used identical guidance materials, and followed identical counseling activity sequences. Equivalent counseling facilities were provided for all counselors. Test, questionnaire, and scholarship data were employed to evaluate the comparative effectiveness and acceptability of counseling given the professional counseled and the student counseled groups. Student counselors were found to be as effective as professional counselors on all criteria of counseling effectiveness. Furthermore, freshmen counseled by student counselors made significantly greater use of the information received during counseling, as reflected by first-semester grades and residual study problems. It was concluded that carefully selected, trained, and supervised student counselors provide a practical and productive addition to the college's guidance program.

A s a result of constantly increasing enrollments in institutions of higher learning, many administrators have found it necessary to enlarge and revise current college counseling programs. The major objective has been to provide the necessary environment and services for the fullest development of each individual's intellectual potential. The demand for expanded guidance activities, however, has usually been restricted by financial and personnel limitations.

At most colleges, the increasing number of freshmen arriving on campus each fall makes it virtually impossible for each to receive early attention from personnel workers and faculty members. A survey recent-

This study was supported by a grant from the Hogg Foundation for Mental Health, The University of Texas, Austin.

PERSONNEL AND GUIDANCE JOURNAL, 1966, vol. 44, no. 7, pp. 738-743.

ly completed by the authors (Brown & Zunker, in press) indicates that college personnel programs are increasingly utilizing upperclassmen to assist in the early orientation of freshmen to the college community. Because of this increasing reliance upon student-counseling-student procedures, the productivity, acceptability, and feasibility of student-to-student counseling needs to be systematically evaluated. Consequently, the purpose of this study was to compare the effectiveness of carefully trained student counselors with the effectiveness of certified school counselors in providing academic adjustment guidance to beginning college freshmen. Specifically, comparative evaluations were made on the following: effectiveness of the counseling in communicating information about academic adjustment problems and solutions, impact of the counseling upon subsequent academic achievement, and acceptability of such counseling by the counselees.

The comparisons were made within a specially structured counseling program designed to provide academic adjustment guidance for entering college freshmen. A comprehensive description of this guidance program has been published elsewhere (Brown, 1965a). Guidance services that require professional training, such as personal-social adjustment counseling, vocational guidance, and psychotherapy, were not included within the structure and scope of this counseling program.

PROCEDURE

Two female and two male professional counselors were selected and trained for the research project. Each of the four professional counselors met the following selection criteria: (1) was certified as a school counselor by the Texas Education Agency; (2) was at least 10 years older than the typical entering college freshman; (3) was recommended by two professors who were primarily responsible for directing their professional training for counseling certification; (4) was presently employed as a teacher or counselor and had at least five years of professional teaching and/or counseling experience; (5) was advanced professionally to the master's degree level.

Eight upperclassmen students, four males and four females, were selected and trained as student counselors for the research project. Seven of the students selected had sophomore classification while one had junior standing. Only one of the student counselors had previous experience as a student academic counselor prior to the fall semester 1963.

All selectees were trained in the regular student counselor training program conducted during the spring and fall semesters by the Testing and Guidance Center at Southwest Texas State College. The total training time consisted of 50 clock hours; 40 hours of initial instruction during the spring semester and 10 hours of reviewing during the fall semester. The training program utilized lectures, demonstrations, discussion periods, and practice exercises, as appropriate, to familiarize trainees with the materials and procedures employed in the college's program of academic adjustment counseling for entering freshmen. The four professional counselors and eight student counselors completed identical training programs.

The 1963–1964 freshman class at Southwest Texas State College furnished the research population. The research utilized experimental and control samples drawn from the total freshman class. One hundred and sixty entering freshmen, half males and half females, received the academic adjustment guidance from same-sex professional counselors. The 80 men and 80 women comprising this experimental sample were randomly selected from the 154 female and 187 male occupants of two selected freshman dormitories. Equivalent guidance from same-sex student counselors was given to all other freshmen residing in college housing. A control sample of 80 men and 80 women was subsequently drawn from those students counseled by student counselors. Students counseled by professional counselors were matched as closely as possible with students counseled by student counselors on the following variables: (1) sex, (2) age, (3) scholastic ability, (4) study orientation, and (5) high school quarter rank. The American College Test and the Survey of Study Habits and Attitudes (Brown & Holtzman, 1965) were employed to assess scholastic ability and study orientation, respectively.

Counseling of the control and experimental groups was accomplished in the counseling rooms provided in each dormitory. For all essential purposes, the dormitories and counseling facilities were equivalent for the two groups.

The guidance activity sequence employed in the investigation is outlined in TABLE 1. Specifically, there were four sequential counseling activities as follows: (1) Survival Orientation, (2) Test Interpretation, (3) Study Habits Guidance, and (4) Study Skills Survey. It should be noted that the group size for Survival Orientation was larger (N = 20) than that for the second and third sessions (N = 4) or the final meeting (N = 1).

EVALUATION CRITERIA

The Effective Study Test (Brown, 1964) was used to assess growth in study skills through a comparison of test-retest differential scores obtained through pre-counseling and post-counseling administra-tions. The Effective Study Test provides the following 25-item subscales for measuring a student's knowledge about effective study techniques: (1) Reality Orientation Scale—measures realism in undertaking the development of effective study habits; (2) Study Orientation Scale—measures knowledge about efficient time utilization and study site organization; (3) Writing Behavior Scale—measures knowledge about efficient note-taking and report-writing techniques; (4) Reading Behavior Scale—measures knowledge about efficient textbook reading and reviewing techniques; and (5) Examination Behavior Scale—measures knowledge about efficient test-preparation and test-taking techniques. Finally, a Total Study Effectiveness Score provides a single overall measure of the student's insight into efficient study methods and the factors influencing their development.

Comparison of scores on the Study Skills Surveys (Brown, 1965b) administered after all counseling was completed provid-

TABLE 1

Guidance Activity Sequence

Meeting Number	Time Period	Size of Group	Length of Meeting	Activity
1	Sept. 16 to Sept. 27, 1963	20	2 hours	Survival Orientation: Briefing session on college survival facts, academic adjustment problems, scholastic achievement standards, effective study behavior, and student assistance resources.
2	Sept. 30 to Oct. 17, 1963	4	2 hours	Test Interpretation: Counseling session on factors determining scholastic success, results of standardized ability and achievement tests, current study habits and attitudes, time budgeting problems, environmental variables influencing study efficiency, college rewards and frustrations, personal-social adjustment problems, the give and take of dormitory life, and the factors influencing peer-group affiliation.
3	Oct. 21 to Nov. 7, 1963	4	2 hours	Study Habits Guidance: Counseling session on how to read and remember textbook material, take lecture and reading notes, write themes and reports, and prepare for essay and objective examinations.
4	Nov. 25 to Nov. 27, 1963	1	$1/_2$ hour	Study Skills Survey: Counseling session on appropriate corrective action for residual study organization, techniques, and motivation problems identified for students receiving unsatisfactory mid-term report.

ed additional data for assessing changes in study organization, techniques, and motivation. The Study Skills Surveys provide three 20-item checklists to which the individual responds by answering yes or no. The checklists are designed as a self-report procedure in which the student indicates his existing study problems. The following three 20-item scales comprise the inventory: (1) Study Organization Survey—a checklist of problems in organizing study time and study environments; (2) Study Technique Survey—a checklist of problems in reading textbooks, taking class notes, preparing themes and reports, preparing for tests, and taking examinations; (3) Study Motivation Survey—a checklist of problems in motivating study and accepting college academic demands.

Counselee reactions to critical aspects of the program were obtained from a 60-item Counseling Evaluation Questionnaire. Using a five-point response continumm (strongly agree, agree, undecided or uncertain, disagree, strongly disagree), each counselee indicated his acceptance or rejection of the counselor, the counseling materials and procedures, and the counseling objectives and results.

Counselee retention of information given during counseling was assessed by a 60-item Counseling Comprehension Test. Twenty questions, each to be answered true, undecided, or false, were provided for each of the three two-hour counseling periods. Questions on the Counseling Comprehension Test covered material other than that included on the Effective Study Test.

Earned course grades at the end of the 1963 fall semester were used to evaluate counseling productivity. Two indices of scholastic success were computed—the point-hour grade ratio and the quality-point total. A four-point scale (A = 4 and F = 0) was employed in computing both measures of academic achievement. The quality-point total is computed exactly like the grade-point ratio except that the student's point-hour values are summed instead of averaged.

ANALYSIS OF RESULTS

Results of the statistical analyses are reported in TABLES 2–7. Fisher's t test for

TABLE 2

Comparison of Test-retest Differential Scores*
Earned by Professional Counseled (PC) and
Student Counseled (SC) Freshmen on the
Effective Study Test

	Males		Females		Total	
	PC	SC	PC	SC	PC	SC
M	3.9	4.0	4.0	4.2	3.9	4.1
SD	10.3	9.4	5.6	5.4	8.2	7.6
t		.07		.30		.12
p		<.10		<.10		<.10

* Obtained by subtracting each counselee's pre-counseling score from his post-counseling score.

correlated means was employed in comparing differences between professionally counseled and student counseled freshmen on the following criteria: (1) test-retest differential scores obtained from precounseling and postcounseling administrations of the Effective Study Test; (2) total scores on the Counseling Evaluation Questionnaire, Study Skills Surveys, and Counseling Comprehension Test obtained through post counseling administrations; and (3) initial academic achievement as measured by first-semester point-hour ratios and quality-point totals. Each table reports the means and standard deviations for professionally counseled and student counseled freshmen, together with the resulting t test values and significance levels obtained when comparing the two groups. Data for each sex and for the combined group are presented in each table.

TABLE 2 reveals that professional and student counselors did not differ significantly in their ability to communicate information about effective study procedures, as measured by a comparison of test-retest differential scores from the Effective

TABLE 3

Comparison of Counseling Evaluation
Questionnaire Scores for Professional
Counseled (PC) and Student Counseled (SC)
Freshmen

	Males		Females		Total	
	PC	SC	PC	SC	PC	SC
M	41.0	55.8	35.0	63.8	39.9	59.8
SD	32.5	22.6	33.0	26.1	31.0	24.7
t		2.78		6.09		5.89
p		>.01		>.01		>.01

91

TABLE 4

Comparison of Study Skills Surveys Scores
for Professional Counseled (PC) and Student
Counseled (SC) Freshmen

	Males		Females		Total	
	PC	SC	PC	SC	PC	SC
M	38.4	38.2	38.9	41.8	38.7	40.1
SD	9.6	9.7	9.8	7.9	9.7	9.0
t		.11		2.04		1.16
p		$<.10$	$>.05$	$<.02$		$<.10$

Study Test. This is the only criterion on which the hypothesis of no difference in counseling effectiveness is supported.

TABLE 3 indicates that student counseled freshmen evaluated the counseling program significantly higher than did professionally counseled freshmen. Responses to items on the Counseling Evaluation Questionnaire clearly reveal that the counselees believed they received more useful information for the counseling program when the material was presented by student counselors.

The number of study organization, techniques, and motivation problems remaining after counseling, as measured by the Study Skills Surveys, indicated that female freshmen counseled by student counselors made significantly better use of the study skills knowledge acquired during counseling. However, TABLE 4 does not show a comparable difference for male counselees.

From TABLE 5 it may be seen that student counseled freshmen of both sexes retained significantly more of the information communicated about topics other than effective study procedures. As measured by the Counseling Comprehension Test, counselee retention of information given

TABLE 5

Comparison of Counseling Comprehension
Test Scores for Professional Counseled (PC)
and Student Counseled (SC) Freshmen

	Males		Females		Total	
	PC	SC	PC	SC	PC	SC
M	40.3	43.1	42.7	44.5	41.7	43.8
SD	6.7	5.8	4.7	5.2	5.8	5.5
t		2.84		2.88		4.04
p		$>.01$		$>.01$		$>.01$

during the three two-hour counseling sessions was highest when the information was transmitted by student counselors.

TABLES 6 and 7 report, respectively, a comparison of grade-point ratios and quality-point totals earned by professionally counseled and student counseled freshmen during their first semester in college. Inspection of TABLE 6 reveals that the differences were not significant when grade-point ratios for males and females were analyzed separately. However, when male and female counselees are combined, a significant difference in favor of student-to-student counseling is obtained. TABLE 7

TABLE 6

Comparison of First-Semester Point-Hour
Ratios Earned by Professional Counseled
(PC) and Student Counseled (SC) Freshmen

	Males		Females		Total	
	PC	SC	PC	SC	PC	SC
M	1.8	2.1	2.3	2.5	2.0	2.3
SD	.8	.9	.8	.6	.9	.8
t		1.79		1.77		2.50
p	$>.10$	$<.05$	$>.10$	$<.05$		$>.01$

TABLE 7

Comparison of First-Semester Quality-Point
Totals Earned by Professional Counseled
(PC) and Student Counseled (SC) Freshmen

	Males		Females		Total	
	PC	SC	PC	SC	PC	SC
M	27.4	32.0	37.1	39.0	31.3	35.5
SD	14.1	14.8	14.0	10.6	14.7	13.2
t		2.30		1.25		2.63
p	$>.02$	$<.01$		$<.10$		$>.01$

reveals a significant difference in favor of the student counselors for male counselees, but not for female counselees. However, as in the case of grade-point ratios, when the male and female counselees are combined, the significance of differences in quality-point totals is even more in favor of the student counseled freshmen.

CONCLUSIONS

Three conclusions appear warranted by the research results. First, student counse-

92

lors were as effective as professional counselors on all criteria of counseling productivity employed in this study. In fact, the student counselors achieved significantly better results than did the professional counselors on the majority of variables used to evaluate counseling outcome. Second, the student counselors received greater acceptance from counselees than did the professional counselors, and were thus able to evoke better retention of most information communicated during counseling. Finally, freshmen counseled by student counselors made greater use of the information received during counseling, as reflected by earned grades and residual study problems.

From the findings of this study it appears reasonable to conclude that the use of carefully selected, trained, and supervised student counselors will provide a practical and productive addition to the college guidance program, thereby relieving professionally trained personnel workers of many routine duties. The research results should not, however, be construed to suggest that student-counseling-student proce-

dures can be employed to replace the work of professional counselors. It must be recognized that student counselors require effective training and supervision and that their usefulness is limited to carefully selected, nonsensitive guidance activities.

REFERENCES

BROWN, WILLIAM F. *Effective study test.* San Marcos, Texas: Effective Study Materials, 1964.

BROWN, WILLIAM F. Student-to-student counseling for academic adjustment. *Personnel Guid. J.*, 1965, 43, 811–817. (a)

BROWN, WILLIAM F. *Study skills surveys.* San Marcos, Texas: Effective Study Materials, 1965. (b)

BROWN, WILLIAM F., & HOLTZMAN, WAYNE H. *Survey of study habits and attitudes: college level.* New York: The Psychological Corp., 1965.

BROWN, WILLIAM F., & ZUNKER, VERNON G. Survey of student counselor utilization at four-year institutions of higher learning. *J. Coll. Stu. Personnel* (in press).

ZUNKER, VERNON G. *A comparison of the effectiveness of student and certified counselors in a selected program of academic adjustment guidance.* Unpublished Ed.D. dissertation, Univ. of Houston, August, 1964.

IV. THE EFFECT OF THE VOLUNTEER EXPERIENCE ON STUDENTS

ATTITUDE CHANGE IN COLLEGE STUDENTS AND CHRONIC PATIENTS:

A DUAL PERSPECTIVE [1]

JACK M. CHINSKY   AND   JULIAN RAPPAPORT

Assessment was obtained of both initial attitudes and attitude change among college students and chronic patients participating in a hospital companionship program. Student attitudes toward a number of mental health concepts were initially similar to two student control groups. Patient expectations of college students likewise were similar to patient controls. At the conclusion of the program, students manifested significantly more favorable attitudes toward patients and less favorable attitudes toward the mental hospital; patients saw the students as more nurturant than they had initially expected. A "social hierarchy" hypothesis is advanced to partially account for the reported success of similar companionship programs.

A growing awareness of the shortage of professional mental health manpower (Albee, 1959) and of the ineffectiveness of traditional treatment approaches for large numbers of patients (e.g., chronic schizophrenics) has led to a search for new approaches to mental health problems. The use of nonprofessionals has been among the most promising of these new approaches. Housewives, hospital attendants, retired oldsters, and many other nonprofessional groups are being used in an ever-expanding number of settings and treatment situations (Cowen, Gardner, & Zax, 1967; Ellsworth, 1968).

[1] This paper is partially based on the authors' PhD dissertations. Portions of this paper were presented at the meeting of the Eastern Psychological Association, Philadelphia, April 1969, and the Midwestern Psychological Association, Chicago, May 1969. The study was supported in part by the Maurice Falk Medical Fund, Pittsburgh, Pennsylvania; the Department of Psychology, University of Rochester; the Department of Psychology, University of Illinois; and the University of Connecticut Research Foundation. The authors wish to express their gratitude to Emory L. Cowen who served as chairman of the dissertation committee for both authors. Special thanks are offered to Carolyn Norris, Judy Park, and Michele Francis, all of whom aided in the collection, scoring, and analysis of the data.

JOURNAL OF CONSULTING AND CLINICAL PSYCHOLOGY, Dec. 1970, vol. 35, no. 3, pp. 388-394.

A frequent example of this type of programing, arising from the understaffed, overcrowded conditions of many state hospitals, has been the use of college students as companions or group leaders in these institutions (Chinsky, 1968; Holzberg, Knapp, & Turner, 1967; Poser, 1966; Rappaport, 1968). One of the many by-products of such programs has been that students often report favorable changes in attitude toward both self and mental patients following participation (Holzberg, Gewirtz, & Ebner, 1964; Scheibe, 1965). Attitudinal changes of the patients involved in these programs, however, have never been systematically examined.

The purpose of this study was to evaluate initial attitudes and attitude change among both the students and the patients involved in such a program. With regard to the students, the aim was to further explore the impact of program participation on attitude change, as well as to compare initial volunteer attitudes with those of nonvolunteers. An attempt was made to separate students' attitudes toward mental patients from their attitude toward the various components of the hospital, including nurses, psychologists, and the institution per se.

It was hypothesized that the experience of working as a volunteer in a mental hospital leads to more favorable attitudes toward self and mental patients, and to less favorable attitudes toward the institution. The latter prediction is based on the premise that volunteer programs of this nature acquaint the college student with some of the unfavorable conditions under which the chronic patient lives, including overcrowded wards, poor physical facilities, lack of treatment, etc.—in short, the conditions which have been described by other observers of large mental institutions (e.g., Goffman, 1961). Initial student volunteer attitudes were also compared to those of demographically and motivationally comparable nonvolunteers to determine if the former are more idealistic, as had been

95

found in an after-school program conducted by Cowen, Zax, and Laird (1966).

A second purpose of this study was to explore the other side of the coin—the expectations and perceptions which chronic patients have about the college students. How do these perceptions change as a result of the experience of contact with such students? Further, how are such students seen in relation to the professional staff?

Rioch (1966) has suggested that one reason for the success of college students in hospital programs is the manner in which they are perceived by the patients. Referring to a companion program reported by Poser (1966), she states that

one possible factor in the positive results obtained by the nonprofessionals was that the patients cooperated more readily with people who were felt to be closer to themselves in the social hierarchy, that is, close to the bottom of the ladder [p. 292].

Professionals in the hospital are frequently in high-status, administrative roles. They might easily be viewed by the patients, especially those on the "back wards," as socially distant, authoritative persons. Seeing the students as closer to themselves in the social hierarchy, the patients might feel more willing to interact with them in a meaningful and open way.

METHOD

Subjects

Students. Thirty college students (15 males, 15 females), participating in an undergraduate seminar and practicum course in community mental health (Cowen, Chinsky, & Rappaport, 1970) offered at the University of Rochester, served as the student experimental group. All but one of these students was a psychology major; the age range was 18–22 years. Two student control groups were used: the first (Student Control I) included 30 students, demographically comparable to the student experimental group, not enrolled in the course; the second (Student Control II) consisted of 30 students, drawn from a large introductory psychology course, who were younger and more diverse in background than either the student experimental or Student Control I groups.

Patients. Patient Ss were 320 chronic patients, an equal number of each sex, hospitalized at Rochester

96

State Hospital, Rochester, New York. All met a threefold demographic criteria: (*a*) ages 21–59, (*b*) neither organic nor mental retardate (most were diagnosed chronic schizophrenic), and (*c*) hospitalized at least 12 months continuously. Mean length of hospitalization was 13.24 years, mean age, 47.04 years. Two hundred and fifty-six patients served as experimentals and 64 as controls. Of these, 268 completed an initial interview, 259 a posttest interview, and 227 (173 patient experimentals and 54 patient controls) completed both.

Experiment I: Student Attitudes

Procedure

Each student in the experimental group met at the hospital individually with a group of eight patients, twice weekly, for approximately 30 hourly sessions conducted over the course of five and one-half months.

The Adjective Check List (ACL) (Gough & Heilbrun, 1965) and an adaptation of the semantic differential (Osgood, Suci, & Tannenbaum, 1957) were administered separately to each of the three student groups on three separate occasions: (*a*) at the beginning of the program, (*b*) one month after the student experimental group began working in the hospital, and (*c*) during the final week of the practicum.

Students were asked to check those adjectives on the ACL which best described the "typical mental hospital patient" (Turner, Holzberg, & Knapp, 1967). Independent scores obtained from the "favorable" and "unfavorable" scales were used. The semantic differential consisted of nine concepts, each rated on 14 scales. The concepts used were "myself," "mental patients," "mental hospital," "volunteer groups," "psychologists," "nurses," "average person," "mental illness," and "psychotherapy." The 14 scales on the semantic differential are listed in Table 1. The favorable adjective on each scale was determined by at least 80% agreement of five independent raters. A random ordering of scales and concepts was used; concept scores were obtained by summing scale ratings in the favorable direction.

Results

Table 2 presents preprogram means and sigmas for the three student groups on the 11 attitude measures. A 1×3 analysis of variance computed on each of the measures revealed group differences in initial attitude toward three of the semantic differential concepts: "average person" ($F = 5.10$, $df = 2/87$, $p < .05$), "mental patient" ($F = 10.40$, $df = 2/87$, $p < .01$), and "mental illness" ($F = 3.91$, $df = 2/87$, $p < .05$).

Examining these differences among the student groups more closely, it was found that Student Control I had more favorable initial attitudes to-

TABLE 1
SEMANTIC DIFFERENTIAL SCALES

Favorable	Unfavorable
Effective	Ineffective
Good	Bad
Healthy	Sick
Relaxed	Tense
Friendly	Unfriendly
Interesting	Boring
Pleasant	Unpleasant
Understandable	Mysterious
Helpful	Harmful
Warm	Cold
Safe	Dangerous
Strong	Weak
Active	Passive
Predictable	Unpredictable

ward the concept "average person" than did both the experimental ($t = 3.28$, $p < .01$) and Student Control II groups ($t = 2.27$, $p < .05$). Control I also had more favorable attitudes toward the concept "mental patient" than did the experimental ($t = 3.24$, $p < .01$) or Control II groups ($t = 4.67$, $p < .01$). The experimental group did not differ from Control II on either of these two concepts. Control II had a less favorable attitude toward the concept "mental illness" than the experimental ($t = 2.16$, $p < .05$) or Control I groups ($t = 2.81$, $p < .01$). The experimental and Control I groups did not differ significantly in attitudes toward this concept. Thus, the three significant Fs found between the three student groups were due to control group differences. The experimental group was not systematically different in initial attitude from both of the control groups simultaneously on any of the measures.

A 3×3 two-way factorial analysis of variance with repeated measures was used to assess differential attitude change among the three student groups. The analysis of variance for attitude change toward the "typical mental patient" on the favorability scale of the ACL revealed a significant Group $\times$ Time interaction ($F = 5.56$, $df = 4/174$, $p < .01$). Although the three groups were identical on the premeasure, the analysis indicated a significant increase in the favorability of the volunteers' attitudes toward the concept.

A structurally comparable analysis was performed, using the ACL unfavorability index as criterion. Once again, the three groups were initially similar but diverged with a significant drop in unfavorability scores for the experimental group over time (Group $\times$ Time: $F = 7.67$, $df = 4/174$, $p < .01$). Thus, participation in the program resulted in a significant increase in ACL favorability and decrease in ACL unfavorability of attitudes toward patients.

A similar analysis of variance, this time based on the semantic differential concept "mental patient," also revealed a significant interaction effect (Group × Time: $F = 5.06$, $df = 4/174$, $p < .01$) demonstrating, once again, differential improvement in attitudes across time favoring the experimental group. This datum parallels the preceding for the two ACL scales.

Another analysis of this same type, with the semantic differential concept "mental hospital" as criterion, showed that the experimental group attitudes toward the mental hospital became significantly less favorable with time (Group × Time: $F = 9.02$, $df = 4/174$, $p < .01$).

An analysis by scales on the semantic differential concepts "mental patients" and "mental hospital" allows for a more specific examination of attitude change toward these two concepts. Using the same factorial design on each of the scales, it was found that the experimental group saw the mental patient as significantly more pleasant, less harmful, more predictable, more friendly, and more passive. The latter change was opposite in direction to the overall favorable change in attitude toward the mental patient. The mental hospital was seen as significantly more passive, more cold, less helpful, less good, less pleasant, less interesting, less friendly, and less effective.

No differences in attitude change among the three groups were found on the remaining seven concepts. An analysis by scales for each of these concepts likewise revealed no systematic difference in attitude change for the three groups.

TABLE 2

Mean Values and Standard Deviations of Initial Attitudes for Student Experimental, Student Control I, and Student Control II Groups

Attitude concept	Student experimental		Student Control I		Student Control II	
	M	SD	M	SD	M	SD
Adjective Check List						
Patient–favorable	16.4	9.0	16.1	9.4	16.5	8.4
Patient–unfavorable	82.2	14.7	80.4	14.5	81.1	18.2
Semantic differential						
Nurses	75.7	9.7	80.0	10.0	78.2	8.4
Volunteer groups	77.0	7.4	74.5	8.8	75.8	10.6
Mental illness	44.4	8.1	45.0	6.6	40.2	6.2
Average person	64.2	10.2	71.4	5.7	66.8	9.3
Psychotherapy	70.8	7.3	67.8	8.2	66.7	9.3
Psychologists	75.5	8.2	75.5	7.2	71.5	8.6
Myself	73.8	7.0	76.4	8.0	74.9	10.9
Mental patients	46.7	7.8	52.3	5.1	43.7	8.4
Mental hospital	60.8	10.5	64.6	10.2	59.8	8.5

Note.—$n = 30$ for each group; total $N = 90$.

Experiment II: Patient Attitudes

Procedure

In an effort to evaluate the patients' perceptions of college students, a technique, simple enough for chronic schizophrenics to follow, was developed during a pilot study (Rappaport & Chinsky, 1968), and individually administered on two separate occasions. This measure of patient expectations and perceptions (PEP) includes 25 statements (see Table 3) such as "He advises you"; "He is critical"; "He senses your feelings." Eighteen of the items are modifications of those listed by Apfelbaum (1958) as most characteristic of patient descriptions of therapists. Six items fall on each of three empirically derived clusters: the therapist as nurturant, as a model, or as a critic. In addition, seven items were added, on a face-valid basis, some of which might test the hypothesis that patients perceive themselves in the "social hierarchy" as closer to nonprofessionals than professionals.

Each patient, both experimental and control, was individually administered the PEP prior to the onset of the program. The statements were read aloud to the S, in a structured interview fashion. The interviewer first read the item, and then asked if it best described a doctor or a college student, alternating presentation of the alternatives. Following this, members of the patient experimental group were assigned to meet with one of the 30 volunteers. Patient controls were a demographically matched group who had no contact with the college students. All patients were readministered the PEP, by interviewers who had no knowledge of whether the patient was experimental or control, at the conclusion of the program. For purposes of data analysis, the patient experimental group was divided into two subgroups: those who attended at least two thirds of the group meetings (attenders) and those who attended less than two thirds (nonattenders).

Results

Item analysis. Responses to the 25-item PEP scale were analyzed in several ways. Since none of the 268 Ss completing this form during the pretest interview was known to have had prior contact with a college student volunteer, initial reactions concerning college students, unlike reactions to physicians, are essentially stereotyped expectations. Pretest scores may be seen then as comparisons between these two groups, based on expectations rather than actual contact. For any item, the expected frequency of endorsement for doctor or college student was assumed at pretest stage to be 50% (if expectations about these two groups did not differ). Differences in perception of these two target groups were tested, item by item, using chi-square analyses. These results are reported in Table 3. Nineteen significant differences in item-endorsement frequency were found. Doctors were perceived by significantly more patients to be giving of advice, well adjusted, hardworking, sympathetic, friendly, gentle, considerate, self-confident, interested in the patient, eager to help, liking of the patient, and liked by the patient. College students were seen more frequently as hard to please; and, congruent with the "social hierarchy" hypotheses, were judged by significantly more patients to be "fun to be with," and "like the patient."

Following assignment of patients to experimental or control groups, pretest items were analyzed in a 2×2 contingency table to test for differential perceptions of physicians and college students across groups. Table 4 demonstrates that experimental and control patients did not differ on a single item at the pretest point. This same analysis, repeated for posttest data (see Table 4) indicated five significant differences between patient experimentals and controls. Thus, a proportionally greater number of patients in the experimental group now saw college students as giving of advice and

TABLE 3

PRETEST DISTRIBUTION OF ALL PATIENT ENDORSEMENTS FOR EACH ITEM OF THE PEP

Item	Frequency of doctor endorsement[a]	Frequency of college student endorsement	x^1
1. He advises you. (N)	226	41	130.26***
2. He is well adjusted. (M)	175	93	25.01***
3. He is critical. (C)	130	138	.24
4. He senses your feelings. (N)	234	34	149.25***
5. He is calm. (M)	217	51	102.82***
6. He is blunt. (C)	128	140	.51
7. He encourages you. (N)	218	50	105.31***
8. He gets along well with others. (M)	148	120	2.93
9. He is clear headed. (C)	191	77	34.02***
10. He is easy to get to know. (N)	130	137	.18
11. He works hard. (M)	179	89	30.22***
12. He is hard to please. (C)	115	153	5.39*
13. He is sympathetic. (N)	217	51	102.82***
14. He is friendly. (M)	158	109	8.60**
15. He is bossy. (C)	124	143	1.49
16. He is gentle. (N)	215	52	100.36***
17. He is considerate. (M)	209	58	86.21***
18. He is self-confident. (C)	175	92	25.80***
19. He is a lot like you.	91	176	27.06***
20. He is interested in you.	217	50	104.45***
21. He is eager to help you.	217	49	106.11***
22. He likes you.	171	96	21.06***
23. He is fun to be with.	82	185	39.73***
24. You like him.	165	102	14.87***
25. You would like to be like him.	148	120	2.93

Note.—N = nurturant cluster; M = model cluster; C = critic cluster.

[a] Total frequency may vary from item to item since some patients could not always make a forced choice for some items.

* $p < .05$.

** $p < .01$.

*** $p < .001$.

gentle, while fewer saw them as critical, hard to
please, and bossy than did the patient controls.
Collectively, these findings indicate a positive shift in
patient perceptions of college students by the end of
the program.

Each item also was analyzed, separately by experimental and control, for changes in frequency of
endorsement for doctors or college students from
pretest to posttest. Within each group the expected
posttest frequency, by item, for doctor or college
student, was assumed to be the established pretest
frequency (corrected for slight posttest decreases in
N). Table 5 indicates that for the patient experimental group there was a significant shift on 18 of
the 25 items. Significantly more patients described
college students at the posttest stage as more likely
than doctors to give advice, sense their feelings, give
encouragement; and to be calm, sympathetic, gentle,
considerate, interested in them, eager to help them,
like themselves, fun to be with; as well as liking
them and liking to be with them. In addition, sig-

TABLE 4

Pretest and Posttest Chi-Squares for Patient
Experimental versus Patient Control Groups'
Endorsement of Each Item of the PEP

Item[a]	Pretest χ^2	Posttest χ^2
1	.14	5.45*
2	.11	3.02
3	.64	5.92*
4	.07	.02
5	.78	1.11
6	2.30	1.67
7	.13	.35
8	1.78	.06
9	.01	.09
10	.00	.17
11	.00	.05
12	.58	4.53*
13	.10	.60
14	.52	.02
15	.14	6.63*
16	.02	3.85*
17	.36	3.08
18	.00	.24
19	.25	1.85
20	.58	2.74
21	.40	1.83
22	.26	2.17
23	.77	2.21
24	.07	1.50
25	.01	1.84

Note.—N for pretest was 268; N for posttest was 259.
[a] Items appear in Table 3.
* $p < .05$.

nificantly fewer patients saw college students as critical, blunt, hardworking, hard to please, and bossy.

For the patient control group there were only 4 of a possible 25 significant changes. These increases were in the direction of greater college-student endorsement for these items: sense your feelings, calm, giving of encouragement, and eager to help. In each of the latter instances, the expected cell frequency for college students was less than 10, thus making even slight changes in observed frequencies statistically significant. However, even including these four changes, the patient control group remained basically stable on most items, whereas the patient experimental group changed markedly in the direction of more favorable attitudes to college students.

Cluster analysis. Finally, to evaluate the foregoing changes in patient perception more globally, the first 18 items of the PEP were grouped for analysis according to the clusters originally described by Apfelbaum (1958): nurturant, model, or critic (six items per cluster). Cluster scores were obtained by summing the frequency of endorsement for *college students* across all items within each cluster. Each cluster had a potential range of scores from 0 to 6.

For this analysis the patients were grouped[2] into attenders, nonattenders, and controls. The three cluster scores were each analyzed for change by group from pretest to posttest. A 3×2 analysis of variance for repeated measures demonstrated a significant interaction of Group $\times$ Time such that there was a significant increase among attenders, but not nonattenders or controls, in the perception of college students as more nurturant than physicians (Group $\times$ Time: $F = 4.97$, $df = 2/213$, $p < .01$). Structurally similar analyses for the model and critic clusters revealed no significant differences among groups.

DISCUSSION

With regard to the students, preprogram data indicate that the student experimental and control groups did not differ in idealism and were, indeed, roughly comparable in initial attitudes to mental health concepts. Significantly more favorable attitudes toward "mental patients" and less favorable attitudes toward the "mental hospital" followed participation in the volunteer program. Volunteer

[2] N for patient controls $= 54$; N for nonattenders $= 54$; N for attenders $= 119$ (11 were randomly eliminated from the analysis of variance in order to make the cells proportional).

changes in self-concept, measured by the semantic differential, did not occur, perhaps because such perceptions were initially quite favorable. Absence of change on this and other semantic differential concepts contraindicates the possibility that a generalized favorability response style (e.g., Rundquist, 1966) was the source of the observed attitude changes.

An increase in favorable attitudes toward mental patients replicates the findings of Scheibe (1965) and Turner et al. (1967) working in previous state hospital projects. The findings also complement those for the patients.

These objective attitude changes were quite consistent with personal observations of, and comments by, volunteers who came to perceive patients more favorably as they got to know them better, while more and more seeing the limitations of the hospital and attributing the patients' conditions to such shortcomings. Over time, many volunteers increasingly viewed patients as real, sometimes warm, and even likable people—much differently than the stigmatized view of mental patients associated with the stereotype of mental illness (a view to which many volunteers, themselves, may have ascribed before patient contact began). They came to see these people as within the confines of an inefficient treatment hospital—an old, crowded, and depressing custodial institution.

The physical surroundings were a major and chronic source of concern to volunteers. Volunteer meetings, for example, had to be held in the basement because there were no other places available for such contacts. The question "How could a person be well in such a place?" was frequently asked by volunteers. Similar concerns have been verbalized by considerably more experienced students of the large mental institution (e.g., Goffman, 1961). Perhaps such concerns, generated by nonprofessional programs such as this one, can contribute to constructive social change to improve the conditions of the large state mental hospital.

Examining the impact that the students had on the patients may provide some clues as to the effectiveness often reported for programs of this nature (e.g., Anker & Walsh, 1961; Poser, 1966; Rappaport, 1968). As mentioned above, one explanation for the reported success of nonprofessionals as mental health workers is the view that such individuals are seen by patients as closer to themselves in the "social hierarchy" than are professionals (Rioch, 1966), thus facilitating the development of meaningful interpersonal relationships. Cowen (1967), speaking to this same point, has reasoned that this may be a "central element in a variety of helping approaches, for example 'AA' . . . Recovery Incorporated . . . or Synanon . . . where efforts are made to reduce the social distance factors [p. 428]." Even before contact with them was established, chronic patients saw college students, more than physicians, as "like themselves" and "fun to be with," items suggesting less perceived social distance between patients and students. In addition, while control patients' perception of college students remained stable over time, patients who regularly attended the group meetings (attenders) shifted their perceptions from pretesting to posttesting such that they came to see college students as more nurturant.

The above finding is most meaningful when one considers the nature of the format of the test instrument used to assess these perceptions. Patients were forced to endorse doctors negatively in order to endorse college students positively. Many expressed anxiety about this during the testing sessions, particularly since they were tested by people who they considered to be hospital personnel. Despite this potential stress, a significant number of patients shifted their endorsements in a direction more favorable to college students. Seemingly, many patients felt positively enough about their relationship with a college student to express such changes in their view,

TABLE 5

PATIENT EXPERIMENTAL AND PATIENT CONTROL GROUP
CHI-SQUARES FOR CHANGE IN FREQUENCY OF EN-
DORSEMENT FOR COLLEGE STUDENTS ON EACH
ITEM OF THE PEP

Item[a]	Patient experimental group χ^2	Patient control group χ^2
1	18.98[b],***	2.35
2	.24	1.73
3	13.02[c],***	.36
4	18.79[b],***	10.48**
5	22.36[b],***	6.00*
6	4.56[c],*	2.51
7	31.95[b],***	7.51*
8	.22	.89
9	3.01	.17
10	3.77	.29
11	6.06[c],*	1.04
12	10.56[c],***	.50
13	23.87[b],***	.58
14	3.48	2.96
15	18.16[c],***	.13
16	34.44[b],***	.13
17	33.96[b],***	2.77
18	.39	1.43
19	1.92	.01
20	22.01[b],***	1.94
21	27.72[b],***	4.01*
22	5.01[b],*	.01
23	6.63[b],*	2.77
24	15.26[b],***	1.14
25	6.09[b],*	.12

[a] Items appear in Table 3.
[b] Represents change in direction of more endorsement for college students.
[c] Represents change in direction of less endorsement for college students.
* $p < .05$.
** $p < .01$.
*** $p < .001$.

even though it may have been somewhat anxiety producing to do so.

As mentioned above, prior studies have demonstrated positive attitude change toward mental patients in college students who participated in volunteer programs; similar changes were found for students in this study. What had not been previously demonstrated, however, was change on the part of the patients. That such attitude change took place in chronic hospitalized schizophrenics is perhaps a major clue to understanding the effectiveness of nonprofessionals in similar settings.

Guerney (1969), for example, has argued that nonprofessionals are probably more important social reinforcers or "significant others" for patients than are professionals. This study lends some support to his argument.

Taken together, the attitudinal changes of both the students and the patients justify continued development of this form of community mental health program.

REFERENCES

ALBEE, G. W. *Mental health manpower trends.* New York: Basic Books, 1959.

ANKER, J. M., & WALSH, R. P. Group psychotherapy, a special activity program, and group structure in the treatment of chronic schizophrenics. *Journal of Consulting Psychology,* 1961, 25, 476–481.

APFELBAUM, B. *Dimensions of transference in psychotherapy.* Berkeley: University of California Press, 1958.

CHINSKY, J. M. Nonprofessionals in a mental hospital: A study of the college student volunteer. Unpublished doctoral dissertation. University of Rochester, 1968.

COWEN, E. L. Emergent approaches to mental health problems: An overview and directions for future work. In E. L. Cowen, E. A. Gardner, & M. Zax (Eds.), *Emergent approaches to mental health problems.* New York: Appleton-Century-Crofts, 1967.

COWEN, E. L., CHINSKY, J. M., & RAPPAPORT, J. An undergraduate practicum in community mental health. *Community Mental Health Journal,* 1970, 6, 91–100.

COWEN, E. L., GARDNER, E. A., & ZAX, M. (Eds.) *Emergent approaches to mental health problems.* New York: Appleton-Century-Crofts, 1967.

COWEN, E. L., ZAX, M., & LAIRD, J. D. A college student volunteer program in the elementary school setting. *Community Mental Health Journal,* 1966, 2, 319–328.

ELLSWORTH, R. B. *Nonprofessionals in psychiatric rehabilitation.* New York: Appleton-Century-Crofts, 1968.

GOFFMAN, E. *Asylums.* Garden City, N. Y.: Doubleday, 1961.

GOUGH, H. C., & HEILBRUN, A. B., JR. *The Adjective Check List manual.* Palo Alto, Calif.: Consulting Psychologists Press, 1965.

GUERNEY, B. G. *Psychotherapeutic agents: New roles for nonprofessionals, parents, and teachers.* New York: Holt, Rinehart & Winston, 1969.

HOLZBERG, J. D., GEWIRTZ, H., & EBNER, E. Changes in moral judgment and self-acceptance as a function of companionship with hospitalized mental patients. *Journal of Consulting Psychology,* 1964, **28**, 299–303.

HOLZBERG, J. D., KNAPP, R. H., & TURNER, J. L. College students as companions to the mentally ill. In E. L. Cowen, E. A. Gardner, & M. Zax (Eds.), *Emergent approaches to mental health problems.* New York: Appleton-Century-Crofts, 1967.

OSGOOD, C. E., SUCI, G. J., & TANNENBAUM, P. H. *The measurement of meaning.* Urbana: University of Illinois Press, 1957.

POSER, E. G. The effect of therapists' training on group therapeutic outcome. *Journal of Consulting Psychology,* 1966, **30**, 283–289.

RAPPAPORT, J. Nonprofessionals in a mental hospital: College students as group leaders with chronic patients. Unpublished doctoral dissertation, University of Rochester, 1968.

RAPPAPORT, J., & CHINSKY, J. M. Nonprofessionals as mental health workers in a state hospital setting: A preliminary report. Paper presented at the meeting of the Eastern Psychological Association, Washington, D. C., April 1968.

RIOCH, M. J. Changing concepts in the training of therapists. *Journal of Consulting Psychology,* 1966, **30**, 290–292.

RUNDQUIST, E. A. Item and response characteristics in attitude and personality measurement: A reaction to L. G. Rorer's "The great response-style myth." *Psychological Bulletin,* 1966, **66**, 166–177.

SCHEIBE, K. E. College students spend eight weeks in mental hospital: A case report. *Psychotherapy: Theory, Research and Practice,* 1965, **2**, 117–120.

TURNER, J. L., HOLZBERG, J. D., & KNAPP, R. H. Effects of companionship with mental patients on students' stereotype of the typical mental patient. Paper presented at the meeting of the Eastern Psychological Association, Boston, April 1967.

ALTRUISTIC ATTITUDES, BELIEFS ABOUT PSYCHIATRIC PATIENTS, AND VOLUNTEERING FOR COMPANIONSHIP WITH MENTAL HOSPITAL PATIENTS

Edward H. Fischer

A major purpose of this study was to show the degree of relationship between humanitarian attitudes and beliefs about mental patients, on the one hand, and volunteering for a companionship program for mental hospital patients, on the other.

The following attributes were measured in a group of incoming students who had been given an appeal to join a companionship program for mental patients: (*a*) *intention* to participate in a helping relationship with a mental patient who, according to the hospital staff, could benefit by having a visitor; (*b*) *generalized attitudes* of social responsibility and concern about helping others; and (*c*) *specific beliefs* about mental patients and mental illness. These variables correspond to conative-affective-cognitive elements in attitude theory; some degree of consistency can be expected among them, e.g., for intentions to be positive where both attitudes and beliefs are also favorable (Insko & Schopler, 1967).

More concretely, beliefs about patients may function like a kind of cognitive screen that affects the correspondence between attitude and intention. Potential volunteers who hold negative beliefs, e.g., that patients are dirty, dangerous, and unpredictable and unlike "normal people," will tend to shy away from a program intended to bring them into contact with such individuals, despite their altruism. The inclination of Ss who do not have unfavorable views of mental patients to take part in the program will vary according to the positiveness of their helping attitude. It was thus hypothesized that attitude and intention are in closer agreement for Ss holding benign beliefs than for those holding negative beliefs about patients.

METHOD

Subjects. The respondents were 329 new students at Middlesex Community College, who met in August, prior to their first classes. The official reason for the assembly was to meet college officials and find out about class schedules.

PROCEEDINGS OF THE ANNUAL CONVENTION OF THE AMERICAN PSYCHOLOGICAL ASSOCIATION, 1971, vol. 6, (pt. 1), pp. 343-344.

109

Procedure. The appeal for volunteers was given vocally, by the author, and printed on sign-up forms. The sign-up form contained a 400-word explanation of the purposes and logistics of companionship and a four-category item for students to indicate interest or noninterest in joining the companion program. Instructions made it clear that responses to the item determined who would be contacted later, when the program began.

The attached questionnaire consisted of the attitude scales used to postdict intentions, a Social Desirability test comprising the 17 most discriminating Marlowe-Crowne items (Goldfried, 1964), and a demographic information sheet (sex, birth order, religion, and social class data). The attitude inventory included four scales, derived by factor analysis, which assessed helping, social responsibility, nontraditional humanitarian (essentially sex progressivism) views, and attitude toward criminals (Fischer, 1970). The helping and social responsibility attitudes were of most interest in the current study; the nontraditional and criminal scales were given as control measures to see if the former two factors correlated more strongly with volunteering, as would be expected.

Fourteen belief statements about mental patients and mental illness also were given. Ellsworth (1965) found that scores of psychiatric aides, on this beliefs scale, were highly correlated with patients' perceptions of the aides' behavior toward patients.

All attitude items were presented in a four-place agree-disagree response format. The scales were keyed so that a high score meant prohumanitarian attitude or benign beliefs about patients.

RESULTS AND DISCUSSION

Table 1 gives the mean scores for Ss who indicated positive or negative intent to join the program for each of the predictor-scale variables. Volunteers scored significantly higher in the altruistic direction on all humanitarian attitudes except for the nontraditional scale. Volunteers also held more benign beliefs about mental patients. However, there was no apparent difference between the two groups on the Social Desirability test.

The relationships between demographic variables and willingness to sign up for companionship were evaluated by chi-square tests. The only significant factor was sex. Women showed a much greater inclination to volunteer ($\chi^2 = 25.8, df = 1, p < .0001$).

The largest attitude-intent correlation (Pearson r) ob-

TABLE 1

Mean Attitude and Social Desirability Scores for Students Who
Expressed Positive or Negative Intention to
Join Companion Program

Attitude variable	Intention				t (difference)
	Positive (n = 96)		Negative (n = 233)		
	$\overline{X}$	SD	$\overline{X}$	SD	
Helping	39.3	5.62	34.9	6.00	6.32***
Social responsibility	55.2	5.62	50.3	7.18	6.60***
Nontraditional humanitarian	34.1	4.69	33.2	4.90	1.56
Criminal	46.6	7.57	43.2	8.22	3.61**
Beliefs about patients	40.3	6.51	37.7	6.69	3.27*
Social desirability	9.4	3.45	9.1	6.74	.53

Note.—The attitude differences between positive and negative
intent groups also held within sexes, analyzed separately.
*p < .01.
**p < .001.
***p < .0001.

served was .36, for both helping and social responsibility
scales. Although the .36 coefficient is small, it represents an
appreciably stronger association than the .18 correlation
between beliefs about patients and intentions (t = 3.58 and
3.23 for helping vs. beliefs, and social responsibility vs.
beliefs, respectively; df = 326, p < .002 in both tests).[1]

The attitude-intention correlation was raised to .47
through use of a bastard scale, composed of 17 items that
correlated .20 (df = 327, p < .001) or more with volunteering. The bastard scale included mostly helping and social
responsibility statements; *none* of the beliefs about patients
items met the criterion for inclusion in this best-predictor
instrument.

It should be noted here that the attitude variables were
in one sense not being correlated with behavior, but rather
with volunteering to participate in compansionship at a
future time. However, on follow-up it was determined that
expressed intentions corresponded closely to actual
participation (p < .001). Therefore, the use of intention as
a variable to represent volunteering was quite appropriate.

---

[1] All t and z tests reported were based on two-tailed
distributions.

111

To test the study's main hypothesis, the whole sample was divided into three subgroups (favorable, neutral, unfavorable), on the basis of beliefs about mental patients scores. According to the hypothesis, the highest coefficients should obtain for Ss with favorable beliefs. As can be seen in Table 2, the weakest associations occurred in the favorable beliefs subsample; also, some of the most important correlations (helping, best predictor) were significantly greater for Ss with neutral beliefs. The correlation between best-predictor scores and intentions was .57 within the neutral beliefs subgroup.

Thus, attitudes and beliefs appeared to interact nonlineally with volunteering. Evidently, beliefs about patients per se had little bearing on the other variables studied (e.g., correlation with intentions was .18); but perhaps the beliefs scale represented a personality dimension that mediated variations in the attitude-intent relationship. Curvilinear interactions between personality factors and attitudes have been reported previously (Vacchiano, Strauss, & Hochman, 1969). Unfortunately, this retrospective explanation could not be evaluated directly. However, in another study (Fischer, 1970), the writer found a -.66 correlation between California F Scale scores and nontraditional humanitarianism; the latter measure consists of items such as "A woman who makes her living as a prostitute deserves little kindness or respect from anyone" and had been included in the present inventory. Also, the correlation between nontraditional humanitarianism and beliefs about patients was only .32—therefore, a second mediating variable, fairly independent of the first, could be tried.

TABLE 2

Attitude-Intention Correlations within Beliefs Subgroups

| Attitude variable | Beliefs about patients | | | Favorable vs. neutral |
	Favorable ($n = 107$)	Neutral ($n = 116$)	Unfavorable ($n = 106$)	z (difference)
Helping	.24	.47	.32	-1.95*
Social responsibility	.27	.40	.33	-1.03
Nontraditional humanitarian	.00	.27	.04	-1.98**
Criminal	.25	.12	.17	.99
Best predictor	.36	.57	.47	-1.98**

Note.—Standard deviations were practically identical across belief subgroups for every attitude variable.
$*p < .06$.
$**p < .05$.

Accordingly, Ss were trichotomized again on the basis of nontraditional humanitarian scores and the attitude-intention correlations examined in the new subgroups. The pattern of intercorrelations was very similar to that in Table 2; the largest coefficients were in the neutral humanitarian group, followed by the antihumanitarian and then the prohumanitarian subgroups (smallest coefficients). The precise contents of the moderator scale, then, seemed not to matter. It is quite possible that a latent personality factor common to both scales was the true moderator.

REFERENCES

Ellsworth, R. B. A behavioral study of staff attitudes toward mental illness. *Journal of Abnormal Psychology*, 1965, 70, 194-200.

Fischer, E. H. Consistency among humanitarian and helping attitudes. Unpublished manuscript, Connecticut Valley Hospital, Middletown, Conn., 1970.

Goldfried, M. R. A cross-validation of the Marlowe-Crowne Social Desirability Scale items. *Journal of Social Psychology*, 1964, 64, 137-145.

Insko, C. A., & Schopler, J. Triadic consistency: A statement of affective-cognitive-conative consistency. *Psychological Review*, 1967, 74, 361-376.

Vacchiano, R. B., Strauss, P. S., & Hochman, L. The open and closed mind: A review of dogmatism. *Psychological Bulletin*, 1969, 71, 261-273.

CHANGES IN MORAL JUDGMENT AND SELF-ACCEPTANCE
IN COLLEGE STUDENTS AS A FUNCTION OF
COMPANIONSHIP WITH HOSPITALIZED
MENTAL PATIENTS

JULES D. HOLZBERG, HERBERT GEWIRTZ, AND EUGENE EBNER

The present investigation describes studies undertaken to determine the effects of association with hospitalized mental patients on the personalities of 32 male college students who were compared to a control group of 24 comparable students who had not been involved in this experience with mental patients. The former demonstrate significant positive change in self-acceptance and in moral judgments concerning sexual and aggressive behaviors. The nature of the companionship experience is examined in order to elucidate the reasons for these changes. The implications of students' associations with mentally ill patients in the type of program described in this paper are considered in terms of their impact on students who will be the future leaders of American society.

Since 1957, students from neighboring colleges have been volunteering for service as companions to mentally ill patients at the Connecticut Valley Hospital. The students are recruited from the general college population without regard for their areas of academic specialization. These students commit themselves to serve for a full academic year, coming on a specific afternoon each week to visit and to interact with chronic, mentally ill patients. Each student selects or is assigned to a patient, and this student-to-patient commitment continues until the student completes his academic year. The specific structure of this commitment is a 1-hour visit each week by each student, during which time the student "companions" with his patient, involving him in any activities that seem appropriate, e.g., walks, rides, college sports activities, etc.

Another feature of the students' commitments is their participation in small groups of 8 to 10 students for meetings with a member of the hospital's professional staff for 1 hour subsequent to the students' visits with

JOURNAL OF CONSULTING PSYCHOLOGY, 1964, vol. 28, no. 4, pp. 299-303.

114

their patients. These group meetings serve as the medium through which students are supervised and formally educated concerning the problems surrounding mental illness and hospitalization.

This program of service, formally designated as the Companion Program, originated with a two-fold objective—to provide a socializing experience for regressed, chronic patients and to provide a significant educational experience for college students with regard to mental health problems. It seemed apparent at an observational level that this experience had beneficial effects for patients, subsequently confirmed in a similar program at another hospital (Umbarger, Kantor, & Greenblatt, 1962). However, we were very early struck with the observation that students also were affected in certain significant ways by participation in the program.

An earlier study demonstrated striking changes in students' knowledge about and attitudes toward mental illness, hospitalization, and related problems as a function of participation in the Companion Program (Holzberg & Gewirtz, 1963). However, from discussions with students during their hospital visits and from their written reports, we very early sensed that the impact of this unique social experience transcended these areas of primarily intellectual enlightenment and touched upon basic personality dimensions. These observations suggested the desirability of investigating in a systematic manner aspects of personality which might have undergone some modification as a result of the companionship experience. Although numerous personality factors seemed conceptually relevant to this situation, further examination of the students' subjective reactions as to the kinds of changes they perceived themselves to have experienced suggested two areas of central interest—moral judgment and self-acceptance. Consequently, in the present study we have attempted to evaluate whether there is any systematic change in these variables which can be related to the Companion Program experience.

METHOD

Subjects

Fifty-six undergraduate students from several Connecticut colleges and universities served as subjects. The experimental group consisted of 32 male students who participated in the hospital's Companion Program. The control group consisted of 24 male students from these same colleges and universities who at no time had any connection or involvement with the Companion Program. The subjects ranged in age from 18 to 21 years. Although it would have been desirable to employ controls matched on relevant classification variables, problems of subject recruitment prevented this refinement.

Procedure

Patients of both sexes were selected by or assigned to the students. With few exceptions, these patients were drawn from the chronic services and represented the more stabilized, but institutionalized, segment of the patient population. Although the pathology exhibited by the patient group varied considerably, all patients were in sufficient reality contact to allow some communication with the students. Each student spent 1 hour per week with his patient over a period of approximately 30 weeks, and the same number of hours in group meetings with a professional staff member.

During their first hospital visit, before actually meeting patients, the Companion group was asked to respond to two questionnaires, one covering the area of moral judgment and the other self-acceptance. The students were told only that these tests was part of ongoing research related to the Companion Program. Within this same period, the control students completed the same questionnaires at their schools. These tests were readministered to both groups at the completion of the program, approximately 2 weeks before the spring semester terminated.

The moral judgment questionnaire consisted of 36 items drawn from the Edwards Personal Preference Schedule. The items described various behaviors which could conceivably be viewed as possessing differing degrees of "moral sanction" or endorsement. Examples of these items are: "To participate in discussions about sex and sexual activities," "To tell other people what you think of them." Nine items concerned sexual behavior, 9 others involved aggressive behavior, and the remaining 18 items represented a variety of areas and were used as buffer items. The subject was asked to rate each item on a 5-point scale in terms of "how right" he felt the particular behavior was. The scale ranged from the extremes of "Never Right" to "Always Right," high scores reflecting greater moral tolerance.

The self-acceptance questionnaire consisted of 40

116

items used in the doctoral research of one of our colleagues (Lesser, 1958). These reflected a variety of personality and behavioral characteristics, e.g., "I'm a submissive person," "I am naturally nervous." The subject was asked to make two ratings of each item on a 5-point scale ranging from "Never Characteristic" to "Always Characteristic." The first rating was with regard to how characteristic the item was for the subject as he currently sees himself. He then rated the item with regard to how characteristic it would be for the type of person he would ideally like to be. The numerical discrepancy between the self-rating and the ideal-self-rating was utilized as a measure of self-acceptance. Thus, the smaller the numerical difference between the two ratings, the greater the self-acceptance; conversely, larger numerical differences indicated less self-acceptance.

RESULTS

Moral Judgment

Table 1 presents the analysis of variance of the moral judgment ratings. It can be seen from the significant $(p < .01)$ Trials × Groups interaction that the pattern of change in moral judgment scores differed for the Companion and control groups. To evaluate the specific changes responsible for the significant interaction term, comparisons of the mean scores for each condition were made (Table 2). It should be noted that the groups differed significantly $(t = 2.04, p < .05)$ on the initial testing, with the control group demonstrating more tolerant moral judgment than the Companion group. However, on posttesting, the two groups scored essentially the same $(t = .18, p > .10)$. It

TABLE 1

ANALYSIS OF VARIANCE OF MORAL JUDGMENT RATINGS

Source	df	MS	F
Between subjects	54		
Groups (experimental & control)		128.39	1.46
Subjects in same group (Error)	53	88.12	
Within subjects	55		
Trials (pre & post)	1	25.55	2.13
Trials × Groups	1	89.10	7.44***
Within error	53	11.97	

Note.—One subject was dropped from the control group due to improper filling out of the questionnaire.
*** $p < .01$.

117

TABLE 2

MEAN MORAL JUDGMENT SCORES AND t TESTS

	Pre	Post	t
Experimental	55.83	58.37	2.84***
Control	59.81	58.73	.30
t	2.04**	.18	

** $p < .05$.
*** $p < .01$.

was found that, after their experience as Companions, the experimental group changed significantly ($t = 2.84$, $p < .01$) toward more tolerant moral judgments, while the control group showed no change ($t = .30$, $p > .10$) as a function of elapsed time between testings.

Self-Acceptance

The self-acceptance score for each subject consisted of the sum of numerical differences between "actual-self-" and "ideal-self-" ratings, without regard to the direction of the difference. Table 3 presents the analysis of variance of these scores. The significant interaction term ($p < .01$) reveals that the experimental and control groups changed in different ways. Table 4 presents the comparisons between the mean scores for each condition. It can be seen that the experimental group shows a significant ($t = 2.11$, $p < .05$) decrease in discrepancy scores (indicating greater self-acceptance) following participation in the program, while the control group exhibits a trend ($t = 1.99$, $p < .10$)

TABLE 3

ANALYSIS OF VARIANCE OF SELF-ACCEPTANCE SCORES

Source	df	MS	F
Between subjects	55		
Groups (experimental & control)		83.31	.44
Subjects in same group			
(Error)	54	191.44	
Within subjects	56		
Trials (pre & post)	1	2.78	.09
Trials × Groups	1	255.66	8.29***
Within error	54	30.83	

*** $p < .01$.

118

toward less self-acceptance upon retesting after the period of elapsed time.

DISCUSSION

The results of the current investigation are incisive in indicating that the students participating in the Companion Program demonstrate significantly greater changes in the personality variables measured than the non-Companion control students.

The changes in the moral judgment scale reveal that the Companions became more tolerant in their judgmental evaluations of sexual and aggressive behaviors. It is of interest that the Companions began the year presenting a picture of greater moral severity than the control group, in that they were more disapproving of behaviors relating to sexuality and aggression. This may be related to an earlier study (Knapp & Holzberg,

TABLE 4

MEAN SELF ACCEPTANCE SCORES AND t TESTS

	Pre	Post	t
Experimental	34.03	31.10	2.11**
Control	32.72	35.90	1.99*
t	.09	.35	

*p < .10.
**p < .05.

1963) which found that religious values occupy a more central role in the philosophies of the Companion students compared to non-Companion controls. The fact that the Companions shifted toward greater approval or sanction of sexual and aggressive behaviors suggests that the type of experience provided by the program may have facilitated the relaxation of initially more prohibitive value systems. Although, on various grounds, one might expect similar kinds of changes in college students from the maturational and presumably broadening effects of the college experience, it is noteworthy that the control group did not reveal any such change.

On the self-acceptance measure, while it

was found that the two groups did not differ significantly at the beginning of the study, the Companion group shifted toward greater self-acceptance, and the non-Companion group showed a trend toward less self-acceptance at the end of the year. This latter trend is difficult to interpret in view of the diverse factors which might influence such a broad variable in the normal course of the year's activity. This change might be a reflection of heightened tension and anxiety concerning the approach of the final examination period, which coincided with the time of the re-testing. However, regardless of the specific causative factors, it is noteworthy that the Companion group, exposed to the same general environmental campus influences, exhibited an opposite change.

The present findings, together with an earlier study of the Companion Program (Holzberg & Gewirtz, 1963), have thus far demonstrated a cluster of changes in the student companions—changes in the direction of more realistic understanding of mental illness, more positive attitudes toward the mentally ill, greater self-acceptance, and relaxation of prohibitive aspects of morality regarding sexual and aggressive behavior. Although an integrated theoretical understanding of the mechanisms underlying these changes is not yet within reach, it is of interest to speculate upon those aspects of the Companion experience which might most directly engage and influence personality variables such as those herein described.

In his comprehensive study of the American college, Sanford (1962) has drawn a fruitful analogy between the college student and the potential therapy patient, in that both are seeking change and both have a significant potential for change. Pursuing this analogy further provides a basis for assuming that the Companion students comprise a population particularly susceptible to personality change. Some suggestive evidence for this assumption was obtained in a recent study (Knapp & Holzberg, 1963) which compared a group of Companions with a randomly selected student group on their freshman admission tests, which included various personality inventories.

The question of what motivations underlie a student's interest in being a Companion is an important area of exploration. It has not yet been possible to identify a particular constellation of motives although one might suspect a multiplicity of factors operating in all students who volunteer. However, it has been possible to discern a certain sequence of events that typically occurs during the student's Companion participation, as reported by both students and professional leaders.

He begins by feeling anxious about being with the patients, and more specifically his own patient, and about his competence in dealing with him. His initial response to this anxiety is that of unrealistic expectations regarding the effects of his visits on the patient. When these expectations collide with the reality of the patient's condition (usually regressed and long-term hospitalized), he predictably becomes pessimistic and despairing. At this point, the role of the student group and its staff advisor becomes crucial in protecting the student from his destructive feelings of failure. As the year progresses, the student gradually regains his optimism, but now in a more realistic sense. It is our current speculation that the student Companions, as they move from failure and self-depreciation to modest optimism and self-enhancement (reinforced by their becoming aware of subtle changes in their patients), are receiving a very personal experience facilitating positive personality change. A more detailed analysis of the dynamics of change in the student Companions has been recently advanced (Holzberg, 1964).

We are of the belief that the Companion Program, apart from its value for patients, is demonstrating the relevance of experience with mental patients for the nonintellective education of college students, or at least, for one segment of the student population. If there is validity to Sanford's observations that college students often fail to demonstrate

121

the significant personality changes that one should expect, perhaps the incorporation of experiences such as we have described in this paper may be one way to facilitate these changes. The college student emerges from the program with a broadened perspective with regard to a significant social problem. He undergoes a transformation of knowledge and attitudes that is consistent with what is expected of an educated person. He is, in addition, being influenced to become more tolerant and more accepting of himself. Apart from this significance for the student himself is the impact on students who are realistically the future leaders of American society, whose collective voices will influence the shape of things to come in mental health (Holzberg, 1963).

REFERENCES

HOLZBERG, J. D. The companion program: Implementing the manpower recommendations of the Joint Commission on Mental Illness and Health. *Amer. Psychologist,* 1963, 18, 224–226.

HOLZBERG, J. D. The significance of the companionship experience for the college student. Washington, D. C.: United States Government Printing Office, 1964, in press.

HOLZBERG, J. D., & GEWIRTZ, H. A method of altering attitudes toward mental illness. *Psychiat. Quart. Suppl.,* 1963, 37, 56–61.

KNAPP, R. H., & HOLZBERG, J. D. Characteristics of college students volunteering for service to mental patients. *J. consult. Psychol.,* 1963, 28, 82–85.

LESSER, W. The relationship between counseling progress and empathic understanding. Unpublished doctoral dissertation, Michigan State University, 1958.

SANFORD, N. Higher education as a social problem. In N. Sanford (Ed.), *The American college.* New York: Wiley, 1962.

UMBARGER, C. C., KANTOR D., & GREENBLATT, M. *College students in a mental hospital.* New York: Grune & Stratton, 1962.

Companionship with the Mentally Ill: Effects on the Personalities of College Student Volunteers†

Jules D. Holzberg, Robert H. Knapp, and John L. Turner

T HIS PAPER describes an ongoing program that brings into interaction chronically ill mental patients and college students. In essence, the program was designed to facilitate social interaction under benign circumstances between alienated patients who are often considerably older than the students and young men and women who are at the height of their physical prowess, intellectual curiosity, and altruistic dedication. Of prime concern have been the effects of the interaction on patients and students. While our report on the effects on patients rests primarily on anecdotal data, effects on students are empirically demonstrated. The results are interpreted in this paper in terms of four hypotheses derived from observations and reactions of the students.

Some six years ago one of the authors appended a field-work experience to an undergraduate course in abnormal psychology. This was designed to enrich the course content by permitting each student in the course to visit the local state mental hospital and to become acquainted with a mentally ill patient during a single semester.

This field work, begun innocently as an adjunct to an educational experience, has led to a formalized program, the Companion Program described here, which involves students from seven colleges.[1] Essentially, the program has provided a blend of service to mentally ill patients and education for students, while at the same time providing a "natural" experiment for the study of the effects of this interaction on the participants. Participation in the program is now open to all students of all seven campuses, and not just to students taking a particular course or majoring in a specific area.

Each student choosing to participate in this program selects or is assigned to a mentally ill patient, almost invariably schizophrenic, who has been in the hospital at least one year and who has minimal involvements with family and friends in the community and limited relationships with other patients in the hospital. No attempt is made to match student and patient on any variables, including sex and age. It is entirely fortuitous whether a group of patients selected for a group of students happens to consist of men, women, or both. The same applies to the ages of patients, although the bulk of patients selected is older than the students because of the criterion of chronicity.

Each student makes weekly visits to the patient throughout the academic year, meeting with him or her for at least one hour a week, engaging in whatever activities the student judges the patient to be interested in, subject only to considerations of good taste and the transactions appropriate between two compan-

[1] Jules D. Holzberg, Harry S. Whiting, and David G. Lowy, "Chronic Patients and a College Companion Program," *Mental Hospitals* (1964) 15:152-158.

† This paper grows out of research supported by a United States Public Health Service project grant MH-01499.

PSYCHIATRY, 1966, vol. 29, vol. 4, pp. 395-405.

ions. Exploration of the hospital grounds is a common activity in early visits. Sometimes it is the patient who takes the initiative in orienting the student to the hospital. He may escort the student on visits to the chapel, the occupational therapy facilities, the movie house, the library, the greenhouse, and other areas of the hospital.

A frequent activity is just talking. For most of the students, this is the most usual mode of relating to friends. They talk while taking walks through the hospital grounds, drinking coffee at the hospital canteen, listening to music in the music department, and so on. The content of their conversations varies, covering areas of mutual interest: how each spends his usual day, their backgrounds, how the patient feels about leaving the hospital, and so on. If a patient reveals an interest in a specific academic area, this may become the subject of discussion, as in the case of the student whose patient-companion shared his interest in mathematics. Sometimes the student may bring to the patient something he has expressed an interest in, such as drawing materials or a particular book. However, talking is not always a comfortable medium of interchange for many of these patients. This may lead the students to play games with them, such as checkers, cards, or pool, or to engage in such activities as tossing a ball around outside. One student with a patient-companion who was not a talker found that they could spend time throwing pebbles at a tree from varying distances. The patient's demonstration of his obvious skill in this activity presumably made him more relaxed with the student, and he became more talkative on subsequent visits. A patient who tends to spend many of his daytime hours on the wards is encouraged by the student to leave the ward during his visit. If in the opinion of the ward staff the patient is too disturbed to leave the ward, the student may spend the entire hour with the patient on the ward. Occasionally a patient resists the student's desire to go outside, sometimes out of fear, sometimes out of negativism;

but it is a rare companion experience which is limited solely to visits on the ward throughout the year, even if the patient is residing on a closed ward.

Not infrequently students take their patients to visit the university nearby. They may explore the university grounds together, have dinner at a fraternity house, or attend a concert. They may talk with faculty members—for example, when one patient expressed an interest in anthropology, his student-companion arranged for him to meet a professor in that department.

Thus, considerable latitude is provided the students in terms of their activities with patients. Very little structure is provided by the professional staff, and it has been our experience that little structure is needed. The students have manifested their sensitivity and basically good judgment throughout the history of the program.

In addition, each student meets every week with eight to ten other students for a group discussion led by a mental health professional. Just as there is wide latitude in the activities engaged in by patients and students, there is considerable diversity in the form and content of these group sessions. Essentially, the professional group leader has a three-fold function: supervision of the student's work with the patient, support of the students at times of anxiety, and education of the students in relation to mental health problems. Although group leaders vary in the degree of their directiveness in conducting group meetings, there is a similarity in the content of the discussions. In the early part of the year, the meetings tend to focus on the anxieties demonstrated by the students. For many of them this is their first experience with formally designated mental patients and their first in a mental hospital. It is rare that these discussions emerge from overt statements of fear. More often the discussions begin with questions raised by the students concerning how they should deal with problems arising from their involvements with the patients. Thus, the student may not verbalize his fears about being on a ward with patients but may pose the problem in terms of how he can persuade a reluctant patient to go off the ward with him.

Once the anxieties of the students diminish, the group discussions tend to focus on understanding the individual patients, with specific reference to what may be happening in their relationships with the students. In varying degrees, each student hopes that he can in some way help his patient. Thus, they may express concern about what they talk about and how this may affect the patient—for example, "Should I ask the patient about his family?," "Should I tell him about my family?," and so on. The student may express concern about the patient who is behaving seductively, or showing resistance, or sharing his fantasy life as in hallucinations. The group discussions focus on helping the student to understand the patient as a person, not as a specimen of psychopathology.

As the relationships between patients and students develop, the students become interested in didactic content relating to general issues of mental illness and hospitalization. Some students seek clarification of such administrative matters as the basis and methods of hospitalization, the various roles of the professionals, and the running of a mental hospital. Other students are more conceptually oriented and seek to understand theories of etiology and treatment and the criteria for the definition of mental illness.

At times, students express concern about patient separation and termination. Discussions center on helping the student to understand these phenomena and their meaning to the patient so that the student may be able to help the patient in facing these potentially traumatic episodes—although they are often more traumatic for the student than for the patient.

To date, our research interest has been directed to three general questions: (1) What is the effect on patients of this unusual dyadic relationship between a mentally ill patient and a college student? (2) What are the qualities that identify the students who volunteer for this program? (3) What are the effects on college students of participation in this novel social engagement?

Partly because this program grew out of an educational objective, the focus of our research has been principally on the latter two questions, pertaining to students. It would be incorrect to infer from this an absence of research interest in the significance of the program for the patient. In fact, we have collected psychological test data on patients in the Companion Program and on a comparable group of patients who have been recommended but who could not be accepted into the program because of an insufficiency of students. We hope this year to have information as to how the patient's psychopathological picture, ward behavior, and social awareness are affected by this experience. A recent study compared 14 companion patients and 30 control patients who were able to complete a Minnesota Multiphasic Personality Inventory. While we cannot be certain that these two populations are representative, it is of interest to us that the companion patients showed a significant decline on the depression scale; in addition, a decline on the paranoid scale barely missed statistical significance.

Most of our current information on the patients, largely derived from anecdotal data, tends to suggest that the introduction of young, intelligent students on a nonprofessional basis has been a positive influence on patients. We have been impressed by the extent to which patients desire the companionship relationship and seek to maintain it. We have had frequent reports of patients becoming more verbally interactive than they have been known to be in many years. Ward personnel have reported that patients show increased self-confidence and a greater interest in their surroundings. Both students and ward personnel have noted that many patients show positive changes in their personal appearance and in their social behavior. While it is hardly likely that the relationship between student and patient-companion affects the core of the schizophrenic process, there have been persistent reports that certain patients show less disturbance in their thinking and considerable improvement in their mood.[2] Greenblatt and Kantor have reported that a similar program at Harvard University resulted in the discharge of patients who had been in the hospital for at least five years.[3] Unfortunately, the absence of data on a control population limits the significance of this type of information, since the onset of college volunteer programs coincides with many changes in institutional policies, such as the open door policy and the use of ataractic drugs.

With regard to the second question, we have carried through systematic studies of companion students and carefully selected noncompanion controls. These have included comparisons between the companions and their controls on psychological tests and on educational, familial, and socioeconomic variables. In the main, the companions differ very little in psychological health or intellectual abilities from the controls. There are small differences in the test data suggesting that student-companions are somewhat more sensitive to others, more idealistic, more altruistic in their attitudes, less involved with worldly success, and more responsive to religious values. There are also small differences on educational and demographic variables, but they do not point to a conclusion that the student-companions are atypical. In fact, it can be stated more positively that there are very few bases on which companions and controls differ.[4] Certainly this study and its replication reject the suspicion that the program is a refuge for morbid and unstable personalities seeking a bizarre adventure.

The third question—namely, the effects on students of participating in the program—has received the major emphasis thus far in our research effort. For several years, we have studied companion-students and a group of student controls at the beginning of the academic year and again at the end. We have compared changes occurring in the companions with changes occurring in a representative group of noncompanion students during the same interval, with the following results: (1) The companion-students manifested a "stirring up" of their attitudes, became more knowledgeable about the problems of mental illness, and began to harbor more enlightened and informed opinions concerning these than did their control counterparts.[5] (2) The companion-students showed a reliable increase in self-acceptance during the course of the year, whereas the control group showed an opposite trend almost of the same magnitude.[6] (3) The companion-students showed a significant movement in the direction of greater moral tolerance toward sexual and aggressive behavior, while the control group showed a slight but nonsignificant movement in the opposite direction.[7] (4) The companion-students increased in introspectiveness and self-examination.

Thus, in summary, the companion-students tended to acquire more enlightened attitudes concerning the field of mental illness, became more self-accepting of themselves and more tolerant of others, and showed a tendency to increased self-awareness and self-examination. We feel that these changes are not merely superficial and hope that they are more than temporary. In fact, some of us who are working with these students are of the opinion that the research to date has not

[2] Carter C. Umbarger, James S. Dalsimer, Andrew P. Morrison, and Peter R. Breggin, *College Students in a Mental Hospital*; New York, Grune & Stratton, 1962.

[3] M. Greenblatt, "A Role for the Voluntary Organization in the Work of Mental Health Institutions"; D. Kantor, "Impact of College Students on Chronic Mental Patients and on the Organization of the Mental Hospital," in *College Student Companion Program: Contributions to the Social Rehabilitation of the Mentally Ill*; Connecticut State Department of Mental Health, Hartford, Conn., 1962.

[4] Robert H Knapp and Jules D. Holzberg, "Characteristics of College Students Volunteering for Service to Mental Patients," *J. Consulting Psychology* (1964) 28:82-85.

[5] Jules D. Holzberg and Herbert Gewirtz, "A Method of Altering Attitudes Toward Mental Illness," *Psychiatric Quart. Suppl.* (1963) 37:56-61.

[6] Jules D. Holzberg, Herbert Gewirtz, and Eugene Ebner, "Changes in Moral Judgment and Self-Acceptance in College Students as a Function of Companionship with Hospitalized Mental Patients," *J. Consulting Psychology* (1964) 28:299-303.

[7] See footnote 6.

yet identified the truly profound changes that may have occurred; some students have from time to time described such changes in group meetings and in unsolicited comments written after they have left the program. Our continuing research, we hope, will lead us to identify these basic changes, which at times are described by the students almost as one might describe a "religious conversion." We also hope eventually to answer the question of the long-term implications of these changes, even though we cannot imagine a profound change which is merely temporary. As one contribution to this problem, we have evaluated the returns of a questionnaire that was mailed to a large group of alumni who were members of the Companion Program during their undergraduate years. Their responses confirm the high value which companions attach to the companion experience retrospectively.

In contemplating the known changes in the students, we have been challenged to attempt some conceptualization that would explain their occurrence. In a sense, there has been a complex of personality changes, changes not unlike those reported in psychotherapy. Is it possible to conceptualize the nature of the interpersonal and intrapsychic experience that can explain these changes and thus direct the future of our research enterprise? In attempting this, we have emerged with four theoretical speculations that we believe deserve further examination and study. These hypotheses should not necessarily be viewed as competing, since it is apparent that there is much overlap between them. It will be the purpose of the rest of this paper to present these four formulations.

A HEIGHTENED SENSE OF PERSONAL COMPETENCE

Our first formulation views the personality changes in the students as a function of a heightened sense of personal competence. It has seemed to us that many of the students began their companionship year with numerous fears of a diverse nature. Some of these fears centered about the mental hospital and the usual stereotypes of the "insane asylum" that unfortunately are still a part of our culture. Other fears arose from students' conceptions of mental patients as having a characteristic potential for aggressive and sexual actions with which the students might not be able to cope. Some students feared that they themselves might do something which would affect the patient adversely. Less explicit, but surely present in some students, were fears about their own psychological health, and anxiety lest they reveal pathological aspects of themselves to others.

After several weeks, many of these fears became attenuated. One of the students described his initial fears and their gradual dissipation as follows:

I believed that mentally ill people are violently disturbed and need to be closely confined and watched. I was frankly afraid that something could happen to me, but I was uncertain what this something was. I was also afraid of what I might see the first time I saw the patients. I remember trying to lose myself in the group of students when we first went onto the ward, and clinging to a fellow student. I think I did not want to even look at the patients for fear of what I might find. When I did begin to look around, I was not repelled as I thought I would be. Rather I was depressed by what seemed to me to be a picture of lost and unhappy people. I remember telling myself that this was not for me, that I would not return next week. But I did, God knows why! And I am glad because I would never have learned how unrealistic my expectations and my fears were. I can't remember when it happened, but my sense of discomfort about visiting at the hospital diminished very rapidly.

However, within several months there emerged what seems like a more basic fear—fear of their own incompetence in helping the patients, many of whom were regressed schizophrenics with long-term hospitalizations. We observed the students setting unrealistic goals for themselves—they expected to "cure" their patients and return them quickly to the community from which they had been ejected. This period of unrealistic optimism soon yielded to the bitter reality of chronic schizophrenia, and many of the students became self-devaluative and felt that they had truly failed. The sense of frustration was described by one student:

My patient was a middle-aged woman who told me that she had been hospitalized for the first time about a year before my first contact with her. She was open in her talks with me, answering my questions freely and equally freely asking me questions in turn. She was married to a man somewhat older than herself and had two children. She very early spoke of her interest in wanting to leave the hospital so that she could return to her family. She seemed as normal as many people I have known, and I was touched by her genuine feelings of wanting to be with her family. I wanted to be of some help to her and became really excited that perhaps I could really help her to get out of the hospital. I was sure she had just been overlooked by a busy staff—I would try to put her in contact with the right person. I discussed this with my group leader and he encouraged me to talk to one of the social workers. This was just before the long Christmas vacation. I was really excited—so excited that I talked more about my patient to my family over vacation than about any other matter.

I could not wait to get back to school to see the social worker. When I met her, I was terribly shocked to learn how little I knew about my patient and how seemingly hopeless it was to think that she could be discharged. She had actually been in and out of the hospital for the past seven years, and her current hospitalization was about one year ago. Each time she left, she returned to her husband, who was described as a well-meaning, hardworking factory worker. However, when she got home, she would become like a child, spend most of her time in bed, expecting her husband to cook for her and the family, and quarreling incessantly with her children. The husband had now reached the point where he could not develop any enthusiasm for her coming home. I cannot remember ever feeling so depressed and so utterly frustrated. It was clear I had misjudged the patient and her problems. I wanted to help, but one form the help could not take was to get her out of the hospital and back to her family. I resented the patient for misleading me but most of all I resented my ineffectuality.

White has indicated how success in dealing with and influencing people is significantly related to one's sense of competence and hence one's self-esteem.[8] The student, within this context, finds it impossible to produce the intended effect —that is, the patient does not get well quickly, and the student cannot escape the reality of his patient's continued hospitalization. The awareness of the discrepancy between intention and accomplishment is experienced as a threat to his sense of personal competence and thus results in lowered self-esteem.

Partly as a function of his experience in the group sessions and partly because of the amazing resiliency of youth, the student makes his way through his fears and his failures and comes to realize the role of his unrealistic optimism in creating his own sense of despair. He then begins to accept more modest goals for his patient, goals that are more possible of attainment. A student emerging from such a period of frustration said:

I now realize that my patient is doomed to live out much of his life in a hospital-like place. He really doesn't want to leave even though I try to encourage him to think along these lines. His family does not want him. I don't think they would care if he died. I can now see that while I felt it was terrible for him to remain here, he was secure because he had found a niche for himself. Once I could accept this, it was less painful for me. I saw my visits as less an opportunity to cure him and more to provide a lonely man with an hour of friendly companionship each week. I guess this is not to be sneered at!

We thus have speculated that the students, in working through fears centering on their sense of competence, finally emerge from the experience with feelings of human efficacy rooted in a sense of accomplishment which is more realistically anchored. We thus believe that the positive changes in some of these students may be viewed as the product of a heightened sense of personal competence.

The Development of an Expanded System of Personal Constructs

Our second formulation views the changes in the students as a function of an expanding and flexible system of personal constructs.[9] It has become apparent

[8] Robert W. White, "Motivation Reconsidered: The Concept of Competence," *Psychol. Review* (1959) 66:297-333.

[9] George A. Kelly, *The Psychology of Personal Constructs. Vol. I, A Theory of Personality; Vol. 2, Clinical Diagnosis and Psychotherapy*; New York, Norton, 1955.

from communications with students that a number of them emerged from the companion experience feeling that they had "made friends" with their patients. Students have many reasons for entering the program: intellectual reasons centering on wanting to learn about abnormal behavior and mental hospitals, vocational reasons concerned with preparing for a vocational goal such as clinical psychology or medicine, altruistic reasons such as wanting to be kind to an unfortunate person, therapeutic reasons pertaining to the wish to help a patient get well. Some students indicate that they are motivated for reasons of self-examination—to learn more about themselves or to get help for their own personal problems. Only a few students entered the program to "make a friend." However, there are a number of students who have been surprised to find that they draw great satisfaction from their experience because they have become real friends with their patients, persons quite unlike them in social and economic backgrounds, intellectual and educational levels. The satisfaction may arise from the student's feeling that he occupies an important place in the patient's life and, conversely, that the patient has become important to him. The student may tell the patient personal things about himself and value highly the patient's opinions about him and his life experiences. This finally culminates in the student's being able to relax and be himself with the patient. He then begins to talk about genuine feelings of affection for the patient. A student who had this type of experience commented:

I was one of those students who was interested in mental health work, probably clinical psychology, maybe social work. I started in the Companion Program hoping to learn about mental illness, but there was a little private thought that maybe I could begin my "therapeutic" practice now. My patient was selected for me because I couldn't make up my mind. He was a 52-year-old man, had been in the hospital for 12 years, and was a schizophrenic, I later learned from a psychiatric aide. Even with my limited understanding I could soon see that psychotherapy, at least what I knew about it, couldn't touch this man. He rarely talked, his chief communication being "Yes" or "No" in response to my questions. The first few weeks I was never sure he even wanted to see me. I remember asking my group leader if I should transfer to another patient, but he encouraged me to continue.

I am not sure I know when it began, but I felt myself feeling sorry for this man, forgotten by his family and living all to himself. As I began to feel sorry, I felt that I wanted to get to know him better, why this had happened to him. At about the same time, I noticed that he was changing in his attitudes toward me. He would smile when I arrived for my visit. Later, he began to shake hands when I would arrive. I took him to the campus one afternoon and we walked around the grounds. I really looked forward to my visits and began to worry about what would happen when the year ended. There was no question in my mind that I was concerned about him, and I had the feeling that his smiles and handshakes meant a similar concern for me. I think I now for the first time understand why the program is called "companion," because I think we have become friends of a sort. Sure, this is not a friendship such as I have with fellows at college, but there are different kinds of friendships. One can be friends with parents, brothers, and schoolmates; these are friendships of different qualities, but friendships nevertheless. I think I am correct in saying that my patient and I became friends. Incidentally, I plan to visit him in the fall even though I will not be in the program again.

We have begun to feel that for certain students there has been an enlargement of the range of persons with whom they now recognize they can establish friendships. It seems as though the student starts the year with a rigid and limiting set of personal constructs, but during the year things happen that are defined as impossible by this rigid construct system —particularly, the *patient* becomes a *person,* the *outsider* becomes a *friend.* These "impossible" developments dramatically demonstrate that something was wrong with the earlier construct system, and the student is compelled to reorganize it. As a consequence, he becomes open to a wider range of possible ways of classifying other persons and of possible ways in which he might relate to them. This expanding and liberalizing of construct systems is our second formulation to account for personality change in the students.

The Clarification of Self-Definition

Our third formulation views personality change in the students as a function of the clarification of their self-definitions and identities.[10] We have observed with regularity the phenomenon of the student who entered the program with naive anticipations that the patients would be frightening, but later complained that he could not perceive anything abnormal about his patient once his fears about patients had diminished. This has happened with such frequency that it may in fact be universally true of all of our students. This development initially may have taken the form of the student's inquiring as to why the patient was hospitalized, but usually has emerged more clearly as an anguished plea from the student that the patient ought not to be in a mental hospital. Not infrequently, the student has voiced the complaint, as well as the fear, that he does not see the patient as in any way being different from himself.

Perhaps some digression here is appropriate in order to stress our belief that one of the students' major therapeutic contributions lies precisely in this failure to perceive the patients' psychopathology. Of all the people who interact with the patient in the hospital—his family, his friends, the hospital staff—it is probably the student alone who perceives and therefore relates to the patient as if he were in fact *not* mentally ill. We shall not elaborate this issue further, since it is not central to our major thesis here.

While we cannot as yet be certain about this, it seems probable that the student is distressed by being unable to articulate the difference between himself and the patient, and that the usual concerns of the adolescent identity problem loom with special force. These students, in spite of their good intellect and well-developed physical prowess, must be recognized for what they are—essentially adolescents, still in the process of developing as in-

dividuals and searching for their unique and discrete identities.

The component of self-definition that emerges as a result of the companionship experience is a redefinition of self which significantly alters the intense anxiety of seeing oneself as identical to a chronically ill mental patient. It is clear that the students have emerged from the experience recognizing their differences from the patients, while still recognizing that they and the patients are members of the human race. They can recognize the patient's pathology at the end of the year and can observe his deviance; yet they are not repelled by this difference. There is, we speculate, considerable reassurance in the recognition of this difference, and also a clearer, more decisive sense of self. For some students, this redefinition of self seems to underlie the positive personality changes. One student for whom the issue of self-definition seemed particularly acute commented:

My patient took the business of withdrawal really seriously. This was obvious from the very beginning, but I could not see why this made him a patient in a mental hospital. I am not a very gregarious person, and I have met some students who were just as serious about their withdrawal. I think it is understandable why this should have puzzled me and bothered me. I don't think I am mentally ill; in fact, I know I am not. I still think that it is not fair to label my patient as mentally ill. I realize he is afraid to leave the hospital, but wouldn't I after 17 years? One of my friends, half seriously, in discussing my patient stated that he was afraid to leave college and go out into the world. So because he has the necessary intellect, he has decided to go on to graduate school and enter the academic profession. I guess he is suggesting that he, too, has elected to withdraw from the real world. But my friend is not mentally ill, and I hope no one is going to suggest that he should be in the hospital. In some ways, I respect my patient for a certain integrity that he displays. In turning his back on the world, he is doing what many students would like to do. After all, it is a pretty crazy world.

There is still another problem in self-definition that we have only just begun to recognize. The student initially meets the patient with whatever social masks he usually wears and whatever interpersonal strategies he usually employs. Be-

[10] Erik H. Erikson, *Childhood and Society;* New York, Norton, 1950.

cause such behavior is habitual, it *feels* natural to the student. But with the patient it does not work. Unlike the student's usual associates, the patient responds to the student's one-upmanship, flirtation, or characteristic line with dismay, confusion, and hurt. The result is that suddenly the "natural" is no longer natural, the act feels like an act, the mask slips and is recognized for a mask. A problem of self-definition emerges— if *this*, which I thought was my natural self, is not I, who am I? Out of this crisis, if it is resolved, comes a kind of real self, at once more genuine and more considerate than the self presented to one's usual associates. The fact that this self exists is reassuring. One student alluded to this issue as follows:

My patient is a lot of fun. She seems so different from the other patients I have met who are companions to other students. She has a sense of humor, at times a little sharp and digging. So much so that I used to feel uncomfortable at the beginning of the year. A group of students and their patients would go each week to the canteen where we would sit and drink coffee. Of course, conversation was our chief contact with each other. Every now and then I would offer a serious comment that I felt was meaningful, only to have my patient say something humorous that cut me down and made others laugh. I remember vividly the day we were sitting around and I offered the comment that it must be dull to live in a mental hospital. My patient retorted, "How would you know unless you tried it?" Everyone laughed and I suppose I was embarrassed. I remember feeling an intense dislike for my patient, but I subsequently thought about it and realized how right she was. It was a little pompous for me to offer such an opinion, and she cut me down to size. I hope I have learned something from her—people on the outside are too controlled to let you know when you're off base.

Sullivan observed that doing psychotherapy with schizophrenics is a significant route to profound self-knowledge.[11] He had in mind a similar thing—these patients' remarkable capacity for unmasking, or, at least, of making one aware of the masks one wears. This may be one of the unique contributions of schizophrenic patients to our students—sub-

jecting their identities to strain and testing, which leads to their reorganization, consolidation, and clarification.

THE ATTAINMENT OF EMOTIONAL CATHARSIS

Our fourth reflection upon the consequences for the student-companion of participation in the program does not preclude the validity of what we have said before, but rather seeks to tie the companion experiences of certain of the students to ancient and largely neglected doctrines of personality change derived from the Aristotelian theory of tragedy. We shall first restate the nature of the experience reported by many of the students.

They enter the Companion Program at a young and impressionable age and are thrust into intimate association with disordered, frequently anguished, and unfulfilled people. They pass some months as companions, undergoing a wide range of emotional involvements, including compassion and indignation. They often respond profoundly to what they see as the tragedy of the patient's condition, his rejection by family and friends, and the waste of his human potential. They often react with feelings of despair. One student described such reactions with poignant feelings:

Paul is a 22-year-old man, not much older than myself. He is the loneliest person I have ever known. If left alone, he would sit in his favorite chair staring out of the window on the ward and at the sky throughout his waking hours. He never smiles, but he doesn't look sad either. He is just alone. I have been told that he was a child schizophrenic and in many institutions before coming to this hospital. His father died in an automobile accident when he was four. This was supposed to have affected his mother mentally and she is described by the group leader as probably psychotic. Paul first began to show his illness when he was in second grade. He was a shy child, frail in physique, and for this reason often picked on by other children. He never was known to have a friend. They tell me he has an IQ of at least 110, and I know enough from my psychology courses that this is probably a low estimate. On more than one occasion, I compared myself to him and it is a heartbreaking comparison. I have had a happy family, a life filled with friends, and an opportunity to develop my abilities. Paul

[11] Harry Stack Sullivan, *Schizophrenia as a Human Process;* New York, Norton, 1962.

probably doesn't remember his father, has a sick mother, never had a friend, and his intelligence is withering for lack of stimulation. I feel so empty and so small that I should have had so much and not be able to give anything to someone who needs it.

At the conclusion of their experience, many of the student-companions find a new depth and a new poise in the manner in which they regard both themselves and others. Many describe their experience as quasi-religious in nature, though few are able to give it a lucid, rational formulation, except to say that they have somehow derived a great, if intangible, human benefit from their encounter.

In the history of mankind, the spectacle and the contemplation of tragic misfortune are associated with the highest forms of art and religious experience. In Christian civilization, many of the great art works are devoted to spectacles of anguish, the Crucifixion itself being the most ubiquitous, but the sorrowing of the Virgin and the martyrdom of saints following the same motif. Moreover, the contemplation of these cruel and tragic spectacles has been credited in this religious tradition with cleansing and ennobling the human spirit. In many cultures and in multitudinous forms, the tragic spectacle is cherished as a religious symbol and psychologically therapeutic agent of first importance.

Aristotle, in his *Poetics* and elsewhere, discusses this phenomenon. He defines tragedy as follows:

A Tragedy is, then, the portrayal of an imaginary chapter of heroic life, complete and of some length, in language sweetened in different parts in all known ways, in dramatic, not narrative form, *indirectly through pity and terror* righting mental disorders of this type [italics ours].[12]

Aristotle then proceeds to discuss the requirements of the tragic hero, plot, form, and so on. But the most important part of the definition from our present point of view is contained in the last phrases, which have also been translated, ". . . and by exciting pity and fear it gives a

healthy outlet to such emotions." His disciple, Proclus, expands somewhat on this as follows:

Tragedy and comedy . . . contribute to the cleansing away of the passions, which cannot be altogether repressed, nor on the other hand safely indulged, but need some moderate outlet. This they obtain at such dramatic performances, and so leave us untroubled for the rest of the time.[13]

This makes yet more explicit the doctrine of the therapeutic effects of tragedy.

Precisely what is meant by the word "catharsis" has been subject to some dispute. The prevailing opinion seems to regard the word as referring peculiarly to cleansing, but with distinctly medical allusions. Thus, Margoliouth sees it as a very literal extension of the doctrine of homeopathic therapy, ubiquitous in classical medicine.[14] Specifically, and in terms of the humoral doctrines of the age, fear and terror dominate the soul when cold is ascendant over warmth. The treatment for the cold soul is to expose it to cold so that the outer cold may draw away the inner.

These quaint medical doctrines may no longer have utility or credibility, but the notion that the tragic spectacle can effectively dampen anxiety, egocentricisms, and disturbances within a person has real merit as psychological description. The analogy employed by Aristotle elsewhere is that "the great fire without may snuff the candle within"[15]—that is, the spectacle of the suffering hero purges the trifling anxieties of the spectator.

The modern psychologist will doubtless want some more adequate explanation of how this process takes place. Without making a positive commitment at this juncture, we believe that several possible interpretations warrant consideration:

(1) Certain emotions may be extinguished by saturation, just as certain persistent habits may be overcome through excessive practice. This is a mere exten-

[12] *The Poetics of Aristotle*, translated by David S. Margoliouth; London, Hodder and Stoughton, 1911; p. 154.

[13] Frank L. Lucas, *Tragedy in Relation to Aristotle's "Poetics"*; New York, Harcourt, Brace, 1928; p. 26.
[14] See footnote 12; p. 57.
[15] See footnote 12; p. 61.

sion of the so-called Dunlap hypothesis.[16]

(2) It may be that the tragic spectacle permits people to project the sources of their own anxieties onto an outer and objective representation. Thus, it is not "I" who harbors fear and terror, but rather the hero of the tragic spectacle.

(3) It may be that the tragic spectacle permits people to discharge certain sadistic and aggressive energies which are the source of neurotic conflict within themselves, leaving them psychologically disencumbered.

(4) It may be that a tragic spectacle permits people, by identification, to suffer certain unconscious self-punishing experiences, from which they may then disengage themselves with final impunity.

(5) Or it may be that the spectacle of great suffering has the effect of re-anchoring the hedonic frame of reference, making one's own miseries perceptually small compared with those of the tragic protagonist and thus providing a release from anxiety.

Not all of the patient-companions in this program realize this experience, and

it is perhaps worth observing the conditions under which Aristotle would predict failure. According to Aristotle, the tragic hero will prove effective only if he is a person of worth and dignity, and only if his misfortunes outweigh his faults. Aristotle observes that he must never be ludicrous or evil, for then the magic of the tragic catharsis is utterly destroyed. This suggests to us that some companions may have failed to experience the "cathartic effect" because they have been unable to develop sufficient respect and empathy for their patient-companion.

The formulations we have just described are at present in a preliminary form. Their value will depend on whether they can be reduced operationally so as to permit more directed research. A number of the formulations are currently being tested. We anticipate that it is not so much a question of which speculation is the correct one, but rather a matter of determining the various routes by which personality changes occur in the naive and unsophisticated as they enter into an encounter with the mentally ill. It is our current feeling that the Companion Program offers a wide variety of meanings to different persons, with a resulting pluralism in reactions.

---

[16] K. Dunlap, "A Revision of the Fundamental Law of Habit Formation," *Science* (1928) 67:360-362.

ATTITUDES OF VOLUNTEERS TOWARD MENTAL HOSPITALS COMPARED TO PATIENTS AND PERSONNEL*

PAUL D. IMRE

PROBLEM

Recent studies [2, 3, 5] have employed the Souelem Scale to measure attitudes towards mental hospitals with groups of patients and personnel serving as subjects. The use of other types of groups has apparently been restricted since no literature appears to be available at this time. Since the volunteer services of this hospital make an important contribution towards the total milieu therapy of Spring Grove patients and their interaction with personnel is rather active, a sampling of this group would add to the studies previously cited. This study investigated their attitudes.

METHOD

The Souelem Scale was administered to 32 female volunteers during their third orientation session. The obtained mean and variance of this group was compared with that of personnel and non-alcoholic psychiatric patients sampled in an early study [2]. Ryan's methods [4] for multiple comparison of variances was employed and the means of the three groups were analyzed by means of Edwards' [1] t for heterogeneous variances, when appropriate, otherwise Fischer's t was employed.

RESULTS

The means and variances of the volunteers and the patients are given in Table 1. The volunteer group was significantly less variable on their scores than were the patients. The personnel and the volunteers appear to be randomly drawn from populations with the same variance and means.

The volunteers at this hospital are represented by more then 60 organizations, include 683 volunteers and they contributed over 34,400 man hours to the hospital during the last fiscal year. That this sample should reflect a rather positive

TABLE 1. MEANS AND STANDARD DEVIATIONS OF THREE GROUPS ADMINISTERED THE SOUELEM ATTITUDE SCALE

	Hospital Personnel	Volunteers	Non-alcoholic Patients
M	3.29	3.31	3.86
SD	.32	.26	.89
N	55	32	72

JOURNAL OF CLINICAL PSYCHOLOGY, 1962, vol. 18, no. 4, p. 516.

view of the hospital and very similar to that of employees presents, to some degree, a common favorable attitude which can be used to plan mutually acceptable goals and, in some cases, it may be possible to interchange roles without impeding the effectiveness of a milieu program.

SUMMARY

The Souelem Scale was administered to 32 female volunteers at this hospital and the means and variances were compared with 55 hospital employees, and 72 patients. Hospital personnel and the volunteers were found to be more favorably disposed towards mental hospitals than the patients. The volunteers and personnel appear to be expressing a very similar and favorable attitude towards mental hospitals.

REFERENCES

1. EDWARDS, A. L. *Experimental design in psychological research*. (1960 rev.) New York: Rinehart and Co., 1960.
2. IMRE, P. and WOLF, S. Attitudes of patients and personnel toward mental hospitals. *J. clin. Psychol.*, 1962, *18*, 232-234.
3. KLOPFER, W. G., WYLIE, A. A. and HILLSON, J. S. Attitudes toward mental hospitals. *J. clin. Psychol.*, 1956, *12*, 361-365.
4. RYAN, T. A. Significance tests for multiple comparisons of proportions, variances, and other statistics. *Psychol. Bull.*, 1960, *57*, 318-328.
5. SOUELEM, OMNEYA. Mental patient's attitudes toward mental hospitals. *J. clin. Psychol.*, 1955, *11*, 181-185.

*The author wishes to thank the hospital administration for its cooperation and assistance in the execution of this study.

PERSONALITY CHANGE AS A FUNCTION OF VOLUNTEER EXPERIENCE IN A PSYCHIATRIC HOSPITAL [1]

MARK KING, LEOPOLD O. WALDER, AND STANLEY PAVEY

Four-hundred and sixteen college students were tested for degree of moral tolerance and self-acceptance before and after completing undergraduate psychology courses. Sixteen of the students concurrently did volunteer work in mental hospitals. The within-Ss analysis indicates the volunteer experience did not significantly change the moral tolerance scores, whereas it did result in greater self-acceptance scores. These results only partially support a previous study.

The last decade has been marked by an increasing interest on the part of college students in the problems of the mentally ill. One manifestation of this interest is the establishment on many campuses of volunteer groups which recruit students to spend time on a regular basis in psychiatric facilities near the campus. Umbarger, Dalsimer, Morrison, and Breggin (1962) describe an ambitious program by Harvard University students which seemed to have beneficial effects on patients in a state hospital.

While the volunteer's primary motivation (or at least the one of which he is probably most aware) is to help bring about health change in the patients with whom he comes in contact, change might well be expected to occur in the volunteer too. It is probably true that for the volunteer a mental hospital is a novel and challenging experience, both intellectually and emotionally. Under these conditions, the volunteer is likely to "see" things differently, to become aware of new feelings, and to reassess himself. Empirical investigation indicates that cognitive and emotional changes do result from experience with hospitalized patients. Holzberg and Gewirtz (1963) found that attitudes about mental health and mental illness were modified as a function of volunteer ex-

[1] The computer time for this project was supported in full through the facilities of the Computer Science Center of the University of Maryland.

JOURNAL OF CONSULTING AND CLINICAL PSYCHOLOGY, Dec. 1970, vol. 35, no. 3, pp. 423-425.

perience, and Holzberg, Gewirtz, and Ebner (1964) found that when students had regular contacts with a patient, under professional supervision, changes occurred in the students' moral judgments and in the degree of self-acceptance. At the completion of an academic year of volunteer experience, students in the latter study were more tolerant of sex and aggression and were more accepting of themselves.

The Ss used in the study by Holzberg et al. (1964) were college students. They volunteered for a "companion" program which lasted a full academic year and which included weekly contact with the same patient. An additional part of the program was a weekly group meeting with a supervisor. The group meetings were seen as "the medium through which students are supervised and formally educated concerning the problems surrounding mental illness and hospitalization [p. 299]." Holzberg and his colleagues made no attempt to differentiate the effects of contact with the patients from the didactic group experience. A number of questions remain unanswered, then, about the source of the changes in the students.

The present study is an extension of Holzberg et al. (1964), and attempts to answer one question raised by it—Do changes in moral judgment and self-acceptance occur in volunteers whose experience lacks in both regular supervision and training?

METHOD

Subjects

The sample for this study consisted of 416 students who were enrolled in one of three psychology courses, and who completed both the pretesting and posttesting. Of these 416, 16 were serving as volunteers for the semester. The volunteers used in the present study belonged to a University of Maryland campus organization known as Volunteers for Mental Health. Each semester, volunteers are recruited from the entire campus and funneled to one or another mental health facility in the area of the University. The typical volunteer is at the hospital one evening a week, works with chronically ill patients, and is largely left to his own devices as to what he does with the patients. Some students form a continuing relationship with a single patient, but more commonly the volunteers circulate freely about the ward, chatting or participating in

TABLE 1

ANALYSIS OF VARIANCE: MORAL JUDGMENT RATINGS

Source	df	MS	F
Between Ss	415		
Class (A)	2	2647.25	58.34**
Volunteer (B)	1	878.30	19.36**
A × B	2	1002.39	22.09**
Error	410	45.37	
Within Ss	416		
Testing (C)	1	346.30	12.55**
A × C	2	101.06	3.66*
B × C	1	7.63	.28
A × B × C	2	40.67	1.47
Error	410	27.58	

* $p < .05$.
** $p < .01$.

games or other activities with the patients. As volunteers, they receive no supervision or didactic training, either at the hospital or on campus. In many ways, then, the volunteers from the University of Maryland are engaged in a different program and have experiences different from the "companions" in the Holzberg et al. (1964) study.

Test Instruments

The instruments used to measure moral judgment and self-acceptance were the same as those described by Holzberg et al. (1964). The moral judgment questionnaire consisted of 18 items which tap attitudes toward sex and aggression. The items were rated in terms of "how right" S felt the behavior to be. The self-acceptance questionnaire required Ss to rate 40 self-reference items twice, once in reference to "perceived self" and once for "ideal-self." The absolute sum of the differences between the two ratings was the self-acceptance score.

Procedure

The questionnaires were administered to the Ss in their classrooms during the first week of the semester. They were told that they were participating in a research project, but were given no information about the nature of the study or its design. The second testing took place in the classroom during the last week of the semester, 15 weeks later. Only students present for both the testings are included in the sample. Volunteers in the various classes were identified by checking the list of students going to the psychiatric hospitals with the class lists furnished by the instructors. There were no specific experimental procedures during the 15 weeks between the first and second testings other than participation (or not) in the Volunteers for Mental Health program. The average amount of patient contact for the 16 volunteers was 11 evenings (three hours per

RESULTS

A Type III (Lindquist, 1953) analysis of variance was used. The analysis was set up by class level (freshman to seniors), by volunteer versus nonvolunteer, and by pre–post testing and its interaction as post effects. The principle focus was on the Testing × Volunteer interaction—namely, that volunteers were expected to show greater pre–post change than controls on moral judgment and self-acceptance.

Moral Judgment

Table 1 presents the analysis of variance of the moral judgment scores. While freshman and sophomores scored higher (more tolerance) than seniors, volunteers were higher than nonvolunteers, and pretest scores were higher than posttest scores. The critical Testing × Volunteer interaction was not significant.

Self-Acceptance

Table 2 presents the analysis of variance of the self-acceptance scores. In the volunteers, self-acceptance increased progressively from freshman to seniors, while the nonvolunteers showed decreased self-acceptance from freshman to sophomores and then increased self-acceptance from sophomores to seniors. Most important, the effects of the Testing × Volun-

TABLE 2

ANALYSIS OF VARIANCE: SELF-ACCEPTANCE SCORES

Source	df	MS	F
Between Ss	415		
Class (A)	2	558.99	2.86
Volunteer (B)	1	87.77	.45
A × B	2	785.81	4.03*
Error	410	195.18	
Within Ss	416		
Testing (C)	1	117.15	1.96
A × C	2	108.09	1.81
B × C	1	281.66	4.71**
A × B × C	2	27.41	.46
Error	410	59.83	

* $p < .05$.
** $p < .01$.

teer interaction was highly significant ($p < .01$).

Table 3 presents the means associated with the Testing × Volunteer interaction. The volunteers' mean self-acceptance score became smaller (more self-acceptance) from the first to the second testing than did the nonvolunteers'.

DISCUSSION

In one respect, the present study confirms the findings of Holzberg et al. (1964): The volunteers showed a greater change toward self-acceptance than the nonvolunteers. It would appear that contact with certain kinds of subject matter may be a factor in the increase in the volunteers' self-acceptance. The uniformity for all the groups that change is the exposure to behavior patterns that are presumed to be deviant.

We may compare the findings of Holzberg et al. with the present findings on the moral judgment score change as a function of volunteer experience. Their volunteers were exposed to a group didactic experience with a hospital staff person; those in this study were not. Their volunteers' moral judgment scores changed, whereas the volunteers' scores in this study did not. Perhaps the change toward a more tolerant moral judgment for those who volunteered in the study by Holzberg et al. occurred when they were exposed to the verbal behavior of a psychologist who was trying to teach information about deviant behaviors (and probably more accepting attitudes) rather than the exposure to the hospital patients.

TABLE 3

MEAN SELF-ACCEPTANCE SCORES—
TESTING × VOLUNTEERING INTERACTION

Sample	Testing	
	Pre	Post
Volunteer	38.60	32.03
Nonvolunteer	37.26	36.75

Note.—The lower the score, the greater the self-acceptance.

REFERENCES

HOLZBERG, J. D., & GEWIRTZ, H. A method of altering attitudes toward mental illness. *Psychiatric Quarterly Supplement*, 1963, **37**, 56–61.

HOLZBERG, J. D., GEWIRTZ, H., & EBNER, E. Changes in moral judgment and self-acceptance in college students as a function of companionship with hospitalized mental patients. *Journal of Consulting Psychology*, 1964, **28**, 299–303.

LINDQUIST, E. F. *Design and analysis of experiments in psychology and education.* Boston: Houghton Mifflin, 1953.

UMBARGER, C. C., DALSIMER, J. S., MORRISON, A. P., & BREGGIN, P. R. *College students in a mental hospital.* New York: Grune & Stratton, 1962.

CHARACTERISTICS OF COLLEGE STUDENTS VOLUNTEERING FOR SERVICE TO MENTAL PATIENTS

ROBERT H. KNAPP   AND   JULES D. HOLZBERG

85 male college students volunteering for service as companions to chronically ill mental patients were compared to a group of 85 control students on a number of psychological tests administered during the students' freshmen years. These tests consisted of the Minnesota Multiphasic Personality Inventory, Edwards Personal Preference Schedule, Allport-Vernon-Lindzey Scale of Values, the Scholastic Aptitude Test, and the Terman Concept Mastery Test. Students taking part in the Companion Program are not differentiated from their control counterparts in any clinical respect. There is evidence that the companions are (a) slightly more religiously oriented, (b) more morally concerned, (c) more compassionate, and (d) more introverted than the control students.

Over the past decade, there has developed in a number of colleges and universities a new approach to the problem of the care of the chronically mentally ill (Umbarger, Kantor, & Greenblatt, 1962). This program, as it has developed at Wesleyan University and the Connecticut Valley Hospital, has been called the Companion Program and has involved an arrangement whereby college students volunteer to undertake weekly visits to mental hospitals throughout the academic year for the purpose of bringing comfort and human companionship to mentally ill patients.

Although this new development in the care of the mentally ill cannot be called therapy in the strict sense of the term, it is nonetheless designed to bring to the hospital environment certain new, fresh, and stimulating influences calculated to facilitate at least the social recovery of the patient. Kantor (1963) has reported several studies which have sought to demonstrate that organized social contacts between college students (at Harvard and Radcliffe) and mental patients have indeed resulted in demonstrable improvement in the condition of these mental patients, especially as they appear to relieve symptoms deriving from the environmental poverty of the typical hospital regime. More recently, Holzberg and associates have been able to demonstrate that participation in the Companion Program has had clear and striking effects upon the participating students themselves. Specifically, the experience of participation has led to significant changes in attitudes toward and knowledge about mental

JOURNAL OF CONSULTING PSYCHOLOGY, 1964, vol. 28, no. 1, pp. 82-85.

142

illness (Holzberg & Gewirtz, 1963). In a recent study Holzberg, Gewirtz, and Ebner have demonstrated increased moral tolerance and increased self-acceptance as compared with carefully selected control groups.

As yet unanswered, however, is the question of the characteristics of students who elect to volunteer for the program itself. It is naturally a question of prime pedagogic interest to determine if such persons represent a self-selected and distinctive body in terms of psychological attributes, or whether they are a rather typical cross section of the student population from which they are drawn. Fortunately at Wesleyan University an answer to this problem could be tentatively obtained, for at this institution an extensive testing program involving all students has been in progress for many years. Moreover, the numbers involved in the Companion Program from year to year have been significant, thus providing a basis for the secure statistical comparison of these students with a selected control group.

METHOD

The experimental subjects, numbering 85 males in all, were selected from five classes (1961 to 1965) of the Wesleyan student body. These constituted all of the students who participated in the program during this period. The control subjects who had not participated in the program were selected in the same proportions from each class. They included the next students following each experimental subject in an alphabetical listing of the class. Thus, the control group numbered the same as the experimental, was selected in the same proportion from

TABLE 1

COMPARISON OF COMPANION AND CONTROL GROUP ON THE MINNESOTA MULTIPHASIC PERSONALITY INVENTORY (SCORES K-CORRECTED)

	Companion means	Contol means	t
Hypochondriasis	11.93	11.72	.35
Depression	17.43	16.26	1.23
Hysteria	19.68	18.93	.88
Psychopathic deviate	20.11	19.81	.22
Masculinity-femininity	27.29	27.09	.38
Paranoia	10.27	9.52	1.32
Psychasthenia	26.71	26.22	.58
Schizophrenia	24.91	24.60	.33
Mania	18.13	18.84	1.01
Social introversion	24.00	21.16	1.64*

* $p < .10$.

143

TABLE 2

COMPARISON OF COMPANION AND CONTROL GROUP ON
THE EDWARDS PERSONAL PREFERENCE SCHEDULE

	Companion means	Control means	*t*
Achievement	16.75	16.60	.23
Deference	11.13	10.46	1.14
Order	8.87	9.87	1.49
Exhibition	13.72	14.31	1.23
Autonomy	14.64	14.66	.03
Affiliation	14.96	14.75	.31
Intraception	18.73	16.32	3.30***
Succorance	10.48	10.24	.33
Dominance	16.79	16.64	.19
Abasement	14.47	13.71	.95
Nurturance	14.13	12.76	1.88***
Change	13.68	15.21	2.13**
Endurance	13.62	14.16	.60
Heterosexuality	16.98	17.07	.10
Aggression	12.33	13.32	1.32
Consistency	11.84	11.76	.08

** $p < .05$.
*** $p < .01$.

each class, and only alphabetical listing was permitted to dictate the selection of the control subjects within each class.

From the records obtained at the university, it proved possible to compare our two groups with respect to performance on five standard psychological tests, namely, the Minnesota Multiphasic Personality Inventory (MMPI), the Edwards Personal Preference Schedule (EPPS), the Allport-Vernon-Lindzey Scale of Values (A-V-L), the verbal and mathematical scales of the Scholastic Aptitute Test (SAT), and the Terman Concept Mastery Test (TCMT). In the case of the MMPI, data were not available for the class of 1964 and accordingly comparisons on this test were made on samples of but 65 companion and 65 controls selected from the other 4 years. It should be observed that in virtually all instances these measures were obtained at the beginning of the freshman year while the companions' participation in the program occurred from 1 to 3 years thereafter. It might have been preferable to obtain test scores contemporary with the students' participation in the program, though this procedure would have been most difficult for practical reasons. Furthermore, this may have left unanswered the question of whether some of the characteristics measured by tests might have been influenced by participation in the Companion Program.

RESULTS

In considering the performance of the two

groups on the MMPI, it should be kept in mind that in the case of this test alone there are but 65 subjects in each group. Table 1 lists the means, K-corrected, on the 10 primary scales for each group together with the t values indicating the significance of the difference on each scale.

It will be observed that it does not attain a significant value in the comparison of our two groups on any of 10 scales. Only in the case of the social introversion scale (not properly a clinical scale) does the value of t approach even the 10% level of confidence.

The means of the two groups and the t values representing the significance of their differences on the EPPS are presented in Table 2. It will be observed that on only one of these scales is there a secure difference between the two groups, namely that for Need Intraception, in which our companion group is notably and significantly higher. However, the control group yields a higher mean for Need Change which exceeds the 5% level of confidence, while the experimental group is suggestively but not significantly higher on Need Nurturance. Here, as on the MMPI, the absence of significant differences is perhaps most striking, while those that are confirmed or suggested are consonant with the proposition that the companions differ from the control subjects primarily in qualities of sympathy and compassion.

In Table 3 are presented the means for each of the six scales of the A-V-L and the t values indicating the significance of the differences. In the case of this instrument, the control group is notably and significantly higher in its espousal of economic values, while the companion group

TABLE 3

COMPARISON OF COMPANION AND CONTROL GROUP ON THE ALLPORT–VERNON–LINDZEY SCALE OF VALUES

	Companion means	Control means	t
Theoretical	45.14	47.03	1.50
Economic	33.46	38.09	3.48***
Aesthetic	38.68	37.14	1.12
Social	38.34	35.22	2.60***
Political	42.22	43.57	1.32
Religious	42.15	38.74	2.27**

** $p < .05$.
*** $p < .01$.

145

is higher on the social and religious scales, although the last of these differences does not exceed the one per cent level. The clear inference is that the companion group, again, is characterized by qualities associated with social interests and moral considerations and de-emphasis of the more practical concerns represented by economic values.

Both of the remaining tests are measures of intellectual abilities. For the first of these, the SAT, the means of the two groups, and the resulting t values are given in Table 4. It is clear that while the companion group yields slightly higher means on both the verbal and mathematical portions of this test, the differences are without secure significance. The general conclusion that the two groups are not intellectually differentiated is confirmed by the means and t value presented for the two groups on the Terman. It is evident here that the differences between the companion and control groups on the tests of intellectual ability are altogether without meaning.

In quick summary of the foregoing, it would appear fair to say that students taking part in the Companion Program are not strikingly differentiated from the general student body. Rather, they appear in most respects entirely typical. There is no evidence of clear differences in neurotic disposition or of intellectual ability, though there is some evidence of greater introversive tendencies. Only with respect to certain attitudinal measures are there clear evidences of differences. Thus, on both the Allport and the Edwards, there is some statistically secure evidence that the companions are more intraceptive, morally concerned, and personally compassionate than the control group with which they have been compared.

TABLE 4

COMPARISON OF COMPANION AND CONTROL GROUPS ON
MEASURES OF INTELLECTUAL FUNCTIONING

	Companion means	Control means	t
Scholastic aptitude test, verbal	630.3	618.4	1.11
Scholastic aptitude test, mathematical	663.5	653.1	.86
Terman concept mastery test	93.33	95.07	.40

DISCUSSION

The importance of this study lies in its refutation of any suspicion that the Companion Program has proven a sort of refuge for the morbid and unstable personality seeking either a bizarre adventure or some resolution of personal problems. The evidence seems particularly clear to us that such is not the case. On the other hand, it is suggested that the Companion Program serves as an outlet for certain impulses of human generosity and altruism which is not normally available to students in the college environment. So far as our evidence indicates, the companions are more idealistic in temper, more capable of generosity, less concerned with personal gain, and more responsive to religious values than their associates who have not elected to join this program. Elsewhere, evidence is presented (Holzberg, 1963) to indicate that participants in this program, far from suffering any morbid contamination through their association with chronic mental patients, undergo personal changes of a desirable character. We are thus disposed to find in the present and other evidence cited a justification of the soundness of the Companion Program. We think it has been demonstrated with reasonable confidence that the program does not attract significantly unstable or insecure personalities while it provides educational advantages to the student and probable comfort, if not therapeutic benefit, to the patient.

REFERENCES

HOLZBERG, J. D. The significance of the companionship experience for the college student. In, *Proceedings of conference on contribution to the social rehabilitation of the mentally ill: College student companion program.* Washington D. C.: United States Government Printing Office, 1963, in press.

HOLZBERG, J. D., & GEWIRTZ, H. A method of altering attitudes toward mental illness. *Psychiat. Quart.,* 1963, 37, in press.

KANTOR, D. Impact of the program on patients and institution. In, *Proceedings of conference on contribution to the social rehabilitation of the mentally ill: College student companion program.* Washington, D. C.: United States Government Printing Office, 1963, in press.

UMBARGER, C. C., KANTOR, D,. & GREENBLATT, M. *College students in a mental hospital.* New York: Grune & Stratton, 1962.

EFFECTS OF MENTAL HOSPITAL VOLUNTEER WORK ON STUDENTS' CONCEPTIONS OF MENTAL ILLNESS*

JAMES A. KULIK, ROBERT A. MARTIN, AND KARL E. SCHEIBE

PROBLEM

In recent years, a number of mental hospitals have set up volunteer programs in which students serve as companions and friends to patients. One of the objectives of these programs, beyond their function as an adjunct to therapy, has been to develop a highly informed cadre of ex-volunteer workers who would then comprise an important long term community resource to the mental health professions.

This report represents an evaluation of the extent and manner in which this objective has been achieved by a large volunteer program. The specific aims of this study are to: (1) determine the nature and amount of change in volunteers' scores on a multidimensional measure of mental health attitudes; (2) specify the extent to which volunteers' conceptions of mental patients change in the course of such programs; and (3) determine the extent to which volunteer programs are instructive in terms of knowledge of psychology and mental illness.

METHODS

Subjects. The experimental *S*s were drawn from a group of 265 college students serving in the Connecticut Service Corps (SC) in the years 1965-67. Students participating in this program work approximately 40 hours a week for 8-10 weeks at one of Connecticut's four mental hospitals or at a summer camp for patients. They deal primarily with chronic patients on back wards with a minimum of supervision from hospital personnel.

*This research was completed as a part of the Connecticut Service Corps Research Project and was supported by Grant MH02127-03 from the National Institute of Mental Health. The authors are indebted to Richard J. Wiseman, director of the Connecticut Service Corps, whose willing cooperation made the data collection possible.

JOURNAL OF CLINICAL PSYCHOLOGY, 1969, vol. 25, no. 3, pp. 326-329.

The control group originally included two subgroups. The first of these consisted of 86 students who had applied to the SC, were accepted into the program, but were unable finally to participate. The second control group consisted of 142 college students in summer school programs at four Connecticut colleges and universities. In initial comparisons, it was found that these two groups were similar in their test responses on the inventories included in this study. Therefore, where the two sub-groups were available, their data were combined for analysis.

Because of revision of some test instruments and other changes in testing materials from year to year, the number of Ss varies in different parts of the study. The number of Ss included in specific parts of the study is reported in the results section of the paper.

All SC volunteers were administered an extensive battery of tests and questionnaires during their first week at the hospitals. The battery was about four hours in length and was completed prior to any patient contact. At the conclusion of the 8-10 week program, the volunteers were administered the identical test battery. Control students attending summer school were administered identical test batteries at their respective colleges at about the same times. SC applicants who did not participate in the program were sent the battery of tests to be self-administered, both at the beginning and end of the summer. All control Ss were paid $10 for their participation.

Test Instruments and Analysis. The first part of the study was concerned with change in students' attitudes toward mental health. The test instrument employed was the Opinions about Mental Illness (OMI) [1] scale, measuring a broad range of mental health attitudes. The Ss were asked to rate each of the 66 items of the questionnaire on a seven-point scale ranging from "strongly agree" to "strongly disagree".

Clustering procedures [4] were used to determine the dimensionality of the OMI. Three clusters of items emerged from this analysis.[1] Cluster I deals with the etiology of mental illness. Low-scorers on this cluster tend to see mental illness as psychological in nature while high-scorers emphasize nonpsychological causation. On Cluster II, high-scorers see the function of mental hospitals as curative or therapeutic and low-scorers as custodial. Cluster III deals with the characterization of the mental patient on a normality-abnormality dimension. High scorers on this cluster tend to see patients as normal human beings while low-scorers see patients as abnormal. The internal-consistency reliabilities of the three clusters are moderate (.64 to .70) and the clusters are relatively independent (intercluster r's range from $-.12$ to .22).

In the second part of the research, a more differentiated picture of the mental patient was obtained from the Adjective Check List (ACL) [2] utilizing: (1) Total number of adjectives checked; (2) Number of favorable adjectives checked; (3) Number of unfavorable adjectives checked; (4) Achievement; (5) Dominance; (6) Endurance; (7) Order; (8) Intraception; (9) Nurturance; (10) Affiliation; (11) Heterosexuality; (12) Exhibition; (13) Autonomy; (14) Aggression; (15) Change; (16) Succorance; (17) Abasement; (18) Deference. The scales eliminated from this analysis were those developed empirically, using criterion groups from a normal population. The method of construction of these scales seemed incompatible with the present research design.

The final part of the study dealt with the effects of the program on students' knowledge of psychology. A test consisting of 34 multiple-choice questions was developed to measure students' command of facts and theories in clinical psychology.

In each part of this study, a similar methodology was employed. Change scores were obtained for all Ss. The change scores of experimental and control Ss were then

[1]The items in these clusters and their factor coefficients are included in tables deposited with the American Documentation Institute. Order Document No. 00089 from National Auxiliary Publications Service, 22 West 34 St., New York, N. Y. 10001. Remit in advance $1.00 for photocopies or $3.00 for microfilm and make checks payable to: National Auxiliary Publications Service.

compared by t ratios to determine whether differential change had occurred in the two groups.

RESULTS AND DISCUSSION

Opinions about Mental Illness. Pre and post means for 176 experimental and 142 control Ss were obtained on the three OMI clusters. Preliminary tests of significance were run to determine whether the two groups differed significantly on their responses to the pre test of the OMI. There was no significant difference on any of the three clusters.

The t ratios for differential change were significant for clusters II and III (t values of 10.14 and 2.64 respectively: $p < .01$). On OMI Cluster I, the change in SC volunteers was similar to that of the control group. There is no evidence that participation in the program alters students' beliefs about the nature or cause of mental illness. Change on Cluster II indicates that in the course of the summer program, volunteers came to see the function of a mental hospital as being custodial rather than curative. This change also indicates that students become somewhat disillusioned about the aims of mental hospitals, their personnel, and the capacity of current programs to bring about change in patients. There was also differential change on Cluster III items. After the summer, volunteers tended to look upon mental patients as more like normals, and less deranged and dangerous. While students grew pessimistic about mental hospitals, they become more optimistic about the capacities of mental patients.

Adjective Check List. Included in the analysis of ACL results were 142 SC volunteers and 84 control Ss. Since ACL data were available only on summer school controls, control Ss were drawn completely from that group. Comparisons by t ratios were again run on the results of the pretest. On several of the scales, there was a significant difference between the two groups: Achievement, Dominance, Endurance, Order, Exhibition, and Aggression. This finding may be explained by the work of Hersch, Kulik and Scheibe[3], who found that, prior to the initial testing period, SC members have had somewhat more contact than control Ss with the mental health field, particularly through academic courses, visits to institutions, etc. This prior contact may have affected their initial attitudes toward mental patients.

Again, t ratios were run on the change scores for the two groups. (These results are also on deposit with NAPS.) Both groups tended to check fewer adjectives on the second administration of the ACL. Since this change was not differential, it is probably most easily attributed to increased cautiousness on retest. Examination of change in the number of favorable adjectives checked revealed that the volunteers tended to look more favorably upon the patient at the end of the summer experience. Their change in usage of favorable adjectives was significantly greater than that of the control group. While changes on the unfavorability scale did not attain significance, the direction of the difference is consistent.

Differential changes on the need scales of the ACL fall into three groups. First, changes on scales of Endurance and Order indicate that patients come to be seen by volunteers as more organized and reality-oriented and less confused and dreamy. Second, they are also seen as more capable of friendship and warmth, as indicated by changes on scales of Nurturance, Affiliation, and Heterosexuality. Finally, they come to be seen as more passive and predictable and less threatening. Scores on Deference increase for the volunteers while Aggression, Autonomy, and Change scales decrease.

Knowledge of Psychology. Data on the Knowledge of Psychology test were obtained for 177 SC volunteers and 123 control Ss. An initial t test on the pre scores revealed no significant difference between the two groups. The method of presentation of these results follows that used for the OMI and ACL. There is a significant change in a positive direction in the SC students' knowledge of psychology. Thus, the program appears to be instructive in terms of the basic principles of psychoanalytic theory and clinical psychopathology.

These data support the contention that participation in a volunteer program affects students' conceptions of mental hospitals and mental patients, as well as improving their knowledge of abnormal psychology. Thus, one of the major objectives of establishing such programs is clearly realizable.

SUMMARY

This study was designed to measure changes in mental health-related attitudes and conceptions in college volunteers working in mental hospitals. The changes occurring in the volunteers were compared with those of a control group of college students not in the program. Volunteers changed more than control subjects in their conceptions of mental hospitals and mental patients. The volunteers came to see mental hospitals as custodial institutions and mental patients as having typical human needs. Volunteers also improved significantly in psychological knowledge.

REFERENCES

1. COHEN, J. and STRUENING, E. L. Opinions about mental illness in two large mental hospitals. *J. abn. soc. Psychol.*, 1962, *64*, 349-360.
2. GOUGH, H. G. and HEILBRUN, A. B. *The Adjective Check List Manual.* Palo Alto: Consulting Psychologists Press, 1965.
3. HERSCH, P. D., KULIK, J. A. and SCHEIBE, K. E. Personal characteristics of college volunteers in mental hospitals. *J. consult. clin. Psychol.*, in press.
4. TRYON, R. C. and BAILEY, D. The BC TRY system of cluster and factor analysis. *Multivariate behav. Res.*, 1966, *1*, 95-111.

IMPACT OF WORK WITH MENTAL PATIENTS
ON STUDENT VOLUNTEERS*

Carl Levine

The growing impersonalization of American higher education, partly the result of increased enrollments and oversized classes (to say nothing of faculty preoccupation with other concerns) has led to widespread discontent, dramatically highlighted by the recent student demonstrations at Berkeley.[1] Complaints against "mechanical education" are not new, of course. The failure of the college to educate in any meaningful sense—that is, to inculcate humanistic values as well as facts and skills, to exert upon students the kind of influence that helps bring about significant changes in attitudes and behavior—was amply documented by Jacob in 1957 in a survey devoted mostly to the general education received by students in the social sciences.[2] More recently another observer, discussing the present state of higher education in the sciences, found today's crop of future scientists "overtrained and undereducated."[3] And yet, if one scans the introductory pages of the typical college catalog, one discovers among the administration's statement of goals some such objective as "dedication to build an environment which will contribute to maximum student growth and self-realization."

The potentials for growth in the entering college freshman are, indeed, enormous; when he arrives at college he is, more likely than not, prejudiced, conformist, narrow in outlook—a condition that cries out for change.[4] But four years later, though somewhat more tolerant and sophisticated (not necessarily due to his exposure to college), the most notable change in him, according to Jacob, is in the direction of *greater* conformity: he remains "gloriously contented," "unabashedly self-centered," his

*This study was supported by a Colorado State University Faculty Research Grant.

JOURNAL OF HUMAN RELATIONS, 1966, vol. 14, no. 3, pp. 422-433.

values largely unaffected by either curriculum, teacher, or the method by which he was taught.[5]

Though Jacob's methodology and some of his interpretations have been questioned,[6] later studies have confirmed his findings that a majority of American students are, indeed, self- and family-centered, tend to be materialistic in their values, and express decided unconcern for social problems and the outside world.[7]

In an age characterized by rapid social and technological change, students of the human condition as diverse as Mead, Wheelis, and Snow have for some time now been urging the necessity of radical alterations in our educational programs to meet new needs and to effect basic value changes in the individual and society.[8] Though it would seem logical to look to our institutions of higher learning themselves to undertake needed reforms, nonacademics more than casually acquainted with the academic establishment are frankly discouraged. The typical university, says *Harper's* editor Fischer, "is too hide-bound, too complacent, too deaf to the needs of its students." [9]

Little wonder the student is disaffected. A small number make the headlines with demonstrations, protest marches, freedom rides, sit-ins and, occasionally, police-battling riots and panty raids. The great majority go about their business, uninvolved, indifferent. Mogar found that almost all the groups of college students he had studied showed "some degree of disaffiliation from the world around them, from the religious, social and political concerns of the previous generation"; their dominant attitude, one of "passive withdrawal—by default—and unenacted idealism." [10]

The present article reports an investigation of the changes in attitude and behavior produced in students by a nonacademic, off-campus program, the Weekend Institutional Service Unit (WEISU), which candidly appeals to and puts to work the "unenacted idealism" of today's college youth.

153

This volunteer program, involving work with mental patients at the Colorado State Hospital, is sponsored by the American Friends Service Committee, a Quaker organization, which in its efforts to relieve human suffering and to seek nonviolent solutions to conflict, frequently enlists the services of students in a variety of projects both at home and abroad. In operation for the past four years, the Colorado WEISU program has resulted thus far in almost five hundred weekend-long visits by students from eleven different Colorado campuses.

Scheduled approximately once a month during the school year, a typical WEISU is composed of from ten to twenty-five students, with a faculty couple as leaders. The weekend at the hospital begins on Friday evening around the supper table, with orientation provided by various members of the institution's personnel, and ends on Sunday afternoon, following a lively question-and-answer evaluation period conducted by one of the staff psychiatrists and the director of social services. During their stay the students live at the hospital and work on assigned wards under the supervision of nurses and attendants; their activities with patients are principally recreational and social: games, conversations, walks, group singing, dancing, etc.

Study of Effects Upon Students

This study is based on mailed questionnaires received from 138 respondents (128 students and 10 adult volunteers, mostly faculty), constituting 46 per cent of all participants; their visits to the hospital totalled 248, which were approximately 50 per cent of all the visits made. Only 126 of the *student* questionnaires (two were incomplete) have been included in the tabulations. With regard to the evaluation of changes in students' attitudes and behavior as a result of their WEISU experiences, one limitation of the study is that no base point exists from which change can be measured; it also lacks a number of crucial comparison and control groups. The most apparent include comparable groups of young men and women not attending college, as well as of college students who did not participate in the program.

A further caution should be noted: although McDonagh and Rosenblum have indicated that greater confidence should be placed by researchers in the reliability of mailed questionnaires (as compared with interviews),[11] the probability is, in the case of the present WEISU study, that there is a measure of bias reflected in the answers of students who had found working with mental patients an unusually stimulating and meaningful experience, and felt they needed to give evidence of their gratitude by responding. (Many took the trouble, in the less structured essay information they supplied, to express "thanks for the opportunity" provided them by WEISU.)

The students who signed up to participate in one or more weekends at the hospital, travelling from campuses as far away as 50 to 180 miles, were an entirely self-selected group—adding whatever biases are related to the impulse to participate. Applicants were not screened; nor was work with mental patients a requirement for any of their college courses. Recruitment efforts were usually in the form of announcements in the college paper or posters on bulletin boards, describing WEISU both as a work-study project, and as an opportunity for the volunteer to help mental patients "as a concerned friend."

Findings of the Survey

Although in the beginning it was generally assumed by hospital staff and patients that most, if not all, of the WEISU participants were professionally motivated, that they were psychology and sociology majors and the like (who else would give up a perfectly good weekend to spend it with the mentally disturbed!), that, in a word, their interest was self-serving, Table I indicates that barely more than one-third of the volunteers had signed up because they had viewed the experience as potentially beneficial with respect to their future career. As for the opposite, the idealistic motive, it is interesting to note that though in keeping with

Quaker philosophy recruitment publicity stressed the humanitarian aspect of WEISU, only 5 per cent of the men and 12 per cent of the women students gave the equivalent of "to help others" as their reason for participating.

TABLE I

MOTIVATIONS OF STUDENTS* WORKING WITH MENTAL PATIENTS IN
WEEKEND INSTITUTIONAL SERVICE UNIT PROGRAM

In Per Cent

QUESTION
"Why did you decide to participate?"

	Men	Women
100% =	(39)	(87)
	(31)	(69)
Professional interest	36	34
Curiosity; it sounded interesting; etc.	46	38
To help others	5	12
Persuaded by friend	3	2
Mixed motives; not sure	10	14

* Fields of study were social sciences, 42 per cent; biological sciences, 15 per cent; education, 15 per cent; humanities, 10 per cent; science, 8 per cent; business, 3 per cent; undecided or not stated, 7 per cent.

In contrast to these two motivational extremes, the interest of the greatest segment of students (46 per cent of the men and 38 per cent of the women) was largely unfocused; typically they said, "it sounded interesting," or "thought I could learn something about mental health," or simply gave "curiosity" as their reason for volunteering. One in eight was not quite sure why he had participated, or had mixed motives. One of the latter, a young woman who had participated several times, suggested the change in student attitudes (indicated by Tables II and III) when she replied, "At first I came out of curiosity, later to understand and help."

A desire to satisfy curiosity is, of course, characteristic of the young, and of the inquiring mind in particular. Curiosity, Flexner believes, is perhaps the outstanding attribute of modern thinking.[12] A different interpretation, however, and quite another insight into student motivations, are suggested by the replies respondents gave to a question not included in the tables in which they were asked to tell how they had anticipated their first arrival at the hospital: 52 per cent reported they had looked forward to the experience "with excitement"; of the nonprofessionals, 31 per cent had felt some form of fear or apprehension of anxiety—"I almost did not come because of fear and uneasiness," one youth said. These reactions, signifying expectation of and possibly a desire for some promising off-beat personal experience, corroborate Naegele's finding that the rebellion of modern youth often takes the form of "emphasis on personal experience and exploration" rather than of political radicalism.[13]

Students' change of attitude toward mental illness in general and toward their own potentially dangerous emotional tensions and drives in particular is indicated in Table II, which shows that the nonprofessionally motivated men were influenced to a greater degree than the students who were presumably more sophisticated (II, A), but that the professionally motivated men gained more insight into their own psychological identity (II, C) than their fellow students. Not surprisingly, there was less change of attitude experienced by all volunteers with regard to a concrete problem situation (the "oddball" on campus) than toward mental illness in the abstract, or toward their own psychological problems.[14] The findings indicate that the least sympathetic of all four categories of students toward the conspicuous nonconformist on campus was the professionally motivated woman, suggesting either a less serious commitment on her part to her stated future career, or premature expression of the impersonal professional stance and the greater rigidity often observed in career women.[15] By contrast, the nonprofessional female student rated consistently higher than her sister on all these questions, perhaps due to the fact that a significant number (one in eight) were motivated by humanitarian concerns.

TABLE II

CHANGE IN STUDENT ATTITUDES FOLLOWING WEISU EXPERIENCE
In Per Cent

QUESTIONS

A. "As a result of WEISU, have you experienced any change in attitude toward mental illness in general?"

B. "As a result of WEISU, have you experienced any change toward the 'oddball' on campus?"

C. "As a result of WEISU, have you experienced any change toward yourself, your own motivations, drives, tensions?"

	Professionally Motivated		Others		Total
	Men	Women	Men	Women	
100% =	(14)	(30)	(25)	(57)	
A. Yes*	79	64	84	79	76
B. Yes*	65	40	48	61	54
C. Yes*	86	67	64	75	72

* The direction of change indicated in the unstructured part of the replies was predominantly toward more liberal and acceptive attitudes, e.g., "am less rejecting of others," "better able to understand causes," "try to avoid stereotyping," "am more self-accepting and thus more able to cope with my problems."

In most cases personal confrontation with the mentally ill was an experience so powerful ("three years later, I still remember the experience vividly," a volunteer wrote) that students were for once shaken out of their customary preoccupation with self ("with the little me I am usually so wrapped up in," as one girl put it) and were stimulated to further study or reading on the subject of mental illness (Table III, A). The experience was meaningful, said another student, "not only because it made me more understanding and sympathetic toward the mentally ill, but because it gave me an increased realization of what it is to be human." Attesting to this realization of their common humanity is the fact that a significant number of students (42 per cent of the total) had further communication with individual patients after WEISU, mostly via brief letters or cards, some by visiting or sending gifts (Table III, B).

TABLE III

FURTHER INTEREST IN MENTAL ILLNESS AND MENTAL PATIENTS FOLLOWING WEISU EXPERIENCE

In Per Cent

QUESTIONS

A. "Have you, because of WEISU, done additional study or reading on the subject of mental illness?"

B. "Have you had further communication with patients since WEISU?"

	Professionally Motivated		Others		Total
	Men	*Women*	*Men*	*Women*	
100% =	(14)	(30)	(25)	(57)	
A. Yes	84	67	28	53	55
B. Yes	43	37	36	47	42

Further broadening of students' sympathies as an indirect result of their WEISU experiences to the point of prompting participation in other forms of social service is indicated in Table IV, which shows that 37 per cent of the total were stimulated to volunteer for a variety of other community and individual service projects; e.g., work with disadvantaged minorities in the slums of Denver and Fort Collins (Colorado), service as a nurse in a summer camp for mentally retarded children, joining the Peace Corps, etc. Another 15 per cent said they hoped or intended to participate in similar types of social activity "when a suitable opportunity presents itself," or "as soon as I can find the time."

The progression indicated in Tables II through IV (from change of attitude toward mental illness and the mentally ill to a personal commitment to ameliorative social action in a wider framework) suggests the possibility of transference or extension from attitude change in one field of human need to generalized behavior change in another, where the value patterns are similar. If this is true, the educational implications of attitude-changing experiences (and, more important, the possibilities for subsequent carry-over) are indeed intriguing. There is nothing new, of course, about the "education through experience" type of college course designed to make learning more meaningful by taking the student out of the classroom and into the field and having him confront his subject or material face to face.[16]

TABLE IV

PARTICIPATION IN SOCIAL ACTION FOLLOWING WEISU EXPERIENCE
In Per Cent

	QUESTION				

"Have you, as an indirect result of WEISU, been stimulated to participate in other community (or individual) service activities?"

	Professionally Motivated		Others		Total
	Men	Women	Men	Women	
100% =	(14)	(30)	(25)	(57)	
Yes	43	30	32	42	37

Antioch College's integrated work-study program, as well as courses such as Haverford's field studies in Sociology, and Amherst's in American Civilization (in which students do door-to-door canvassing in political campaigns), indicate that students' attitudes are often challenged as a result of personal experience. Such programs as these, however, are fairly limited, available mostly in smaller schools where the curriculum can be hand-tailored to fit the needs of small groups of students—though in the last few years, it should be noted, the National Commission on Cooperative Education has encouraged more colleges and universities to undertake work-and-study projects of benefit to both community and student.[17] However, as far as attitude and behavior changes in students are concerned, we have had almost no objective information as to the effects of these programs. "The truth is," Wilson observes in *Antioch College Reports,* "we don't know what we're doing. Nor will we know until such time as we can say what changes are wrought by whom." [18] Furthermore, we can only guess at the inhibiting effects of "required" courses and financial remuneration (students are generally paid for the work they perform in work-study projects) with respect to attitude and behavior change as compared with the effects produced by completely voluntary programs such as WEISU.

Jacob, after surveying a number of educational projects of the personal experience or social action type, finds the reports on the outcomes of these programs "mainly impressionistic." Though sympathetic with regard to their objectives, he is forced to conclude that "the carry-over into personal behavior and the effect on individual value judgments have not been adequately appraised." [19] The same complaint about the paucity of research in this field was voiced by Festinger in his address to the meeting of the American Psychological Association in 1963; he went on to speculate about the relationship between opinion change and resulting behavior, and suggested that in order to produce a real behavior change "an environmental change must also be produced which, representing reality, will support the new opinion and the new behavior." [20]

If we truly seek to alter student attitudes in the direction of more humanistic values and behavior, we cannot escape the fact that the environmental change to which Festinger alludes must represent a more ideal "reality" than the one the student now encounters in college; indeed, it will need to be quite different from our present unideal academic reality with its competitiveness, its rigidities, its conformity-producing orthodoxies. One cannot help wondering what would happen if the student's latent idealism and curiosity were seriously challenged, if he were given as much freedom and responsibility for his own education as he was capable of assuming. A good deal of further investigation is needed to determine the conditions most favorable to attitude and behavior change in the student, without which meaningful education can hardly be said to take place.

1. See Nathan Glazer; "What Happened in Berkeley," *Commentary*, XXXIX (February, 1965), 39-47.
2. Philip E. Jacob, *Changing Values in College* (New York: Harper & Brothers, 1957).
3. J. A. Gengerelli, "The Education of Future Scientists," *Journal of Higher Education*, XXXV (February, 1964), 65.
4. Nevitt Sanford, "Higher Education as a Social Problem," in *The American College: A Psychological and Social Interpretation of the Higher Learning*, ed. N. Sanford (New York: John Wiley & Sons, Inc., 1962), pp. 10-30.
5. Jacob, "Summary of Findings," *op. cit.*, pp. 1-11.
6. Among others, by David Riesman, "The Jacob Report," *American Sociological Review*, XXIII (1958), 732-38; J. Bushnell, "Student Values: A Summary of Research and Future Problems," in *The Larger Learning: Teaching Values to College Students*, ed. M. Carpenter (Dubuque, Iowa: Little, Brown & Company, 1960), pp. 45-61.
7. Rose Goldsen and others, *What College Students Think* (Princeton, N.J.: D. Van Nostrand Company, Inc., 1960); Robert E. Mogar, "Value Orientations of College Students," *Psychological Reports*, XV (December, 1964), 739-70.
8. Margaret Mead, *New Lives for Old* (New York: William Morrow and Company, Inc., 1956); Allen Wheelis, *The Quest for Identity* (New York: W. W. Norton & Company, Inc., 1958); C. P. Snow, *The Two Cultures and the Scientific Revolution* (Cambridge: Cambridge University Press, 1959).
9. John Fischer, "Is There a Teacher on the Faculty?" *Harper's* CCXXX (February, 1965), 28.
10. Mogar, *op. cit.*, p. 766.
11. E. C. McDonagh and A. L. Rosenblum, "A Comparison of Mailed Questionnaires and Subsequent Structured Interviews," *Public Opinion Quarterly*, XXIX (1965), 131-36.
12. "Institutions of learning should be devoted to the cultivation of curiosity, and the less they are deflected by considerations of immediacy of application, the more likely they are to contribute not only to human welfare but to the equally important satisfaction of intellectual interest which may indeed be said to have become the ruling passion of intellectual life in modern times." (Abraham Flexner, "The Usefulness of Useless Knowledge," *Harper's*, CLXXIX [October, 1939], 544-52.)
13. Kaspar D. Naegele, "Youth and Society," *Daedalus*, XCI (1962), 57. In the same issue of *Daedalus*, which is devoted to "Youth: Change and Challenge," Kenneth Keniston similarly notes that "many college students have a kind of *cult of experience*." ("Social Change and Youth in America," pp. 159-60.)
14. Incidentally, the problem of student mental and emotional crack-up in college is a serious one. The amount of research in this field, however, has been termed "pathetically small." To too many college administrators, the emotional problems of the student are "of small significance indeed." (Dana L. Farnsworth, *Mental Health in College and University* [Cambridge, Mass.: Harvard University Press, 1957], p. 181.)
15. In the remotivation of mental patients, one of the difficult problems is overcoming "the emotional distance" between them and the hospital staff, largely female. See Otto von Mering and Stanley H. King, *Remotivating the Mental Patient* (New York: Russell Sage Foundation, 1957).
16. See Royce S. Pitkin and George Beecher, "Extending the Educational Environment: The Community as a Source for Learning," in *Higher Education: Some Newer Developments*, ed. Samuel Baskin (New York: McGraw-Hill Book Company, Inc., 1965), pp. 174-95.
17. James W. Wilson and Edward H. Lyons, *Work-Study College Programs* (New York: Harper & Brothers, 1961).

18. Everett K. Wilson, "Effecting Change in the College Student: Who Teaches What?" *Antioch College Reports*, No. 4, March, 1963.

19. *Op. cit.*, p. 97.

20. Leon Festinger, "Behavioral Support for Opinion Change," *Public Opinion Quarterly*, XXVIII (1964), 404-17.

V. OTHER PARAPROFESSIONAL ASSISTANCE

THE NONTRADITIONALLY TRAINED MENTAL HEALTH WORKER: FAD OR FUTURE?[1]

Jacqueline C. Bouhoutsos

The shortage of professional personnel in the mental health fields, the economic necessity of creating new jobs for the unskilled, the desirability of having translators of the poverty ethos for the middle class clinicians—these are but some of the reasons adduced to explain the current proliferation of programs for the training of mental health nonprofessionals.[2]

In Los Angeles, for example, there was one academic program to train nonprofessional individuals in 1968.[3] In 1970, such courses are either operative or are scheduled to begin in almost every one of the local two-year colleges. Similar programs are springing up across the nation, designed to train special segments of the population, using a multitude of methods and teachers from different disciplines and aimed at producing a variety of mental health workers.

A parallel development of training efforts has been observed in community agencies, where large numbers of indigenous or poverty people, housewives, ministers, or other groups are now being trained as nonprofessional mental health workers.

Most of the studies in the literature on the training and/or use of nonprofessionals have been theoretical discussions of the way in which such individuals could or should be used, or descriptions of a particular training or agency program. There have been inadequate data available regarding extent and type of current agency *use* of the nonprofessional in the delivery of mental health services. This study was designed to provide such information.

Method of Inquiry

A two-page questionnaire was directed to the intake social workers of the 90 psychiatric out-patient services, both public and private, in Los Angeles County and to 30 such facilities in Cleveland, Toledo, and Salt Lake City.

Subsequently, the study was extended to include a second group of 59 agencies in the Los Angeles area offering counseling, but not necessarily psychiatric services. An additional specific public sample was selected from the large public service agencies located in Los Angeles County, which include the Probation Department, California State Service Centers, and the Department of Public Social Services. Personal interviews were conducted with personnel in these agencies when it became apparent that the data obtained could not be handled quantitatively.

[1] This investigation was made while the author was a resident fellow at the Center for Training in Community Psychiatry, Los Angeles. It was designed in collaboration with Janice Bradley, MSW, who has generously agreed to allow use of the data, but who should not be held responsible for conclusions drawn.

[2] Mental health professionals are defined in this study as psychiatrists, clinical psychologists, psychiatric social workers, and psychiatric nurses; mental health nonprofessionals as those not in the above group who "attempt to improve the psychological adaptation of clients."

[3] "Project Grow" at California State College, Los Angeles.

PROFESSIONAL PSYCHOLOGY, Fall 1970, vol. 1, no. 5, pp. 455-459.

TABLE 1

Results of Questionnaire

Agencies employing mental health agents	Los Angeles psychiatric out-patient (39%)	Los Angeles counseling (44%)	Out-of-state psychiatric (14%)
Primary function of mental health agents	Teaching 53% Social work 17% Recreational 15% Vocational 10% Other 5%	Teaching 22% Social work 67% Other 10%	Teaching 0% Social work 31% Other 69%
Nonacademic training for agents preferred by	55%	72%	50%
Salary range per month	$330-$1000	$300-$920	$380-$659
Agencies now using mental health agents, desiring more	95%	73%	100%
Agencies not now using but interested in further exploration	50%	61%	56%

Note.—Total number of questionnaires sent out was 117. Sixty-five percent, 119, were returned.

Types of Workers

Most of the studies of nonprofessional mental health workers have concentrated on selected groups of individuals, such as the "volunteer," the "indigenous" nonprofessional, or the mature housewife therapist. Imaginations have been piqued by the innovative social experimentation of Rioch, Riessman, True, and others. But there has been a need for a comprehensive view of the nonprofessional within the framework of the total delivery of services in the mental health field not limited to specific experimental areas.[4]

[4] Because of limitations of space, neither the voluminous statistical material nor a full discussion can be presented. The original paper may be obtained by writing the author at the Motion Picture Association, 8480 Beverly Boulevard, Los Angeles, California 90048.

This study has revealed four types of nonprofessional mental health agents now in use. The first, and by far the largest, group is made up of individuals in the public agencies who, although they fall within our definition of "nontraditionally trained," nonetheless are considered professionals by their agencies. These number roughly 6,000 in the four agencies which made up our "public sample." Although this sample was excluded from Table 1, any discussion of the delivery of services must recognize them as an integral part of the system. This group is college-trained, with an undergraduate major in various fields, but generally with little educational background in the behavioral sciences. From personal interviews, they appear to be a horizontally mobile, dissatisfied group, held together by agency identification and characterized by general discontent, high anxiety level, and feelings of inadequacy.

The second largest group is composed of "indigenous" nonprofessionals. We found such federally funded positions throughout our sample, in both public and private agencies. Because of changes in funding, the demise of some programs and the instituting of new ones, the lack of any central information on the variety of placement settings, and the fact that the positions are temporary and often part-time, the identification of either specific numbers or a comprehensive description of their function is virtually impossible.

Members of the third group have been called the "ubiquitous" nonprofessionals, for want of a better term; they are usually college-educated, middle-class, and privately employed.

The fourth category is made up of people from other professions, such as teachers, ministers, recreation workers, and others who "attempt to improve the psychological adaptation of clients."

Concepts of Function

Two distinct concepts emerge from an observation of the ways mental health agents are used in agencies. One model utilizes mostly "other professionals" and the "ubiquitous" agents to do what was formerly reserved to the professional. The training for such individuals seems to have been deeply influenced by crisis theory and features careful selection of individuals for training and a teaching method which stresses techniques and includes field work, with little emphasis on theory. The usual format is a structured training program of three to five weeks in an agency, requiring from five to 16 hours per week. Trainees are assigned cases early in their training and are supervised carefully.[5]

The second concept, which is primarily demonstrated in the indigenous group, is based on differentiating those tasks requiring technical knowledge and professional judgment from tasks requiring primarily referral or supportive services. Training programs for these individuals vary from weekly lectures, films, or discussion workshops to attempts to teach very specific techniques quickly, thus enabling an untrained person to begin functioning immediately on the job. Little selection is done; there is general acceptance of any applicant for the program, with active recruitment sometimes necessary to fill some of the funded positions so that they will not be lost from the budget request lines.

There is disagreement among mental health professionals about the validity of both concepts of the utilization of non-professionals and their related training models. Concern is expressed about lowering the overall quality of service and about the effectiveness of a piecemeal approach, and a lack of comprehensiveness. While some mental health professionals advocate screening, intake, and crisis therapy with clients as appropriate activities for nonprofessionals, others maintain that these functions are critical and require a high degree of skill, experience, and professional judgment. Strong feelings of rivalry and threat enter into attempts to differentiate essential professional functions from the activities of mental health agents.

---

[5] Several Los Angeles agencies now offer services by lay individuals trained in this model. Many of the programs hiring mental health agents, particularly among the psychiatric services, are utilizing them to do clinical evaluation and treatment services, as well as to conduct group therapy.

Perhaps the most severe limitation is that both training models require extraordinary amounts of time in teaching and supervision. Agencies which have looked to nonprofessionals to alleviate the shortage of professional personnel have found that those scarce professionals they do have must give up part of their direct service activity for supervising, teaching, and consulting with the nonprofessionals. This is a frequently expressed source of annoyance to agencies, and one of the often cited reasons for not employing nonprofessionals.

Training Sites

One might hypothesize, then, that if the agencies were given the choice of the ways to have their nonprofessionals trained, they would choose an academic program in contrast to agency-based programs, since this would not involve utilization of their own agency personnel as teachers, and would provide a supply of personnel at least minimally cognizant of mental health principles. We find, however, from the data that this hypothesis is not substantiated. There is a marked preference for nonacademic training. This finding is substantiated by the lack of positions available in local agencies to graduates of the local mental health worker programs at community colleges, and by the lack of agency-academia communication and cooperation in the training of individuals.

Universities across the nation have been reluctant to train professionals for service delivery (the declining training programs for clinical psychologists is an example), and the state colleges have followed suit. On the other hand, we see an increasing number of students looking for the kind of intensive educational experiences in the human services which can help them find meaningful careers in the mental health fields, without limiting their vertical or horizontal mobility.

Many community colleges have moved toward setting up such courses to train individuals at the beginning level. But articulation with state colleges or with universities has not as yet been possible, so that vertical mobility is limited, except along traditional educational lines. Also, the sources of employment for graduating students of community college programs--the community agencies, as we have seen—appear to be resistant to accepting graduates as employees, preferring to train their own workers, yet complaining bitterly about the increased work load for their limited staff of professionals.

Perhaps one of the reasons for this complaint may be the discomfort on the part of the professionals in undertaking activities which they do not feel are part of their basic function, and in which they themselves have not been trained, such as teaching and supervision. Another reason may be the traditional distrust of undergraduate programs as preparation for service.

It has long been recognized that mental health professionals alone cannot hope to meet the problems of all troubled individuals, and that perhaps they are not even best suited to deal directly with certain kinds of socio-economic-political problems. There has been a growing trend toward the deployment of professional skills into more indirect functions such as training, supervision, consultation, planning, and program evaluation. These are areas where the majority of professionals have had little experience and even less training. Thus, there is an urgent need for evaluating current training models, not only at the lower, entering level, but all along the health-welfare spectrum, to avoid the lacunae in the delivery of services which exist side by side with the proliferation of training programs.

REFERENCES

Riessman, F. Some specific recommendations for training nonprofessionals. Unpublished manuscript, 1965. (Mimeo)

Rioch, M. Pilot project in training mental health counselors (Report No. 1254) Washington, D.C.: Public Health Service.

True, J. E. An experimental program for training subprofessional personnel in mental health: Problems and prospects. Paper presented at the meeting of the American Personnel and Guidance Association, Lafayette, Indiana, 1967.

The Role of Nonprofessional Volunteers in a Suicide Prevention Center

Sam M. Heilig, M.S.W.
Norman L. Farberow, Ph.D.
Robert E. Litman, M.D.
Edwin S. Shneidman, Ph.D.

An important current focus of interest in the mental health field has been the development of theory and principles of community mental health and community psychiatry. Bellak (1964) has called this development the third major revolution in the history of psychiatry. He defines community psychiatry as "the resolve to view the individuals' psychiatric problems within the frame of reference of the community and *vice versa*." (p. 5). A significant aspect of this development has been the involvement of the community and its members in the concern for its own mental health. The citizen as well as the mental health professional can exert a personal, positive force toward the mental health of his community.

More specifically, roles are now being developed in which the citizen can play an active role, including direct therapeutic interaction with emotionally disturbed individuals. This conception of the citizen's role is markedly different from the approach in past years when the volunteer's activities had been considered ancillary and indirect.

COMMUNITY MENTAL HEALTH JOURNAL, 1967, vol. 4, no. 4, pp. 287-295.

REVIEW OF LITERATURE

Review of the literature indicates that volunteers have been used in the mental health field in a limited way for a long period. Traditionally the volunteer has been used in mental hospitals for entertainment, providing gifts, and clerical activities. A major contribution of volunteer programs has been to establish a bridge between mental hospitals and the community, both in giving patients a link with the outside world and helping enlighten communities about mental illness.

Volunteers have also been used in court as an aid to relatives of patients appearing for commitment (Lee, 1962). Bellak (1964) covers many of the newer developments in the field. These include use of volunteers in halfway houses, sheltered workshops, committees to contact employees, and as key persons in imparting psychiatric understanding to target groups in the community, such as clergy, police, lawyers and others. Maya Pines (1965) describes the work of volunteers in mental health centers in slum areas of New York where people indigenous to the area and familiar with the culture are used to work directly with people who need help.

The use of nonprofessional volunteers to perform the same functions as trained persons had not been attempted in any organized way until Rioch's et al. (1963) extensive project to train lay people to perform a psychotherapeutic function. The program demonstrated successfully (1) that it was possible to add to the source of manpower in a mental health field by using a hitherto unexplored group (housewives); (2) that it pointed out another avenue of transition from one phase of life to another for the middle-aged woman; and (3) that it was possible to offer adequate preparation to do psychotherapy with on-the-job training.

In the United States there are also self-help groups of volunteers in organizations that serve mental health functions; AA is probably the best known of these. Some centers for suicide prevention have used nonprofessional volunteers with great variations in success.

The report that follows, of the selection, training and use of lay volunteers to provide direct clinical service in evaluation and handling of suicidal crises, most closely parallels the project described by Rioch. The volunteers have been used to support a professional team of psychiatrists, psychologists and psychiatric social workers in the Suicide Prevention Center of Los Angeles.

PROCEDURES FOR SELECTION

The volunteers were referred to the Center from several sources, primarily by the Los Angeles County Mental Health Association and by members of the staff and professional colleagues. The primary procedure for selection of the volunteer was the interview. The volunteer was seen by at least three professional persons on the staff of the Center and evaluated by each. The volunteer was accepted only if all three agreed on the suitability. In addition, the candidates were ask to take the MMPI and to write out an autobiography.

170

CRITERIA FOR SELECTION

No prior set of criteria existed at the time the program was initiated for appropriate selection of volunteers in such activities. As a result, some criteria were set up a priori and used as general guidelines. These were: maturity, responsibility, motivation, sensitivity, willingness to accept training and supervision, and ability to get along well in a group.

The main criteria were maturity and responsibility. Persons working with individuals in a suicidal crisis need to be able to view such situations in their proper perspective and to provide the caller with a feeling of depth of experience and understanding. Stability in occupation and interpersonal relationships and evidence of good judgment in dealing with serious crises in their own lives was sought.

Motivation was evaluated primarily in terms of the reasons the candidate was applying for such activity. Most often, it was a combination of children in school, having time and a need for further self-development, and an unwillingness to become involved in the usual run of teas, bridge games or charity affairs. Usually the person did not see suicide, per se, as focally interesting, but rather was attracted by the prospect of working directly with people and by what seemed to be a real opportunity to learn and develop. Motivation was also examined in terms of willingness to give time and effort consistently over a long period. This was required not only for the training period but also for the subsequent work schedule.

Sensitivity to the multiple levels on which humans function and ability to recognize and respond to different feelings was important. It was not necessary for the person to know the details, but there had to be an awareness that dynamics in self and others existed.

Inasmuch as the candidate would be required to interact constantly with staff and other volunteers, the ability to work as a member of a team and to get along well with a group was another selection criterion. Persons judged to be disruptive, hypercritical, complaining, or rigid and not able to adapt readily to new situations were excluded early.

An important characteristic was the ability to accept training and supervision. Such persons indicated they did not know all the problems involved but were willing to learn. Certain volunteers were avoided. These were especially people looking for a way to gratify their own needs and to push their own individual conceptions of human problems and their solutions. Their investment was frequently in such areas as astrology, hypnotism, spiritualism, numerology, graphology and others. Often such persons were emotionally disturbed themselves, rigid, inflexible and tenuously organized. It was felt that such persons would not serve the agency, they would use it.

VOLUNTEERS SELECTED

Out of 16 applicants who went through the screening process, 10 were selected. All were women; men simply were not available during the daytime when the Center planned on using the volunteers.

The women were primarily in their 30's and early 40's. All were married and had children who were grown or in school. All were in the middle or upper class socioeconomically. One woman had recently worked as a nursery school teacher, the rest were housewives. Two had had recent office experience.

In regard to spouses' occupations, two were skilled craftsmen, three ran or owned successful businesses, two were physicians, one was a psychiatrist, and the remaining three were a lawyer, a banker, and an engineer. Although the women were not selected on this basis, all had some college training, six having received a bachelor's degree. In general, their college education was in the liberal arts. None had any prior training or experience in mental health work. An interesting feature of the group was that six of the ten women had a satisfactory experience in psychotherapy. One of the women was still in active treatment and it was with her therapist's approval that she participated in the program.

Of the six not used, three were evaluated as unsuitable. Two wanted immediately to take over the program and to direct it. They were semi-professionals, having had some professional training and experience although not enough fully to qualify at a professional level. One woman was considered unsuitable because of immaturity and low threshold for anxiety. Three otherwise suitable candidates were unable, because of family and other commitments, to contribute the investment of time and energy required.

171

THE TRAINING PROGRAM

The training program was also considered a period for further evaluation, especially of motivation both by the Center and by the volunteers. The training program consisted of two major divisions, a formal lecture and discussion program, and an in-service training apprenticeship. The formal lecture and discussion program was held two days a week for five weeks. All of the regular staff of the Center participated, allowing the group the opportunity to hear various points of view of many disciplines. The last hour of each day was used for group discussion of the material presented. It became an hour in which the group often aired their own feelings about suicide and death.

The content of the formal presentations covered three main areas: (1) theoretical material about the meaning of suicidal behavior, (2) methods and techniques for handling the suicidal crisis, and (3) case histories and clinical material. In the theoretical area, concepts such as communication, ambivalence, significant other, reaction to death and dying, and other areas pertinent to suicide were discussed. In addition, basic aspects of personality, adjustment, and defense mechanisms were presented. In the area of methods and technique, emphasis was placed on the problems of establishing and maintaining rapport in a telephone interview, evaluation of the suicide potentiality, identifying and focusing on the significant problems, assessing personality strengths and weaknesses, utilization of personal and community resources, and initiation of a helpful action.

One useful procedure in the training was to listen to a call being taken by one of the regular staff. During the fifth week several of the volunteers began to take their own calls under supervision, which they would then bring back to the group for discussion.

Following the five-week training program, the volunteers were assigned to work one day each week. One member of the staff served as supervisor and teacher for two volunteers, and the volunteer discussed each case with her supervisor before making a disposition. The professional supervision served mainly as a teaching and supportive arrangement for the volunteer, but also offered the staff an opportunity for continued evaluation of the work of the volunteers.

During this apprentice-training experience, all the volunteers met once weekly for group discussion of cases, the program, and their own feelings and reactions to the work. A cohesive, enthusiastic group feeling developed which was in marked contrast to the earlier meetings during the formal training program. The women became quite enthusiastic about the work and were eager to learn more. After several weeks they asked not only for suggestions for continued reading, but also for more lectures on such topics as personality development, interviewing technique, neurosis and mental illness, and the process of therapy.

With the continuing interest in learning and growth experience, the volunteers were invited to sit in when a staff member interviewed in person the patient they had talked with on the telephone. After some months, some women began to see an occasional patient in the office and to provide brief counseling service in selected cases. In addition, if a volunteer showed a special interest in any of the activities of the Center, an effort was made to include them. For example, some women helped in several of the on-going research projects, and one volunteer sat in as a regular observer in a group therapy. It seemed to be especially important to allow the volunteer to expand her interests and activities and not to restrict her to a routine function.

Several women volunteered to work more than one day per week. Four women came in two days a week, and one woman came in three days a week. All were invited to participate in the regular Friday morning staff meeting of the Center, and many did.

INTERACTION WITH STAFF

The volunteers interacted well with the regular professional staff both in working relationships and in informal contacts. They all used staff members readily for supervision and consultation on cases. If the assigned supervisor was busy, the volunteer had little hesitancy in seeking out another professional staff member. Supervisors were rotated for the volunteers every three months to provide exposure to the different styles and points of view of the staff therapists. The volunteers participated in the coffee breaks, informal staff discussions, and group lunches. Nevertheless, they always tended to identify themselves as a group and their closest relationships in the Center were with each other.

In the beginning of the program there was some resistance within some members of the staff to the demands of the training program, felt to be an extra burden in an already heavy work schedule. Doubts were voiced about whether or not the volunteers would be able to do enough work to warrant all the extra effort. Several of the volunteers also asked if it was worth the agency's time to spend so much effort and energy in their training. When the volunteers began to take calls, and there was definite feeling of relief from some of the pressure of clinical work, there was general agreement that the program had been worthwhile. Some of the staff even became interested in developing the abilities of the more eager volunteers and spent extra time in their supervisory sessions with them.

ONE YEAR LATER

During the first year, the volunteers worked eagerly and enthusiastically, handling approximately one third of the daytime calls to the Center. Out of 1,808 new daytime calls for 1965, the volunteers took 680 calls, or 38 percent. Monthly, the highest percentage of calls, 54 percent, was taken in July while the lowest percentage, 22 percent, came in October 1965. In July, many of the regular staff took vacations, throwing more of the case load to the volunteers. In October, new students began to take calls, ordinarily taken by the volunteers.

VOLUNTEERS VIEW

An effort was made to determine the reaction of the volunteers to their first year's experience in the program by asking them to fill out a short questionnaire. Seven of the original 10 filled out the questionnaire. Two had dropped out of the program (demands of the home) and one was ill in the hospital. A summary of the responses follows:

1. "You came to the program with personal desires, expectations, etc. Which have been met and how?" The most frequent response to this question, given by five of the seven volunteers was the hope of making a significant contribution, stated in terms of feeling helpful, being useful and feeling of both giving and receiving. The second most frequent response (4/7) was the hope that some form of self-development would occur through the experience, such as learning new things, developing new skills, being exposed to intellectual stimulation and the like. In some responses it was apparent that a search for feelings of identity was in process, e.g., to express maternal or philanthropic needs.

2. "What expectations had not been met and why not?" None of the volunteers indicated any disappointment in their expectations about the program. One person did express discouragement in feelings about herself as a therapist and the fact that her own aspirations in that direction had not been realized. One volunteer pointed to an intrinsic difficulty in the program, i.e., we set paradoxical roles, altruistic volunteer versus responsibility of the professional. One represented denial of aspirations, the other affirmed them.

3. "How has the work or program affected you? What impact if any has it had on you and your activities, values, thinking, aspirations, and so forth? Most of the answers to this question stressed the feeling that the experience has made them more sensitive and understanding of others' problems. Four responses indicated feeling more tolerant of others and the development of a sense of empathy toward the behavior and feelings of others. Some noted changes that had occurred within themselves, for example, changes in values about what's good or right; coming to terms with death and living, and a growth in learning about the self; a feeling of being a better mother, friend, with more strength in values, thinking and aspirations; more self-confidence in dealing with people; and a reaffirmation of identity based upon acceptance of self and aspirations. Others specifically indicated a rise in confidence in dealing with and meeting other people. It is apparent that many of the women felt the same kind of self-development and growth that occurs in going through an intensive therapy or analysis—tolerance, self-directed questioning, and seeking for further understanding of one's own aspirations, desires and motivations.

174

The most frequent suggestion for improvement was for continued training either through presentation of cases or formal lectures. There were suggestions for more frequent evaluation of their work. One person stated that the availability of staff was the most important aspect for her and would be for new volunteers. Another talked at length about the need of the staff to think through carefully and clearly the definitions of role and limitations of goals for the volunteers. This applies not only to what the volunteers themselves have as their own aspiration, but also what the Center can provide. Thus, the staff needs to be explicit about what the volunteer can expect from the program. Warning should be given to new volunteers that aspirations will be aroused.

Occasionally the need for separation of a volunteer arises. The volunteer should be prepared for this. Six volunteers expressed either explicitly or implicitly the wish to continue working in the Center. Three of these indicated that they wished at the same time to return to school and receive more professional training. Two volunteers saw within their continuing work at the Center the possibilities of new learning experiences, such as with group therapy and help in future training of volunteers. One volunteer was uncertain about her future role.

After 18 months in the program five volunteers were still available for a repeat MMPI. When first and second MMPI's were compared, what stood out was the *lack* of marked changes. None of the volunteers showed any significant changes in character, some showed some changes in behavior—mostly in the direction of greater sensitivity to others—and more energy, while practically all showed some change in the presentation of self. They all seemed to be more open about themselves and to display less need to be "good."

SOME PROS AND CONS

The volunteers showed strengths in particular aspects of the suicide prevention work. They did well in obtaining necessary information about the patient and in mobilizing the patient's resources during the crisis. They did not hesitate to make the time-consuming effort to enlist family and friends, and to contact personal physicians, ministers and therapists, when available.

The volunteers frequently offered a relationship to the patient which was on a more direct, friendly level than that of professionals. This seemed especially important in those cases in which contact rather than authority seemed more important. This is similar to experiences of the Samaritans in England, where "befriending" by the worker is seen as most significant in helping suicidal persons.

One special difficulty in connection with the volunteers occurred on days when, for one reason or another, few calls came and there was little work. It was found to be demoralizing for a volunteer to come to the Center and to have little to do. It is interesting in this context to note that on those days when the staff feared the volunteers were being overworked, there was never any complaint from the volunteers. They would, however, not hesitate to complain when they did not have work.

One general disadvantage refers to size of staff and communication difficulties. Adding a significant number of new people to any program of activity complicates many of the organizational and communication procedures. For example, in using volunteers the responsibility for a case might be shared by one or more volunteers and a supervisor, and there was often the simple problem of knowing where the record was when it was needed. Most important was the problem of keeping current in communications about cases that were shared. This is really not a criticism or consequence of volunteers per se, but rather a comment on size. Its relevance is that using volunteers in an organization frequently increases precipitously the number of people involved.

One significant, unanticipated problem emerged, the problem of identity and self-concept. As the volunteers have grown in experience and skills, they have developed as mental health counselors. While they feel hampered by their lack of formal training, this does not lessen their sense of identity with the mental health area. In our Center this feeling was constantly encouraged by attitude and precept so that the volunteers readily adopted the professional stance. Unpaid volunteer status has, therefore, begun to lose appeal for some of the women. Perhaps as a direct result, three persons have returned to school with a professional goal in view.

A partial answer lies in providing a further sense of accomplishment and reward. Recognition might be offered with the establishment of an intermediate level in the professional area which would identify these trained volunteers as capable of giving expert service for payment rendered. Certainly the need for such skills remains high. As shown by Rioch (PHS publication, undated), there is more than enough room for such workers in the hierarchy of mental health activities. The regular staff of any agency must also undertake the task of providing further growth experiences. Some possibilities are: training of subsequent volunteers in the same agency; participation in the clinical activities of the Center, such as brief or emergency psychotherapy, longer term rehabilitative psychotherapy, group therapy, intake and history gathering; involvement in research activities in the agency; and others.

Fundamental to the planning for use of volunteers must be a clear conception of the need they will be asked to meet. The program then can be task-oriented. For example, at the Suicide Prevention Center, the need was to have more help in handling an increasing number of calls from suicidal people. With this need explicit at the outset, enlistment, selection and training could be focused. The volunteer, too, could be clear whether or not she wanted to do this particular work.

Probably the most important was staff interest, enthusiasm, direction and coordination. The staff accepted wholeheartedly the volunteers as persons to be trained, peers, with no sign of fence-guarding, or threat to professional status. The director may be a key factor in that his enthusiasm, or lack of it, influences the morale and attitudes of the group.

COMMENTS

The comments offered above are limited to that agency situation that involves the nonprofessional volunteer working in regular collaboration with a professional staff. The evaluation cannot be applied to volunteers who work in other models of agency functioning, such as self-help groups, where the professionals are used only incidentally in support of their work. Much needs yet to be learned about the optimal structure of the predominantly volunteer staffed agency. The limited experience gathered to date with such widely scattered suicide prevention activities in Pasadena, California, Seattle, Washington, Orlando, Florida, and London, England seems to indicate that a crucial factor lies in strong, enthusiastic and devoted leadership.

In general, it is apparent that nonprofessional volunteers, carefully selected and trained in crisis intervention techniques and personal counseling, can occupy an important place in the field of mental health and make a significant contribution to the mental health of the community.

REFERENCES

Bellak, L. (Ed.) *Handbook of community psychiatry and community mental health.* New York: Grune and Stratton, 1964.

The Development of Standards and Training Curriculum for Volunteer Services Coordinators. Psychiatric Studies and Projects. Washington, D.C.: Mental Hospital Service of the American Psychiatric Association, February 1964, 2 (2).

Lee, D. T. A new dimension for volunteers. *Mental Hygiene,* 1962, 46, 273-282.

Pines, Maya. The coming upheaval in psychiatry. *Harper's Magazine,* October 1965, 54-60.

Rioch, Margaret, Elkes, C., Flint, A. A., Usdausky, Blanche S., Norman, Ruth G., & Silber, E. National institute of mental health pilot study in training mental health counselors. *American Journal of Orthopsychiatry,* 1963, 33, 678-689.

Rioch, Margaret, Elkes, D., & Flint, A. A. Pilot project in training of mental health counselors. Washington, D.C.: U.S. Department of Health, Education and Welfare. *Public Health Service Publication, #1254,* undated.

Training Lay Counselors for Church and Community Mental Health

IN this generation, there have been new horizons charted for church and community mental health. On the one hand, the United States has unleashed a gigantic effort to combat mental illness. Improved institutional custodial care as well as the multiple approaches of community mental health centers seek to renovate the public *status quo* attitude toward the mentally ill. In the 1961 Final Report, the Joint Commission on Mental Illness and Health observed that there was a shortage of professional resources and recommended that a supplementary force of mental health counselors could be trained through short courses and consultation on the job.[1]

But, on the other hand, there has been a spirit of procrastination and hesitation on such a proposal among the traditional mental health professions. As George W. Albee, the 1969 president-elect of the American Psychological Association, declared: "We have talked about the need for training subprofessional people to supplement the efforts of members of the mental health professions, but we have not really begun

DOMAN LUM

to train such people."[2] It would be interesting to speculate about the reasons behind such resistance. However, there is need for an additional 12.000 fully trained helping professionals to serve 200 million Americans. In fact, Emory L. Cowen and Melvin Zax pointed out in 1967 that all available psychologists could be absorbed into college and university teaching alone,[3] so great is the demand.

It is my conviction that sensitive and mature church laymen with appropriate training and supervision are able to be potential resources as volunteers for church and community mental health.

[1] Joint Commission on Mental Illness and Health, *Action for Mental Health*, (New York: Basic Books, 1961). p. 257.

[2] George W. Albee, "The Relation of Conceptual Models to Manpower Needs," *Emergent Approaches to Mental Health Problems*. Emory L. Cowen, Elmer A. Gardner, and Melvin Zax, (eds.), (New York: Appleton-Century-Crofts. 1967), p. 63.

[3] Emory L. Cowen and Melvin Zax, "The Mental Health Fields Today: Issues and Problems," *Emergent Approaches to Mental Health Problems. ibid.*, p. 14.

The church has been engaged in serious and critical introspection of its structures over the past decade. Not only is there a call for church renewal, but there are bold proposals and experiments which signal a relevant reformation where the church is rediscovering its mission in the world. A recent lay effort has been FISH which originated in England and spread throughout various American communities. The members of FISH are committed to Christian involvement and are ready to assist in any emergency. Volunteers are available for baby sitting, housework for the disabled, a hot meal, transportation to a doctor or a hospital, and other practical services. Referrals to appropriate helping agencies and short-term assistance are other functions of FISH.[4]

However, since forty-two per cent of all troubled persons initially contact a minister, there is also a need for a core of competent lay counselors to alleviate the burdens of pastoral supportive counseling. Major theological seminaries, as well as the American Association of Pastoral Counselors and the Association for Clinical Pastoral Education, have established clinical programs for clergymen. However, equivalent theoretical and practical training for laymen on a supplementary level has been lacking. The acceptance of pastoral and lay forces as part of the healing ministry of the church is long overdue. The present responsibility of pastoral counseling is to widen its boundaries to include the layman in a meaningful way. We must recapture the sense of the priesthood and pastorhood of all believers.

There are numerous models of subprofessional manpower which have been employed in various projects throughout the United States. The shortage of mental health personnel has literally forced the creation of the subprofessional in mental hospitals, outpatient clinics, child care centers for underprivileged families, neighborhood recreation programs, school classrooms, welfare institutions for dependent and delinquent children, and neighborhood service centers. The manpower force has been drawn from a cross-section of society: college students and graduates, middle-aged women, high school dropouts and former delinquents, and former welfare recipients of the inner city ghetto.

AMONG the pilot projects demonstrating volunteer training are:

1) *College Students as Companions to Mental Patients in the State Hospital.* At the present time, there are at least 114 state mental hospitals in the United States which have utilized college students as volunteers as well as companions to mental patients. Much of the therapeutic approach is activity-centered therapy such as accompanying a patient into town or talking, reading, walking, playing games, or listening to music on the hospital grounds. The goals of the program generally are the improvement of social communication, skills, and preparation for discharge. In some hospitals, a mental health professional is available to students for supervision of the relationship between the patients and themselves, support as students express feelings, and education regarding mental illness and hospitalization.[5]

2) *Middle Aged Women as Mental Health Counselors in Out-Patient Clin-*

---

[4] For further information on FISH, see Robert Lee Howell, *Fish For My People*, (New York: Morehouse-Barlow, 1968).

[5] Jules D. Holzberg, Robert H. Knapp, John L. Turner, "College Students as Companions to the Mentally Ill," *Emergent Approaches to Mental Health Problems, op. cit.*, pp. 91–108.

ics. Margaret J. Rioch of the Washington School of Psychiatry is a firm believer in mental health careers for warm and sensitive middle aged women. Through the 1960 and 1964 Pilot Projects in Training Mental Health Counselors under the auspices of the National Institute of Mental Health, sixteen women were trained over a two year period which covered observations of individual, family, and group therapy; lectures, courses, and practical case seminars, and field work and supervision. The mental health counselors in the first project handled initial interviewing with a wide variety of patients ranging from adolescent adjustment problems to borderline schizophrenics and psychotics in remission. The second project concentrated on counseling with under-privileged mothers of young children in poverty and family disruption situations.[6]

3) *College Graduates as Mental Health Workers for Socioenvironmental Therapy*. Attendants of state mental hospitals are usually overloaded with custodial care, marginally employable, and poorly educated. They receive low salaries and there is a poor public image of their jobs. At Philadelphia State Hospital, a program was initiated to train college graduates as mental health workers. Six trainees were chosen every six months for a one year program in socioenvironmental therapy which included courses covering: 1) personality theory, psychopathology, and treatment; 2) group dynamics; 3) social institutions; 4) activity skills; and 5) social interaction therapy. The supervision for the training program came from a multi-disciplinary staff who ap-

praised the trainees' performance and techniques.[7]

4) *Dropouts as Human Service Aides for Community Social Service Agencies*. In the spring of 1964, ten young adults began a three month training program to prepare for human service aide positions in child care centers, neighborhood recreation programs, and social research projects under the sponsorship of Howard University's Institute for Youth Studies. The purpose of the program was to raise the personal and educational aspirations of trainees who were themselves high school dropouts and Negro youths from poor central areas of Washington, D.C. The training phase was built around the Core Group which grappled with situations, explored constructive alternatives, and responded in a responsible manner. Through numerous teaching methods, the trainees covered principles of human growth and development, techniques for managing problem children, recognition of emotional problems, the meaning and function of play, observation skills, games and preschool activities, and parent contacts. There were also opportunities to visit outside agencies and institutions and to spend a half day at an on-the-job experience. There were no dropouts from the program, although the staff dealt with some delinquent and criminal involvement. From 1964–1967, one hundred youths have graduated from the project. Supervisors have found them to be valuable additions to community social services. Most astounding is that former negative or even pathological youths began to render the same services at agencies which once helped

---

[6] Margaret J. Rioch, "Pilot Projects in Training Mental Health Counselors," *Emergent Approaches to Mental Health Problems*, *op. cit.*, pp. 110–127.

[7] Richard Sanders, "New Manpower for Mental Hospital Service," *Emergent Approaches to Mental Health Problems*, *op. cit.*, pp. 128–143.

many of them as delinquents and drop-outs."

5) *Ghetto Residents as Mental Health Aides at Neighborhood Service Centers.* Perhaps the most exciting program has been the use of the indigenous non-professional mental health aide in the neighborhood service centers of New York City. Under the leadership of Frank Riessman, the prime mover of The New Careers Development Center, storefronts have sprung up with trained residents of the neighborhood providing a "psychosocial first aid" approach of a listening ear and emotional support for problem-solving predicaments. The Center has available hospital mental health clinics as resources, stresses social activities, and is concerned about an organized action program for the community. There has been legislative action taken to develop the new careers for the poor. The Scheuer-Nelson Subprofessional Career Act of 1966 appropriated seventy million dollars to employ and train untrained and unemployed people as police aides, recreation aides, homemakers, welfare aides, code enforcement inspectors, and other positions. There is literally a mushrooming and a boom across the nation utilizing sub-professionals in the major helping fields.[9]

IN LIGHT of this manpower revolution, how can the church introduce laymen to church and community mental health in a meaningful way? The daily life of an active church lay couple

[8] William L. Klein, "The Training of Human Service Aides," *Emergent Approaches to Mental Health Problems, op. cit.,* pp. 144–161.

[9] Frank Riessman, "A Neighborhood-Based Mental Health Approach," *Emergent Approaches to Mental Health Problems. op. cit.,* pp. 162–184.

illustrates the need for a therapeutic witness.

Jack and Joyce Thompson are a middle aged couple with three children. They have been members of the First Congregational Church for over twenty years, and were married by the minister of the church. Let's go through a typical week with the family. Jack is an insurance district manager who has four men working under him. On Monday, Jack receives a call at the office from the wife of Bill Frazer who is one of his agents. She reports that her husband has been drinking and cannot come to work. Could Jack possibly help Bill, she pleads. After the morning conference, Jack visits his employee at home. Bill greets his boss at the door with a bottle in his hand. There is a brief conversation between the two men. Jack recommends to Bill the Alcoholics Anonymous group at the church, and later calls Bill's wife to assess his condition and to tell her about Ala-Non, a group for the spouses of alcoholics. Jack feels that sound employer-employee relationships are worthwhile to the company, especially when a career is at stake.

The Thompsons have a wholesome marriage and family life. Since Jack and Joyce have participated in a church sharing group, the family gathers together for a Tuesday evening conference after supper, with the father acting as chairman. Relevant problems are aired: Joe's request for the family car this Saturday evening for a date, Mary's personal appearance and her boyfriends, Dennis' gift of a summer camping experience for good grades during his sixth grade year, mother's proposal for new living room furniture, and a fifteen minute telephone call policy introduced by father. Whether the family council grants or denies these requests, there is active communication and an expression of feelings within the family. Furthermore, the family participates as a group on occasional outings and social nights. During the week, Jack and Joyce try to reserve an evening for themselves. They eat at a restaurant, go to a movie, or spend time with another couple and talk over coffee and cake. Every other Wednesday of the month, Jack presides as chairman of the church deacons. Usually there are numerous decisions before the board at every meeting. As moderator, Jack tries to add a therapeutic dimension to the discussion. The feelings of some deacons are easily hurt and misunderstanding often arises when there is a controversial issue. Through probing questions and reflective responses, Jack is able to clarify various opinions. He has grown in his leadership role as mediator. As a deacon, he often calls on sick parishioners, hostile and inactive members, and new persons who have recently moved into the area. Jack must cope with a wide assortment of complex personal problems as he visits those people on behalf of the church.

Joyce Thompson is a busy housewife. However, every Thursday she spends some time with her neighbor, Charlene Johnson, whose husband is in the Navy. Usually Charlene is alone three out of seven months during the year while her husband is aboard ship. She appreciates Joyce's warmth and friendship. They are able to talk over personal matters as they shop, eat lunch, or visit each other's home. Recently, the Rev. Mr. Carlson, pastor of the First Congregational Church, asked Joyce to help him in a pastoral counseling case. It seems that Mrs. Murray, a counselee, was in the process of obtaining a divorce and was quite lonely and depressed. Mr. Carlson felt that Joyce Thompson could be a supportive listener and give encouragement in the transitional period. Church laymen like Jack and Joyce Thompson are a vital resource for church and community mental health. In a meaningful way, they are involved with others because the Christian faith implants a sense of caring.

AFTER graduation from The School of Theology at Claremont, California, I returned to Honolulu, Hawaii, to become pastoral counselor and chaplain of the Salvation Army Men's Social Service Center. In order to maintain contact with my denomination, the United Church of Christ, I also became the director of the Makiki Christian Counseling Center, a pilot project in religion and mental health sponsored by Makiki Christian Church, an eight hundred member U.C.C. congregation located in Central Honolulu. As a part of the educational thrust, we trained a selected group of the Makiki Christian Church laymen as lay counselors. The Rev. Theodore Ogoshi and myself approached thirty-six potential trainees whom we considered to be warm and caring persons and who possessed inner resources for nurturing others. Twelve persons indicated initial interest. They were willing to commit themselves to twelve sessions with the understanding that they would function as lay discussion leaders for a six week Easter study series.

For four months, these selected lay leaders were exposed to lectures, discussions, and role playing in addition to outside assignments. The material for the course covered pastoral counseling: community mental health; Rogerian reflective counseling; group process and leadership; non-verbal communication games; family and marriage counseling; adolescent counseling; counseling the sick and dying, the mentally ill, the suicidal, the alcoholic, and the elderly. In the following months, ten lay counselors who held leadership positions utilized their skills in church visitation, teaching church school, advising youth groups, conducting church meetings, and supporting persons in informal counseling situations. Several were recruited by the pastoral staff to spend part of a day with persons who were mildly disturbed and who required the presence of an understanding friend. Two others became volunteers for The Waikiki Ministry, a detached church-related night mission ministering to the "concrete jungle" scene of tourists, servicemen, and displaced young adults in Hawaii.

Responsible lay counseling presupposes: 1) the screening of potential volunteers; 2) the training of lay counselors on theoretical, practical, and therapeutic levels; 3) the creation of a task-oriented program; and 4) the continuous supervision of a mental health resource leader. These prerequisites for lay participation require the assessment and mobilization of manpower, study and training for specific mission, formulation of concrete structures in church and community, and supportive assistance from an experienced mental health person.

1. *Screening.* From personal contacts and interviews in various churches, there are laymen who are warm and caring persons and who are able to relate to others. Usually these individuals are in contact with their own feelings and reflect a mature style of life. In order to deal effectively with others, the lay counselor needs to be sensitive to underlying feelings, flexible to cope with change and emergency, responsible for others, competent in the role of a helping agent, and aware of over-invested feelings in a therapeutic relationship. Often times, certain vocations bring us into contact with people where

a cool head is necessary for emotional survival. These are some of the characteristics we should look for as we select candidates for training.

2. *Training.* Depending on the specific purpose of the project in mind, lay counselors should be trained in a number of areas which can be applied to situations confronting the church. Built into sessions are discussions of supportive counseling approaches to group discussion, sensitivity training, family counseling, adolescent counseling, marriage counseling, and crisis areas such as sickness, mental illness, suicide, alcoholism, and old age. The recommended outline is three hours per session which deal with: 1) a presentation and discussion on a church and community mental health theme; 2) a laboratory with a counseling demonstration and an evaluation of training practice; and 3) a continuing group experience for sensitivity sharing and personal therapeutic development. During the week, there is an assignment to contact community resources and to read relevant suplementary textbooks. Instruction can be mobilized from a variety of sources: a pastor with clinical training, a mental health professional who is sympathetic with church and community mental health efforts, an ecumenical team approach with several churches that are willing to combine pastoral and lay resources as teachers or various guest mental health lecturers.

3. *Programming.* There are various church-related ministries where trained sub-professionals and volunteers are able to provide manpower as therapeutic agents of the Christian faith. Such structured ministries as undershepherds for the local parish, group study discussion leaders, church visitors for sick persons, coffee house workers, night ministry volunteers, church and com-

munity telephone crisis answering service, vocational missions volunteers to various segments of business and industry, bring laymen into contact with a multitude of problems regarding interpersonal relationships. Likewise, there are unstructured ministries occurring quietly around the community as the church fellowship is dispersed in the world during the week. In many locations, informal lay counseling occurs: persons discussing their problems with sympathetic and sensitive friends in a home, backyard, park, playground, car, bus, train, boat, airplane, restaurant, bar, corridors of a building, and other places where people gather. The lay counselor should assume an informal and unstructured stance and adopt his caring style to numerous strategic situations. He should be a listening post for persons who have confidence in him and share their burdens. At the same time, an alert pastoral staff should analyze the needs of a church and surrounding community with a core of committed laymen. Arising from such discussions may emerge a clear project which will execute a vital ministry.

4. *Supervision.* Lay counseling provides an opportunity for a clinically trained clergyman and a mental health professional to collaborate in a team effort. If at all possible, every local church should budget to make a part-time psychiatrist, psychologist, social worker, or pastoral counselor available on a fee-for-service basis, both for counseling and education. Community mental health professionals can be group therapy leaders for the church, as well as conduct lectures and forums on family life, marriage counseling, mental illness, social and mental health problems, juvenile delinquency, alcoholism, aging, and other crucial areas. In turn, church members can serve as social club sponsors for after-care cases, volunteers for

state mental hospitals, promoters of special mental health activities, and other worthwhile efforts. As lay counselors are trained and participate in church and community mental health affairs, a mental health professional should be available for bi-monthly supervisory conferences with these workers to discuss interpersonal relationship problems which may have occurred in various encounter experiences with people. Lay counselors need periodic support, on-going training, and a sense of direction from competent supervisors as they are engaged in therapeutic relationships.

TRAINING lay counselors for church and community mental health offers a basic exposure to major areas of counseling. It provides structure for vital church missions. It upgrades the role of the layman as therapeutic listener and the role of the clinical minister as coach and supervisor. It fosters a sense of understanding and confidence as the layman relates to a person in crisis. To train lay counselors is not to produce a new breed of "junior psychiatrists." Rather, the lay counselor is able to have some orientation to the problem, offer reflective support, and refer to the proper mental health agency. He should be aware of his limitations as a layman and should work closely with mental health professionals. At best, lay counseling bolsters the manpower potentials of the church for community mental health resource assistants. Only then can various caring ministries of the church or ecumenical cooperative projects be strengthened through competent voluntary forces.

At the present time, there have been recent proposals to develop non-professionals as a third force. For example, William J. Lederer and Don D. Jackson discuss the use of a third party to assist spouses who are involved in self-marital appraisals. These listening and reflective resources are trained to be objective, maintain confidentiality, and describe and interpret the behavior, actions, and messages of husband and wife in a feedback. In their book, *The Mirages of Marriage,* Lederer and Jackson predict that, given the overwhelming number of marriage counseling cases, such therapy will be handled by non-professional counselors in the future.[10] In the field of alcoholism, Eva Maria Blum and Richard H. Blum have introduced the idea of the "change-agent." They state: "The change-agent may be an expert or an ordinary citizen; the alcoholic may consider himself sick or well, a patient or a problem drinker or neither. Still it is 'treatment' as long as someone undertakes to alter another's drinking for the benefit of the community and the patient."[11] According to

them, a wide variety of persons have a constructive impact upon alcoholics. In this sense, the understanding of treatment has been extended to include non-professional members of the community. Moreover, a distinctive aspect of the suicide prevention movement has centered around the non-professional volunteer. At the Los Angeles Suicide Prevention Center, volunteers took 680 calls out of 1,808 new day calls, or 38%, during 1965. As a result of the program, regular staff members were able to pursue other needed areas of the center, provide supervision and consultation on cases, and were enthusiastic in their evaluation.[12]

From these indications, we are on the brink of a new era of mental health training. Pastoral counseling has the opportunity of developing an allied discipline as a theological and therapeutic thrust for the local church: lay counseling.

---

[10] William J. Lederer and Don D. Jackson, *The Mirages of Marriage,* (New York: Norton, 1968), pp. 364, 370.

[11] Eva Maria Blum and Richard H. Blum, *Alcoholism: Modern Psychological Approaches To Treatment,* (San Francisco: Jossey-Bass, 1967), p. 20.

---

[12] Sam M. Heilig, Norman L. Farberow, Robert E. Litman, Edwin S. Shneidman, "The Role of Nonprofessional Volunteers in a Suicide Prevention Center," *Community Mental Health Journal,* Volume 4 (4), 1968, pp. 287–295.

Volunteers Learn Test Techniques

WILLIS H. McCANN, Ph.D.

O UR PSYCHOLOGY DEPARTMENT uses volunteers as assistants in its testing program. We started about three years ago, and have found that the work they do is a challenge to them and an invaluable aid to us. Although we have only six psychologists serving this hospital of more than 2000 patients, the assistance we receive from our volunteers enables us to meet the demands for psychological testing without having to curtail other kinds of psychological services. Yet the volunteers' work in no way involves the practice of psychology by unqualified persons.

The idea of this program developed out of the need to solve two major problems—one hospital-wide, the other concerning only our department. The hospital problem was how best to utilize some intelligent, well-educated, highly motivated volunteers who were dissatisfied with their traditional roles. The psychology department's problem was how to meet the increasing demands for psychological testing without neglecting all other psychological services.

In the spring of 1960, two volunteers expressed their desire to do something that would help to expedite the preparation of patients for psychiatric treatment. They were dissatisfied with spending their time visiting and entertaining patients whose

The following members of the psychology department collaborated with the author in the preparation of this paper: Ellis Shutts, Kenneth West, and Roger Henry, clinical psychologists; Lloyd Gathman, vocational rehabilitation specialist; Nell Donly and Aditha Herzog, volunteers; and Luella Anderson, department secretary. Diane Lund and Millicent Riggs were the volunteers who originated the idea. Other volunteers who participated in the program at one time or another are Patty Gilley, Susan McCord, Ann Rossi, Frances Schmidt, Mary Shipley, and Thala Stalls. Madine Buckey, director of volunteer services, cooperated with the psychology department in making the program a successful one.

MENTAL HOSPITALS, 1964, vol. 15, no. 5, pp. 269-271.

needs for therapy were being neglected because our professional staff was too small. They wanted to do some of the routine work so the professional people would have more time to devote to therapy.

Volunteers With an Idea

These two volunteers offered their services to the psychology department because they believed they could help us to reduce the lag between the time we received test referrals and the time we completed the psychological reports. They proposed that we let them work as testing assistants in our department.

Because they were neither psychologists nor psychometrists, our first impulse was to decline their offer. Lacking professional training, what could they do for us?

They had a ready answer.

They could take care of all the preliminary arrangements preparatory to our testing patients individually or in groups. These would include arranging tables and chairs in the testing area, providing pencils and answer sheets, laying out the test materials selected by the psychologist, and attending to whatever incidentals might arise. They could receive the patients brought for testing, see that they were comfortably seated at the tables, help put them at ease, distribute test materials and answer sheets, and give the appropriate instructions. They could then monitor the test, escort disturbed patients from the room, collect answer sheets and test materials, and supervise the return of patients to their wards. They could return all test materials to the department files, use stencils to score the answer sheets, plot profiles, and maintain records.

These things they could do for six hours a day, one day a week. They were certainly qualified for such work and, in the light of our predicament, their proposal began to make sense.

At that time our department consisted of the chief psychologist, three staff psychologists, and one clerk-typist. We had no psychometrists. Nevertheless, we were receiving more referrals for testing than we could possibly handle. Understandably, the psychologists were reluctant to become full-time test technicians, hence the referrals were accumulating at an alarming rate. The volunteers could not have made their proposition at a better time. We gave it careful consideration and decided, not without some misgivings, to give it a trial. But we expanded on the duties the volunteers had proposed to undertake.

Testing Quickly Learned

At our request, the director of volunteer services assigned these two volunteers to our department. First we taught them the mechanics of giving and scoring the Minnesota Multiphasic Personality Inventory. They learned quickly, and we then taught them to give and score the Raven's Progressive Matrices and the Edward's Personal Preference Schedule. In a short time the volunteers, working under the supervision of a psychologist, were giving and scoring these tests.

We were pleased—and relieved—to find close agreement between the interpretations made from data obtained by the volunteers from these tests and the interpretations made from data obtained by psychologists from the individual Rorschach and Thematic Apperception Tests. With this reassurance we launched the volunteers on a program of group testing for all routine referrals. Special referrals are never delegated to the volunteers.

Routine referrals request information in one or more of six general categories: intelligence, personality, assets and liabilities, dynamics, potential for psychotherapy, and diagnosis. The purpose is to obtain general information for use in the initial screening of patients for various types of treatment.

It has been determined empirically that one or more of the following tests will provide all the information needed to satisfy any routine referral: Bender-Gestalt, Draw-A-Person, Edward's Personal Preference Schedule, Harrower Multiple Choice Rorschach, Minnesota Multiphasic Personality Inventory, Raven's Progressive Matrices, The Peabody Picture Vocabulary Test, The Ammonds Full Range Picture Vocabulary Test, and the written Thematic Apperception Test. The volunteers were trained to give all ten of these tests, and, with the aid of a psychologist, to score all of them except the Draw-A-Person Test and the written Thematic Apperception Test. These two are projective tests which must be scored by a psychologist who understands projective techniques and who is familiar with these particular tests.

Routine referrals never request information in all six categories. Hence volunteers never give the complete battery of tests to any one patient. Only those tests are used which will provide the information requested.

Secretary Can Select Tests—

In the beginning the department secretary assigned each referral to a psychologist. The psychologists rotated these assignments, except that all referrals on juveniles were assigned to the psychologist working in the juvenile program.

It soon became evident to the department secretary, however, that the psychologists routinely designated certain tests for each category of information. Our secretary began to anticipate the tests which the psychologist would order and would routinely select the Raven's Progressive Matrices for the intelligence category. If the patient was an alcoholic or had a history of head injury, she would routinely add the Bender-Gestalt. Eventually she became so adept at anticipating which tests were required that it was no longer necessary for a psychologist to verify her selection prior to the actual testing. If the psychologist writing up the report wants additional test data, he arranges for supplementary testing, either by himself[1] or by the volunteers at their next testing session.

Thus, because we are fortunate in having an extremely capable secretary, the testing program revolves around her more and more. She receives the referrals, checks the type of information requested, notes on the referral form the tests to be used, and schedules the patients. When the volunteers arrive, she gives them a list of the patients they are to test, supplies them with the necessary materials and equipment, and calls for the patients previously scheduled. The volunteers take over at this point and when finished report to the secretary, who arranges for the patients to be returned

---

[1] If he wants data from a test such as the individual Rorschach, the Wechsler Adult Intelligence Scale, or the Wechsler Intelligence Scale for Children, which the volunteers are not qualified to give.

to the wards.

—*Volunteers Can Score Them*

The volunteers then score the tests, calling on a psychologist for assistance whenever they feel the need. The data are turned over to the secretary for filing in each patient's folder. At his convenience, the psychologist gets the folder from the secretary, studies the data, obtains any supplementary test data he may need, and then prepares his report.[2]

Although the working arrangements among the volunteers, the department secretary, and the psychologists are informal, the program itself has become functionally streamlined and operates at a high level of efficiency. We believe this has come about because the program is neither rigidly structured nor overelaborated by specific detailed instructions. The volunteers and the secretary are not reduced to automatons, who must blindly follow a set procedure regardless of what variations changing circumstances may demand. On the contrary, we have capitalized on the critical thinking and sound judgment of our volunteers and our department secretary. We expect them to do a good job, and they, in turn, perform at a level which fully meets our expectations. Some mistakes have been made, but this happens in any undertaking. On the other hand, no damage has been done. The worst that has happened has been the accumulation of more data than we needed, but even this was without cost to us in either time or money.

We feel that the success of our program has come from treating our volunteers and our secretary as the highly intelligent, responsible people they are. Lines of communication are always open in all directions among all involved. As a result, we have an integrated team of test technicians, which adequately meets the demands for routine testing and, at the same time, releases the psychologists for services more in keeping with their professional qualifications.

Without minimizing the importance of the tra-

---

[2]This is not done blind. The psychologist, through initial interviews and orientation sessions with newly admitted patients, is always acquainted with the patient whose test data he analyzes.

ditional volunteer contributions to the therapeutic milieu of the mental hospital, we believe we have demonstrated how some volunteers can contribute even more productively to the hospital program when they are trained to function as psychological test technicians.

Volunteers for Mental Health

Affleck, D. C., Strider, F. D. & Helper, M. M. A clinical psychologist assistant approach to psychodiagnostic testing. Supported by Research Grant No. R11 MH-02024 from Applied Research Branch NIMH (Undated reprint).

Aquiar, Maria, et al. Symposium: "Out reach" An approach to human relationships in the introductory psychology course. Paper presented at meetings of the American Psychological Association, New York, New York, 1966.

Beier, Ernst G., Robinson, Peter, & Micheletti, Gino. (U. Utah) Susanville: A community helps itself in mobilization of community resources for self-help in mental health. Journal of Consulting & Clinical Psychology, 1971 (Feb), Vol. 36 (1), 142-150.

Bouhoutsos, Jacqueline C. (1525 San Vincente Blvd. Santa Monica, Calif.) The nontradionally trained mental health worker: Fad or future? Professional Psychology, 1970 (Fal), Vol. 1 (5), 455-459.

Briggs, E. Convicted felons as social therapists. Correctional Psychiatry and Journal of Social Therapy., 1963, 9 (3), 122-127.

Buckey, Harold M., Muench, George A., & Sjoberg, Bernard M.(San Jose State Coll.) Effects of a college student visitation program on a group of chronic schizophrenics. Journal of Abnormal Psychology, 1970, 75 (3), 242-244.

Carkhuff, R. R. & Traux, C. B. Lay mental health counseling. The effects of lay group counseling. Journal of Consulting Psychology, 1965 29 (5), 426-431.

Chaplan, Abraham A., Price, John M., Jr., Zuckerman, Isadore, & Ek, Jon. (Queens Child Guidance Center, New York, N. Y.) The role of volunteers in community mental health programs. Community Mental Health Journal. 1966, 2 (3), 255-258.

Chinsky, Jack M. (U. Rochester) Nonprofessionals in a mental hospital: A study of the college student volunteer. Dissertation Abstracts International, 1969, 30 (3-B), 1355.

Chinsky, Jack M. & Rappaport, Julian. (U. Connecticut) Attitude change
in college students and chronic patients: A dual perspective.
Journal of Consulting & Clinical Psychology, 1970 (Dec) Vol. 35 (3)
388-394.

Cowen, Emory L. (U. Rochester, Center for Community Study) Broadening
community mental health practicum training. Professional Psychology
1971 (Spr), Vol. 2 (2), 159-168.

Cowne, Leslie J. (Brooklyn Coll., City U. New York) Case studies of
volunteer programs in mental health. Mental Hygiene, 1970 (Jul),
Vol. 54 (3), 337-346.

Cytrynbaum, S. Project Outreach: An approach to human relationships,
experimental learning, and community action in the introductory
psychology. Paper presented at meetings of the American
Psychological Association, Washington, D. C., 1969.

Cytrynbaum, S., and Mann, R. Innovation, work and bicultural teaching.
In P. Runkel, R. Harrison, and M. Runkel (eds) The Changing College
Classroom. San Francisco: Jossey-Bass, 1969, 266-289.

Fieldhouse, Walter. A place for the volunteer in mental health.
Mental Health, 1966, 25 (4), 40-41.

Fischer, Edward H. (Connecticut Valley Hosp., Middletown) Altruistic
attitudes, beliefs about psychiatric patients and volunteering
for companionship with mental hospital patients. Proceedings of
the Annual Convention of the American Psychological Association,
1971, Vol. 6 (Pt. 1), 343-344.

Fischer, Edward H. (Connecticut Valley Hosp., Middletown). College
students as companions to long-term mental hospital patients:
Some considerations. Journal of Consulting & Clinical Psychology,
1970 (Dec), Vol. 35 (3), 308-).

Freund, Diane. Project GROW: Report of a conference on nontradional
training and the future of paraprofessionals, held at California
State College at Los Angeles (5151 State College Drive, Los
Angeles, Calif., 90032), December 11, 1968.

194

Gendlin, E. T. Mental Health Field Worker Training Project.
Preliminary draft of a proposal for joint collaboration of the
Illinois Department of Mental Health and OMAT, U. S. Department
of Labor, Mimeo, Undated.

Gendlin, E., Kelly, J. J., Raulinaitis, V. B., & Spaner, F. E. Volunteers
as a major asset in the treatment program. Mental Hygiene, 1966
50 (3), 421-427.

Heilig, S. M., Farberow, N. L., Litman, R. E., & Shneidman, E. S.
The role of nonprofessional volunteers in a suicide prevention
center. Community Mental Health Journal, 1967, 4 (4), 287-295.

Holzberg, Jules D. (Connecticut Valley Hospital) The companion program:
Implementing the manpower recommendations of the joint commission
on mental illness and health. American Psychologist, 1963,
18 (4), 224-226.

Holzberg, Jules D., Gewirtz, Herbert, & Ebner, Eugene. Changes in moral
judgment and self-acceptance in college students as a function of
companionship with hospitalized mental patients. Journal of
Consulting Psychology, 1964, 28 (4), 299-303.

Holzberg, Jules D., Knapp, Robert H., & Turner, John L. (Wesleyan U.)
Companionship with the mentally ill: Effects on the personalities
of college student volunteers. Psychiatry, 1966, 29 (4), 395-405.

Imre, P. D. (Spring Grove State Hosp., Baltimore, Md.) Attitudes of
volunteers toward mental hospitals compared to patients and
personnel. Journal of Clinical Psychology, 1962, 18 (4) 516.

King, Mark, Walder, Leopold O., & Pavey, Stanley. (Iowa State U.)
Personality change as a function of volunteer experience in a
psychiatric hospital. Journal of Consulting and Clinical Psychology,
1970 (Dec), Vol. 35 (3), 423-425.

Knapp, Robert H., & Holzberg, Jules D. (Wesleyan U.) Characteristics of
college students volunteering for service to mental patients.
Journal of Consulting Psychology, 1964, 28 (1), 82-85.

Kulik, James A., Martin Robert A., & Scheibe, Karl E. (Wesleyan U.)
Effects of mental hospital volunteer work on students' conceptions
of mental illness. Journal of Clinical Psychology, 1969, 25 (3),
326-329.

L'Abate, L. Utilization of technical and subprofessional personnel.
In The laboratory method in clinical psychology: Part IV: Training
for the laboratory method. (Undated mimeograph from the author)

Lawton, M. Powell, & Lipton, Mortimer B. (Norristown State Hosp.,
Norristown, Pa.) Student-employees become companions to patients.
Mental Hospitals, 1963, 14 (10), 550-556.

Ledvinka, James and Denner, Bruce. New directions for student involvement
in the community. Symposium held at the meetings of the American
Psychological Association, Miami Beach, Florida, 1970.

Levine, Carl. (Colorado State U.) Impact of work with mental patients
on student volunteers. Journal of Human Relations, 1966, 14 (3),
422-433.

Lumm, Doman. (Salvation Army, Men's Social Service Center, Honolulu,
Hawaii) Training lay counselors for church and community mental
health. Pastoral Psychology, 1970 (May), Vol. 21 (204), 19-26.

Mace, Douglas L. (U. Rochester) College volunteers as group leaders
with chronic patients: Effects of ward personnel involvement on
ward behavior change. Dissertation Abstracts International, 1970
(Oct) Vol. 31 (4-B), 2287.

McCann, Willis H. (State Hosp. No. 2, St. Joseph, Mich.) Psychologists
discover value of volunteers: I. Volunteers learn test techniques.
Mental Hospitals: 1964, 15 (5), 269-271.

McCaulley, M. H. (Chm) The manpower gap and the elastic psychologist:
New attempts to stretch psychological manpower to meet increasing
demands. Symposium presented at the meeting of the Southeastern
Psychological Association, Atlanta, April, 1967.

Mechanick, Philip, et al. (U. Pennsylvania, Medical School) Concepts
in university mental health services. JAMA, 1969 (Jun), Vol.
208 (13), 2453-2456.

Nelson, Constance B. Veterans Administration Mental Hygiene Clinic,
Denver, Colo.) College students help chronic patients.
Hospital and Community Psychiatry, 1969 (Dec), Vol. 20 (12), 394-395.

Rappaport, Julian (U. Rochester) Nonprofessionals in a mental hospital:
College students as group leaders with chronic patients.
Dissertation Abstracts International, 1969, 30 (3-B), 1365.

Reding, Georges R., & Goldsmith, Ethel F. (U. Chicago) The nonprofessional
hospital volunteer as a member of the psychiatric consultation team.
Community Mental Health Journal, 1967, 3 (3), 267-272.

Reinherz, Helen. College student volunteers as case aides in a state
hospital for children. American Journal of Orthopsychiatry, 1963,
33 (3), 544-546.

Schwartz, Arthur N. (Veterans Administration Center Domiciliary, Los
Angeles, Calif.) Volunteers help build patients' self-esteem.
Hospital & Community Psychiatry, 1970 (Mar), Vol. 21 (3), 87-89.

Sinnett, E. Robert, & Niedenthal, Linda K. (Kansas State U. Student
Health Center) The use of indigenous volunteers in a rehabilitation
living unit for disturbed college students. Community Mental
Health Journal, 1968, 4 (3), 232-243.

Sobey, Francine. (Columbia U., School of Social Work) Volunteer
services in mental health: An annotated bibliography: 1955-1969.
National Clearinghouse for Mental Health Information, 1969, No.
1002.

Spoerl, Otto H. (U. Washington) An activity centered volunteer
program for university students. Hospital & Community Psychiatry,
1968, 19 (4), 114-116.

Umbarger, C. C. Dalsimer, J. S., Morrison, A. P. & Briggin, P. R.
College students in a mental health hospital. New York: Grune &
Stratton, 1962.

Vineberg, S. E. Subdoctoral and supportive personnel in psychology.
Paper presented at a conference on selection, training, and
utilization of supportive personnel in rehabilitation facilities,
sponsored by Arkansas Rehab. Res. & Trng. Center and Assoc. of Rehab.
Centers, September, 1966.

197

Walker, C. Eugene, Volpin, Milton, & Fellows, Lloyd. (Westmont Coll.)
The use of high school and college students as therapists and
researchers in a state mental hospital. Psychotherapy, Theory,
Research & Practice, 1967, 4 (4), 186-188.

Wanderer, Zev, & Sternlight, Manny. (William Healy Sch. Chicago, Ill.)
Psychologist discover value of volunteers: II. Psychology students
work with retardates. Mental Hospitals, 1964, 15 (5), 271-272.

Zunker, V. G. & Brown, W. F. Comparative effectiveness of student
and professional counselors. Personnel and Guidance Journal, 1966,
44 (7), 738-743.

198